John Locke's Liberalism

John Locke's Liberalism

Ruth W. Grant

THE UNIVERSITY OF CHICAGO PRESS

CHICAGO AND LONDON

RUTH W. GRANT is assistant professor of political science at Duke University. The dissertation upon which this book is based received the Leo Strauss Award from the American Political Science Association.

The University of Chicago Press, Chicago 60637
The University of Chicago Press, Ltd., London

© 1987 by The University of Chicago
All rights reserved. Published 1987
Printed in the United States of America

96 95 94 93 92 91 90 89 88 87   5 4 3 2 1

Library of Congress Cataloging in Publication Data

Grant, Ruth Weissbourd, 1951–
    John Locke's liberalism.

    Originally presented as the author's thesis (Ph.D.)—
University of Chicago, 1984.
    Bibliography: p.
    Includes index.
    1. Locke, John, 1632–1704—Contributions in political
science.   2. Liberalism.   3. Authority.   I. Title.
JC153.L87G73 1987   320.5'12'0924   86-30743
ISBN 0-226-30607-0

to my parents

Contents

Acknowledgments

This book has been a long time in the making, and its publication gives me the opportunity to acknowledge my debt to the people who have helped me with my work on it not once, but many times.

The book began as my doctoral dissertation. My interest in the project grew from my graduate studies at the University of Chicago with the late Herbert Storing. From him I learned why liberal constitutionalism, which I already admired, is deserving of admiration.

I owe my greatest debt to another of my teachers, Joseph Cropsey. He provided me with an education in political philosophy, a model of scholarly integrity, and consistent encouragement for my efforts to pursue an independent path.

Nathan Tarcov gave me the benefit of his thorough understanding of Locke's work and also of his thorough reading of my drafts from the first draft of the dissertation to the very last revision of the manuscript for the book. His criticism and conversation have made this a much better book than it otherwise would have been.

I am also indebted to Russell Hardin for insisting to the last that I repair a defect in the original manuscript that needed to be repaired. The comments provided by the readers for the University of Chicago Press also contributed to improve the book.

I prevailed upon my friends Michael Gillespie and Vivien Ravdin to comment on the original draft of each chapter, to listen to endless conversation about Locke, and to provide encouragement during the initial phases of the project. I am deeply grateful to them.

Kathleen Pucci assisted me ably in preparing each version of the manuscript. Anne Crippen prepared the index.

Finally, I wish to thank my husband, Stephen Grant, whose critical reading of my work kept me honest and whose moral support kept me going.

Introduction

Liberal political theory appears at once as a success and a failure. It takes its bearings from the thought that all men have an equal right to govern their actions as they see fit. No man has an intrinsic or natural right to govern another. In other words, men are equal in the sense that they are by nature free. This thought has gained tremendous power since political theories taking it as their premise were formulated in England in the seventeenth century. The basic principle of human freedom and equality is now part of the universal ideology of our times; even the worst of modern tyrannies pays lip service to it. Moreover, this principle has been the premise of most modern political philosophy, though of course men have drawn quite different political consequences from it. Nonetheless, to find a political theory that seeks to justify political hierarchy on the basis of a natural inequality among men, one has to return to the classical writings of antiquity. In these respects the liberal idea has been victorious. Yet from the beginning, theories of liberal government derived from this idea have been seriously criticized. The political conclusions drawn from the liberal premise have not received the same universal acclaim as the premise itself. And the defects of liberalism have seemed so significant that men have been proclaiming its imminent demise for at least a hundred years.

Contemporary critics of liberalism on the left and the right focus on two areas where liberal theories seem most vulnerable; their emphasis on legal formalities and procedural justice and their elevation of the status of the individual at the expense of the community. With respect to the first, liberal theories of government assert that in any free government, and consequently in any legitimate government, the law rules. The proposition that all men are equally subject to the laws and are entitled to equal treatment under the laws is derived from the premise of equal individual rights. But this

1

emphasis on the rule of law as essential to the justice of the liberal state can produce a corresponding emphasis on the forms and institutional procedures required for maintaining legal protections for the individual that critics find excessive and distorting.

For example, when political questions are resolved according to strict legal rules and procedures, there is often little room for a flexible, practical response. A politician with the skills of a statesman might find little opportunity to use them to advantage. Moreover, when political issues are legalistically framed as matters of individual rights, the possibility of an honest confrontation of partisan political groups is diminished. The political argument itself may be distorted by the need to frame the discussion in terms of existing precedents. In general, the legalistic liberal approach appears to put obstacles in the way of realistic political responses to the necessities of a situation or to the forces at work within the society. Liberals often seem to be naively unaware both of the realities of power relationships and of the economic, or cultural, or psychological substratum that shapes political life. Instead they treat the political arena as an independent one, where problems can generally be resolved through improved institutional mechanisms and laws. This criticism is reflected in debates over the study of politics as well. The study of the structures and functions of government bodies in their institutional relationships is said to produce only a superficial understanding that neglects the underlying forces shaping the political realities.

In the most general terms, these criticisms are simply various forms of the charge that liberal theory sacrifices substance for form. The legalistic approach tends to raise the question, Is this action legitimate or authorized? rather than, Is this action good? While the rule of law is introduced as a principle of just government, undue emphasis on legal forms can lead to a politics that fundamentally fails to address problems of justice and injustice.

Long before liberal theory or its critics, political thinkers were well aware of the limitations of the law as the sole means for securing justice in political societies. There is a traditional critique of the law that has much in common with the criticisms later leveled at the particular liberal version of the rule of law. Laws, as general rules, cannot give sufficient guidance for individual situations. Strict adherence to the rules may hinder necessary political action or result in injustice in a particular case where the circumstances warrant a departure from the rule. Laws, as particular conventions, have a lesser status than standards to be found in nature or religion. These particular conventions must give way if they conflict with natural, universal standards of justice. Laws, as commands, cannot encompass those virtues whose nobility derives from their quality as free gifts beyond obligation. When liberalism is criticized for its overemphasis on legal forms and inattention to substantive results, the criticism is a version of the thought that legality cannot be simply equated with justice. Liberals seem to need reminding that the law is in the service of something else; either something lower, in the case of the contemporary charge that the laws of a society merely reflect underlying political realities, or something higher, in the case of the charge shared with traditional thinkers that the law cannot replace what is good or just but is an instrument to achieve justice.

The second area in which liberal theory seems vulnerable to criticism is its emphasis on the primacy of the individual. Because liberal theory begins with individual rights, with individual freedom, the political community appears to be nothing more than a temporary collection of individuals bound together by contract relations that dissolve whenever the association no longer serves its purposes. Liberalism is criticized for its inability to provide a firm foundation for claims of the public good over claims of individual interest. It must find a way to explain how a liberal polity can sustain itself over time and how it can expect loyalty from its citizens. The integrity of the political community is a particularly important matter, not only in explaining the relation of the individual to the society, but also in explaining the relation of the society to its government. Liberalism seems to have difficulty explaining what remains when governments change—what makes a people a people.

Both of these sets of criticisms were present in some form from the beginning of the efforts to develop political theories based on the premise of individual natural rights. John Locke[1] was certainly well aware of them from a variety of sources, including the traditional analysis of the shortcomings of the law, but he addressed them particularly in responding to Sir Robert Filmer's criticisms of

1. John Locke's works will be cited throughout in the following manner: *Conduct of the Understanding*, 2d ed., edited with an introduction by Thomas Fowler (New York: Lenox Hill Burt Franklin, 1971), will be cited as CU followed by a section number.

An Essay Concerning Human Understanding, edited with a foreword by Peter H. Nidditch (Oxford: Clarendon Press, 1975; reprinted with corrections as a paperback, 1979), will be cited as Essay followed by book, chapter, and paragraph numbers—e.g., Essay I.3.4.

Two Treatises of Government, rev. ed., with an introduction and notes by Peter Laslett (Cambridge: Cambridge University Press, 1963), will be cited as 1T followed by a paragraph number when the reference is to the *First Treatise* and 2T followed by a paragraph number when the reference is to the *Second Treatise*.

any theory that laid the foundation for political authority in the consent of the people.

It was Filmer's opinion that consent theories could not adequately explain the individual's obligation to political authorities. If each individual were to remain free until he consented to subject himself to government and to be obligated only for so long as he consented to his own subjection, it would be impossible to establish and maintain distinct political nations. Consent theories could not fully explain how rulers could be chosen, territories claimed, and authority maintained from one generation to the next. It seemed to Filmer that none of these things could be accomplished in practice without violating the principle of individual natural rights, since he thought that the principle of individual right would require both that there be unanimous consent and that consent could be withdrawn at any time at the discretion of each individual. If this latter were correct, the problem of a right of revolution would be insurmountable. There is no real obligation, no possibility of political stability if revolution is always justified on any grounds.[2] Consent theories overemphasize the rights of the individual at the expense of the claims of the political community.

According to Filmer, the final determination of political questions cannot rest with the individual members of the society but must rest with the government. And this means that if there is more than one branch of government, the final determination must rest with one of them. There is no true sovereignty unless this condition is met. An institutional system of a mixed and balanced government where the branches are meant to be coequal is really not a government at all. There is no sovereign unless the king, who is the source of the laws, stands above the law. The problem of sovereignty cannot be avoided by the naive faith that sovereignty can be successfully divided. All members of the society cannot be equally subject to its laws because there must be a ruling will that is paramount. In this way too, by relying on the fiction that the law

2. Sir Robert Filmer, "The Anarchy of a Limited or Mixed Monarchy," in *"Patriarcha . . ." and Other Political Works of Sir Robert Filmer,* edited with an introduction by Peter Laslett (Oxford: Basil Blackwell, 1949), pp. 284–87; idem, "Observations upon Aristotle's Politiques Touching Forms of Government," in *"Patriarcha" and Other Works,* pp. 211, 217–18, 225–26; idem, "Observations on Mr. Milton *Against Salmasius,*" in *"Patriarcha" and Other Works,* p. 256; idem, "Patriarcha or the Natural Power of Kings," in *John Locke, "Two Treatises of Government" and Robert Filmer, "Patriarcha,"* ed. Thomas I. Cook (New York: Hafner, 1947), 1:1–2, 2:5–7. All references to "Patriarcha" will be to the Hafner edition, which is based on the text Locke used. The Laslett edition contains a better text of "Patriarcha," but it is now out of print. All references to other writings by Filmer will be taken from the Laslett edition.

rules, consent theories fail to establish secure grounds for effective political authority.[3]

This is the way Locke was confronted with the challenges facing liberal theorists generally. He had to explain the relations between individual, community, and government in a manner compatible with a stable political order. He had to justify legal and institutional forms and procedures that establish the rule of law. And in so doing, he had to show how the shortcomings of the law could be recognized and overcome without abandoning the principle of the rule of law. He had to show both that the rule of law could be practicable and realistic and that the system of positive laws and lawmaking could be justified in terms of the natural law. The adherence to certain legal forms had to be grounded in a substantive standard of justice.

We find in Locke's political writings a serious confrontation with the problems facing liberal theory then and now, problems that perpetually face liberal theorists because they arise from the starting premise of liberal thought—natural freedom. If men are naturally free and equal individuals, the formation of political community and political authority requires explanation. And if there is to be legitimate political subjection, it must somehow be compatible with natural individual rights. Liberalism finds that compatibility in equal subjection to reasonable laws. Thus the two major problems facing liberal theorists are related because both are inseparable from the premise of liberal thought. Fundamentally Locke, like any liberal theorist, was faced with the task of demonstrating that true political obligation can emerge from a foundation in individual freedom.

Or to put the matter somewhat differently, Locke had the task of justifying both a duty to obey and a right to resist, a right that is inseparable from natural equality and freedom. To accomplish this task requires the ability to clearly distinguish the legitimate from the illegitimate exercise of power. Political theory must identify the standards by which legitimate authority, which ought to be obeyed, can be distinguished from illegitimate power, which ought to be

3. Filmer, "Anarchy," p. 298; idem, "The Necessity of the Absolute Power of All Kings and in Particular of the King of England," in *"Patriarcha" and Other Works,* pp. 215–26; idem, "Observations on Aristotle," pp. 219, 224, 228; idem, "Observations on Hugo Grotius *De Jure Belli et Pacis,*" in *"Patriarcha" and Other Works,* p. 267; idem, "Observations on Milton," pp. 251, 254; idem, "Patriarcha," 1:4, 2:16, 3:3, 8. See also Thomas Hobbes, *Leviathan,* edited with an introduction by C. B. Macpherson (Harmondsworth, England: Penguin, 1968), pp. 236–37, 245–47. Filmer praises Hobbes's *De Cive* on the rights of sovereignty in his "Observations on Mr. Hobbes's *Leviathan,*" in *"Patriarcha" and Other Works,* p. 239.

resisted. And according to Locke, this is the primary task of political theory.

This is the question that dominated Locke's political writing, and it is appropriate that it should dominate the investigation of his political thought. Locke begins the *Second Treatise* with the thought that "he that will not give just occasion, to think that all Government in the World is the product only of Force and Violence, and that Men live together by no other Rules but that of Beasts, where the strongest carries it, and so lay a Foundation for perpetual Disorder and Mischief, Tumult, Sedition, and Rebellion . . . Must of necessity find out another rise of Government, another Original of Political Power, and another way of designing and knowing the Persons that have it" (2T.1). Brute force can be distinguished from rightful authority on the basis of the correct understanding of the origins of political authority. Locke finds those origins in consent, a principle directly derived from natural freedom, and he uses this principle in his effort to define legitimate government. For Locke, liberal government is the solution to the problem of defining legitimate government, because only the liberal state can meet the standards set by the natural law; only the liberal state is compatible with the liberal premise. Locke provides us with a coherent defense of the liberal state, one that takes full cognizance of the criticisms that can be leveled at liberal theory.

But Locke does much more than this. He was particularly conscious of the question of the grounds of his own enterprise as a political theorist. In writing his *Essay Concerning Human Understanding,* Locke examined the problem of what could be known about political right. He defended in the *Essay* the possibility of demonstrative normative political theory. And he defended in the *Two Treatises* the importance of providing such a theory, one that would establish the norms for political legitimacy on the basis of reasoned demonstration.

For this reason, this investigation of Locke's political thought begins with a consideration of his *Essay.* The project proceeds from the question of what political theory can do to what it should do, then moves on to explore how Locke's theory does it and how well. After considering Locke's discussion of the epistemological grounds for the possibility of political theory (chap. 1), I will turn to the *Two Treatises* for the development of Locke's attempt to find the grounds for legitimate political power and the criteria for distinguishing it from illegitimate political power (chap. 2). The investigation is dominated throughout by the question of the grounds for legitimate political authority. Locke bases his normative theory on the equal right of each to preservation, drawing his standards for legitimate government both from natural freedom and from the natural goal of preservation. The discussion then moves on to consider whether Locke's standards are applicable in practice in a manner that can meet the objections raised by Filmer and others (chap. 3). The question here is whether Locke's theory of consent can justify lasting obligation as well as support a doctrine of resistance that is not an invitation to perpetual anarchy.

Finally, I return to Locke's writings on human reason to consider their relation to his proposed solution to the political problem (chap. 4). Locke's description of the political problem begins with the observation that men have no common judge on earth. God does not pronounce judgment during this life. Guilt or innocence cannot be determined by the methods used in England in the twelfth century; trial by battle and ordeals by hot iron or water took physical events as indications of God's judgment. Neither do men receive their just rewards and punishments in this life. If there is to be justice on earth, it will not be because of divine intervention. Men must govern themselves "according to reason" (2T.19). And it is Locke's view of the possibilities and limits of human reason that shapes his view of the possibilities and limits of both liberal politics and liberal political theory.

This procedure for investigating Locke's political thought is guided by the view that Locke's is a demonstrative political theory. It is demonstrative in that it is meant to be read as a series of deductions from clearly stated initial premises. It is argued as if it were a geometric proof. It is political in that its purpose is to define legitimate political authority. The analysis here attempts to follow out Locke's reasoning from its premises and focuses on the political question as Locke defines it.[4]

In taking this approach, neither of the two dominant controversies in recent Locke scholarship will be directly addressed. But the approach does imply a position with respect to each. The first of these controversies arises from the work of C. B. Macpherson, who looked to Locke's theory, among others, for the particular concep-

4. In treating Locke's work as liberal political theory, my approach most resembles the following: J. W. Gough, *John Locke's Political Philosophy: Eight Studies* (Oxford: Clarendon Press, 1950); Willmoore Kendall, *John Locke and the Doctrine of Majority Rule* (Urbana: University of Illinois Press, 1941); Raymond Polin, *La politique morale de John Locke* (Paris: Presses Universitaires de France, 1960); Martin Seliger, *The Liberal Politics of John Locke* (London: George Allen and Unwin, 1968).

tion of individualism that led to the justification of a class state under capitalism.[5] This is a view that gives prominence to Locke's discussion of property in the *Second Treatise* and diverts attention from his discussion of directly political questions concerning the establishment, form, and change of governments. In the discussion of the *Second Treatise* here, the emphases will be reversed. Locke's discussion of property is treated as a necessary component of his reply to certain Filmerian criticisms of his political argument. The context is set by the political question.

The second controversy concerns whether Locke's work must be read with the understanding that he wrote in such a way as to intentionally obscure his thought. This is related to the question whether Locke can be considered a clear and consistent writer or whether his work is fundamentally contradictory and confused. Leo Strauss, identifying certain inconsistencies in Locke's work, interprets them as intentional. He argues that, while Locke wishes to present his theory as part of the natural law tradition, his is not in fact a traditional natural law teaching.[6] In following out Locke's

---

5. C. B. Macpherson, *The Political Theory of Possessive Individualism: Hobbes to Locke* (Oxford: Clarendon Press, 1962), esp. pp. 250–51. See Leo Strauss, *Natural Right and History* (Chicago: University of Chicago Press, 1953), pp. 234–38. Leo Strauss agrees with two of Macpherson's fundamental points: that Locke justifies the unlimited accumulation of property by an individual, and that the discussion of property is central to Locke's thought. For contrasting interpretations of Locke's views on property see John Dunn, *The Political Thought of John Locke* (Cambridge: Cambridge University Press, 1969), pp. 203–41, and James Tully, *A Discourse on Property: John Locke and His Adversaries* (Cambridge: Cambridge University Press, 1980). See *The Locke Newsletter*, no. 13 (Autumn 1982), for discussions of the competing interpretations of Macpherson and Tully with a reply by Tully.

6. Strauss, *Natural Right*, pp. 202–51. For arguments in support of his position see Richard H. Cox, *Locke on War and Peace* (Oxford: Clarendon Press, 1960), pp. 1–44; Willmoore Kendall, "John Locke Revisited," *Intercollegiate Review* 2 (January–February 1966): 217–34; and Michael P. Zuckert, "The Garden Died: An Interpretation of Locke's *First Treatise*" (Ph.D. diss., University of Chicago, 1974), pp. 29–136. For opposing arguments see Hans Aarsleff, "Some Observations on Recent Locke Scholarship," in *John Locke: Problems and Perspectives*, ed. John W. Yolton (Cambridge: Cambridge University Press, 1969), pp. 262–71; Charles H. Monson, Jr., "Locke and His Interpreters," *Political Studies* 6 (1958): 120–33; Patrick Riley, "On Finding an Equilibrium between Consent and Natural Law in Locke's Political Philosophy," *Political Studies* 22 (December 1974): 432–52, esp. 445–47; Seliger, *Liberal Politics*, pp. 32–36, 45–49, 55–62; and John W. Yolton, "Locke on the Law of Nature," *Philosophical Review* 67 (1958): 477–98.

In support of his position, Strauss cites passages from Locke's *Reasonableness of Christianity*, where Locke describes how authors and speakers sometimes intentionally obscure their meaning for good reasons. Strauss's critics question the relevance of these passages for the interpretation of Locke's own work. With the exception of Zuckert, pp. 91–137, the exchange for the most part omits discussion of the many places where Locke emphasizes both that proper writing should clearly and consistently state the author's meaning without metaphor, analogy, or rhet-

reasoning for the analysis presented here, there seemed to be no inconsistencies of the sort that would require the conclusion that apparently contradictory statements are meant to indicate some deeper unifying thought. Most apparent inconsistencies evaporated on further consideration of the context of conflicting statements, their place in the argument, or Locke's word usage. Most often, when I thought I had met with an inconsistency, I had merely misunderstood some portion of the text because I had assumed too readily that I already knew what it meant.

Strange as it may seem, the assertion that Locke's work can be read as a coherent, orderly demonstration, carefully written, is probably the single most unusual claim of the analysis that follows. Most authors seem to agree that Locke's writing is perplexing and imprecise at best, though some find this intentional, others take it at face value, and still others find it unintentional but explicable in the light of unstated assumptions of his thought.[7] Of course I do not claim that Locke's work has no textual inconsistencies or that Locke completely resolves every theoretical problem he addresses. What I do wish to stress is that the *Second Treatise* in particular is a remarkably orderly, systematic presentation of an argument and that many of its apparently confusing pieces become sensible when their place in the whole structure of the argument is recognized.[8] But ultimately, the validity of the approach taken here must be

---

orical flourish and that a reader should approach a work looking for the plain sense of the language and for its chain of logical argument. While Locke took extraordinary care to conceal the fact that he was the author of the political views he published, he often emphasized that the best writing made the author's views directly accessible to the reader and minimized the possibility of confusion or misinterpretation. See CU.20, 29, 32, 42; Essay III.9, III.10, III.11; "An Essay for the Understanding of St. Paul's Epistles, by consulting St. Paul himself," in *The Works of John Locke in Ten Volumes*, 12th ed. (London: Thomas Davison, 1823), 8:21.

7. Macpherson explains Locke's inconsistencies by articulating the "unstated social assumptions" behind his argument. See pp. 1–8. Kendall, *Majority Rule*, also finds Locke's argument sensible only when the "latent premise" is expressed. Dunn, *Political Thought*, sees Locke's Calvinism as the unifying premise that explains what otherwise seems inconsistent. Gough, p. 90, and Laslett, Introduction to *Two Treatises*, pp. 94–95, acknowledge the inconsistencies but seem to accept them without much explanation. Gough seems to find Locke's writing persuasive and clear despite the inconsistencies and lack of originality; pp. 123–24, 196. Again, Polin and Seliger adopt an approach closest to my own, though Seliger sees more surface carelessness and inconsistency than I do. Both conclude that Locke's is fundamentally a coherent theory carefully presented. See Polin, pp. 1–9, 48, 304–5; Seliger, *Liberal Politics*, pp. 34, 39.

8. See Locke's letter to Molyneux, 20 January 1692–93, in *Works*, 1823, 9:303, where Locke notes that when his reader did "observe the design and foundation of what I say, rather than stick barely in the words," he saw that there was no contradiction between two particular passages where there had previously seemed to be one.

judged by whether the analysis provides a convincing explanation of the text.

The approach to Locke's work in the discussion that follows can also be distinguished from two different historical approaches. Some scholars interpret Locke essentially as a progenitor of some political phenomenon found in our own times. They usually identify some negative aspect of life under modern liberal capitalism and look to Locke for its theoretical roots. They seek the fundamental theoretical errors that justify capitalism, colonialism, excessive individualism, or unqualified majoritarianism, for example.[9] This sort of enterprise has the virtue that it highlights the direct relevance of Locke's theoretical work, but it also tends to distort the reading of that work by viewing it through a prism shaped by our own concerns and our own way of perceiving political problems. A question is brought to the reading of Locke phrased in contemporary terms before considering the question as he puts it in framing his own undertaking. A second group of works explains Locke's thinking in terms of the currents of thought that shaped his own intellectual milieu.[10] These are extremely important for understanding

---

9. See Macpherson on capitalism; David Gauthier, "The Role of Inheritance in Locke's Political Theory," *Canadian Journal of Economics and Political Science* 32 (1966): 38–45, and Martin Seliger, "Locke, Liberalism and Nationalism," in Yolton, *Problems and Perspectives,* pp. 19–33, on nationalism and colonialism; Louis Hartz, *The Liberal Tradition in America* (New York: Harcourt, Brace and World, 1955), on the excessive individualism of America's Lockean politics, which produces undue fear of majorities; and Kendall, *Majority Rule,* on the authoritarian character of Locke's doctrine of majority rule democracy.

10. For examples see Dunn, *Political Thought;* Julian H. Franklin, *John Locke and the Theory of Sovereignty: Mixed Monarchy and the Right of Resistance in the Political Thought of the English Revolution* (Cambridge: Cambridge University Press, 1978); and Tully. Franklin and Tully each focus on a particular problem and locate Locke's argument in relation to theoretical treatments of the same problem by his contemporaries. Dunn explains Locke's political theory in general as consistent only on the basis of his Calvinist principles, principles he finds irrelevant today. See Dunn, *Political Thought,* p. 267.

A new historical study appeared in print as this book was being prepared for publication: Richard Ashcraft, *Revolutionary Politics and Locke's "Two Treatises of Government"* (Princeton: Princeton University Press, 1986). The book is an impressive and fascinating account of Locke's activities and writings as a member of a radical political movement. Ashcraft views the *Two Treatises* as "in effect, the political manifesto of this movement" and treats it accordingly as political ideology (pp. 9, 12). Ashcraft's Introduction defends his particular kind of historical approach to the study of political theory.

My own quite different approach is based on the view that though it is necessary to know why an author wrote what he did and for what audience (in order to avoid ahistorical errors at the very least), it is also necessary to consider whether what the author says makes sense. Locke himself argues for the necessity of making political and moral arguments and for the possibility of reaching the truth about political principles on the basis of argument. When an author makes his case in the form of

Locke's place in his contemporary debate and for explaining why certain issues are discussed or discussed in the way they are. Taken alone, however, they can give the impression that Locke's work is so particular to his own time and place that it can be of no more than historical interest to us.

Locke's work will not be treated here as if he were directly addressing our political concerns, but neither will it be treated as if the fact that he was part of a seventeenth-century debate means that his writing cannot be important to us in our own thinking about political issues. Locke's work will be treated instead as an example of liberal political theory, and it will be examined to assess whether it is an adequate solution to the problems facing liberal theories. That assessment involves understanding what those problems are, what tasks liberal theory must accomplish, and what our expectations ought to be for what this sort of theoretical undertaking can accomplish at its best. For anyone who does not wish to abandon the premise of liberal theory—human freedom—these are subjects worth considering.

---

an argument, it deserves to be considered for its cogency as an argument, and particularly so in this case.

On two important points, Ashcraft and I reach the same conclusions through different types of evidence and argumentation: that there is a unity and coherence to Locke's epistemological and political writings, and that Locke's doctrine of resistance is more radical than it has sometimes been taken to be. Chapters 7 and 11 of Ashcraft's book are especially pertinent to my discussions of resistance in chapter 3. See also Richard Ashcraft, "Revolutionary Politics and Locke's *Two Treatises of Government:* Radicalism and Lockean Political Theory," *Political Theory* 8 (1980): 429–86.

1

The Possibility of Political Theory

Introduction

Locke sets out in his major philosophical work, *An Essay Concerning Human Understanding,* to discover what it is possible for men to know and with what degree of certainty. Those areas where demonstrative knowledge is possible are distinguished both from those where men must rely on educated judgment to guide their beliefs and from those that remain entirely dark and inaccessible to human reason. In undertaking to define the limits of reason, Locke intends to show that, while we cannot know all things, our rational faculties are nonetheless sufficient to guide our conduct. Locke's concern in writing the *Essay* is a practical moral concern.[1]

> How short soever their [men's] Knowledge may come of an universal, or perfect Comprehension of whatsoever is, it yet secures their great Concernments, that they have Light enough to lead them to the Knowledge of their Maker, and the sight of their own Duties. (Essay I.1.5)

> 'Tis of great use to the Sailor to know the length of his Line, though he cannot with it fathom all the depths of the Ocean. 'Tis well he knows, that it is long enough to reach the bottom, at such Places, as are necessary to direct his Voyage, and caution him against running upon Shoals, that may ruin him. Our Business here is not to know all things, but those which concern our Conduct. If we can find out those Measures, whereby a rational Creature put in that State, which

---

1. See Peter H. Nidditch, foreword to John Locke, *An Essay Concerning Human Understanding* (Oxford: Clarendon Press, 1975; reprinted with corrections, 1979), pp. xvii–xxi. See also John Locke, MS. c.28 f.8, 14 February 1683, the Lovelace Collection of the Papers of John Locke in the Bodleian Library, Oxford. In criticizing Cicero's definition of wisdom as speculative knowledge, Locke writes that wisdom refers to the "conduct of a man's actions in reference to his own happiness or highest concernment."

Man is in, in this World, may, and ought to govern his Opinions, and Actions depending thereon, we need not be troubled that some other things escape our Knowledge.

This was that which gave the first Rise to this Essay concerning the Understanding. (Essay I.1.6, 7)[2]

By making this case, Locke stakes out a position for himself between two opposing extremes. On the one side are those skeptics who abandon the claims of reason altogether because we cannot know all things with certainty. According to Locke, these men

> intemperately require Demonstration, and demand Certainty, where Probability only is to be had, and which is sufficient to govern all our Concernments. If we will disbelieve every thing, because we cannot certainly know all things; we shall do much-what as wisely as he, who would not use his Legs, but sit still and perish, because he had no Wings to fly. (Essay I.1.5; see also Essay IV.14.1)

On the other side are those who deny the importance of reason by maintaining that the principles guiding our conduct are innate and need not be demonstrated or argued. Locke replies that if there were principles of conduct that were innate and part of the constitution of the human mind, one would expect them to be easily recognizable and to govern everywhere and always. These men fail to explain the possibility of error and of evil, and also the wide variety of customs and conventions according to which men guide and judge their actions (Essay I.1, I.3).[3]

Locke's defense of his own position, that men can govern their actions according to reason, requires him to show that men are capable of acquiring true and certain knowledge of moral principles through the use of the faculties of the understanding; that they are free to guide their conduct according to this knowledge; and that, where certain knowledge is impossible, men are nonetheless able to reach a more or less reasonable judgment on the basis of what can be known. Locke's analysis of the understanding is, then, a defense of the possibility of moral responsibility at the same time that it is an explanation for the wide variety of human practices and

2. Emphasis added. See also Locke's journal for 8 February 1677, printed in Richard I. Aaron and Jocelyn Gibb, eds., *An Early Draft of Locke's Essay: Together with Excerpts from His Journals* (Oxford: Clarendon Press, 1936), p. 86.

3. Thomas A. Spragens, Jr., *The Irony of Liberal Reason* (Chicago: University of Chicago Press, 1981), pp. 52–54; R. S. Woolhouse places Locke in a "tradition of constructive skepticism," *Locke* (Minneapolis: University of Minnesota Press, 1983), pp. 14, 146–48. See James Gibson, *Locke's Theory of Knowledge and Its Historical Relations* (Cambridge: Cambridge University Press, 1917; reprint ed., 1968) for the relation of Locke's ideas to those of his contemporaries.

the role of judgment in human affairs. It is an analysis that depends upon distinguishing thought and knowledge into two sorts: one where principles are accessible to human reason and can be demonstratively known, and the other where practical judgments of probable consequences must guide human action.

Locke's epistemological analysis has a direct bearing on his political thought, and before examining his political writing it is appropriate to ask what he thought men could know about political things and whether he thought political questions could be settled beyond doubt. The answers to these questions will give some indication of what kind of political argument is to be found in the *Two Treatises*. The *Essay* explains Locke's views on the proper methodological approach to political investigations. In addition, the answers provide the background for the substantive inquiry into Locke's political ideas. Locke's political prescriptions ought to be suited to men who are rational in the way that and to the extent that Locke describes men as rational in the *Essay*.

The limits of human understanding, as Locke sees them, give the political problem its particular shape. Politics involves both sorts of thought and knowledge; one where moral principles of conduct can be known with certainty, and the other where practical judgments of probabilities must suffice. We will find that the argument of the *Second Treatise* itself is a demonstration belonging to the first type. It is a reasoned proof of the extent of the rights and duties of men in political communities. But the *Second Treatise* also takes account of the dual character of our understanding in its analysis of political life. In politics, civil law is the bridge between the two realms of knowledge. Legislating is an act of judgment embodying demonstrable natural law principles, but in conventional categories that determine their application to particulars. Though the principles of right governing political life can be known, this does not preclude the need for a common judge whose determinations as to their applicability disputing parties are bound to obey. Locke's conception of government as judge or umpire has its background here. These are intimations of the bearing of the *Essay* on our understanding of the *Second Treatise*. In general, this initial investigation of Locke's epistemology will serve to introduce the investigation of his political thought.

Two Kinds of Understanding

The basics of Locke's epistemology are simple and straightforward. All our ideas originate in experience; either in experience of the external world, which we have through sensation, or in experience of our own thinking and wishing, which we have through reflection. Each of the distinct ideas that are formed in our minds directly from these experiences is an idea of "one uniform Appearance" and cannot be reduced to any component parts. These Locke calls simple ideas, and they include such ideas as solidity, perception, pain and pleasure, cold, soft, and white. These simple ideas are the building materials out of which the mind constructs complex ideas, by combining and comparing, and general ideas, by abstracting one idea from the others with which it might happen to be associated in particular circumstances. This constitutes an exhaustive description of the components of our mental life. Everything that it is possible for a human being to think is either an impression from experience or a modification of such impressions produced by the operations of a few faculties of the mind (Essay II.1–2, 12).

Despite the simplicity of the scheme and the common source for all our ideas, there are significant differences between two major types of complex ideas, differences with important implications for the possibility of moral and political knowledge. Locke distinguishes complex ideas of substances from complex ideas of modes and relations: "The *Ideas* of *Substances* are such combinations of simple *Ideas,* as are taken to represent distinct particular things subsisting by themselves," for example, man, sheep, army, gold. "Modes I call such complex *Ideas,* which however compounded contain not in them the supposition of subsisting by themselves, but are considered as Dependences on, or Affections of Substances; such are the *Ideas* signified by the Words *Triangle, Gratitude, Murther,* etc." Modes may be either simple or mixed, the first if they are combinations of a single simple idea (e.g., a dozen) and the second if they combine several different simple ideas. Ideas of relations are a special type of mixed mode, and they arise by comparing one idea with another—for example, father, whiter, cause and effect (Essay II.12, III.4.1).[4]

The category of mixed modes and relations includes our moral ideas and much of our legal and political ideas as well. Since the ideas of actions are mixed modes, lawmaking involves defining categories of mixed modes (Essay III.5.5). Comparing ideas of actions to rules that are to govern them produces ideas of moral relations. Men judge their actions as sins or duties, criminal or innocent, vir-

4. There is some ambiguity about relations since Locke also says that a great many ideas include some kind of relation. See Essay II.21.3, II.26.6.

tues or vices as they conform to or violate the divine law, civil law, and law of opinion or reputation respectively (Essay II.28). Ethics, divinity, law, and politics are all disciplines dealing primarily with mixed modes (Essay II.22.10–12, III.5.12). When men think about right and wrong in political affairs, the materials for their thoughts are ideas of mixed modes and relations. So to discover what can be known about political things, it would be well to begin by comparing what can be known about mixed modes in general with what can be known about substances. We will find that the latter, the subject of natural science, is the sphere limited to judgment and probabilities, while the former is an area where demonstrative knowledge is possible.

The differences between substances, on the one hand, and mixed modes and relations, on the other, all follow from the basic fact that our ideas of substances are meant to be copies of archetypes with a real existence, "subsisting by themselves," whereas our ideas of mixed modes and relations are themselves archetypes. For example, in forming the idea of gold, we combine ideas of several characteristic properties occurring together in our experience— yellow, malleable, inanimate, and such. We can come to have a clearer idea of gold by adding to the list of qualities as we discover them, for example, the temperature at which it melts. But we can never have a perfectly adequate and comprehensive idea of gold, or any other substance, since it would have to include the infinite ways a given substance can affect and be affected by all other substances. All our ideas of substances are inadequate because they are imperfect copies, and some may also be unreal or fantastic (e.g., the idea of a centaur) if the components of the idea do not in fact coexist in things.

But our ideas of mixed modes and relations cannot be either inadequate or fantastic, since these ideas are arbitrary creations of the mind.[5] In forming ideas of mixed modes, we combine elements that we may never have experienced coexistent in the world. It is possible to have a clear idea of murder or adultery without ever having seen either of them committed and even without any action corresponding to these ideas ever having been committed (Essay II.22, III.5.5, III.6.44–47). It is precisely because there is no supposition that ideas of mixed modes reflect real existences that these

---

5. All simple ideas are also real, adequate, and true, but because they are perfect copies and "agree to the reality of things." Essay II.30.2; see Essay II.30–II.32.

ideas cannot be said to be false or inadequate.[6] Such ideas are not copies, but are patterns formed in the mind by which we order our experience. So long as they are consistently made, that is, not impossible, ideas of mixed modes are all adequate ideas. Because they are arbitrary and conventional, they are complete in themselves, unlike ideas of substances, which are meant to reflect the connection of qualities as they exist in nature and are always imperfect and incomplete (Essay II.22, II.23, II.25, II.30–32, III.5).

We could have perfect ideas of substances if we could know what it is that determines that a given thing will have each of the qualities and powers it has; if we could know the "real essences" of substances. This is not a problem in the case of mixed modes. For example, the "nominal essence" of a triangle, its definition, is a three-sided closed figure. The definition is a complete description of it; all its properties can be derived from its definition. There can be no distinction between its "nominal" and "real" essence. But in the case of substances, knowledge of "real essences" is inaccessible to human reason, according to Locke. Our knowledge is limited to what can be known by experience, and we cannot know by experience how the insensible constitution of things can account for our experience. We find that a certain set of sensible qualities occur together, but we cannot know that they are necessarily connected (Essay II.23.9–13, III.3.15–20, III.6.1–18).[7]

The consequence of this limitation of our understanding is that species of substances cannot be distinguished on the basis of their "real essences." For example, in forming the complex idea of a man, we combine ideas such as rationality, corporeality, a particular shape, and so forth, and unite them by designating the combination by a single word. The combination is the nominal essence of the species "man." But we cannot know any necessary connection among this particular group of qualities. There is an element of arbitrariness in selecting a particular group of qualities as definitive. By naming a set of ideas "man," we set off the species of things that correspond to our idea of man from all other things; the species is man-made.

And men will not all make it in exactly the same way. There is no

6. Ideas of mixed modes can be false only in the sense that one man's idea of "justice," for example, may not correspond to the idea that another man attaches to the same name. Essay II.32.9–12.

7. John W. Yolton, *Locke and the Compass of Human Understanding: A Selective Commentary on the "Essay"* (Cambridge: Cambridge University Press, 1970), pp. 80–82.

clear natural boundary between species that we can discover to settle disputes when men differ as to what constitutes a given species.
Whether a creature born of woman but with a monstrous shape is a
man and whether a changeling is sufficiently human to be baptized
are questions that cannot be answered by reference to natural categories. Although our ideas of substances do group things that are
similar in nature, they are nonetheless arbitrary in the sense that
they create species with definite boundaries that do not correspond
to natural boundaries or to natural "real essences" (Essay III.3,
III.6, IV.4.14–17).

The number and kinds of species men create are also arbitrary,
both in the case of substances and in the case of mixed modes. In
Jamaica, where men have never seen ice, there will be no word, and
hence no species "ice" as distinct from "water" (Essay III.6.13). Or
men may combine the idea of killing with the idea of the relation of
a father to create the distinct species of action called patricide, but
there is no more connection in nature between the two than there is
between the idea of killing and the idea of the relation of a neigh-
bor, a combination for which we do not create a distinct species of
action (Essay III.5.6–7). The categories with which the mind operates are artificial categories.

The question that arises at this point is whether the mind, operating within the limits Locke describes, is capable of any real understanding. What can be known on the basis of propositions constructed from words and ideas of substances and mixed modes
when the first are necessarily inadequate and the second are
arbitrary?

Knowledge of a substance is the perception that particular
qualities coexist in the same subject. But this is truly knowledge,
that is, certain, only when the subject is present to the senses. Not
knowing the real essences of things, we do not have universal
knowledge of substances; we cannot know the necessary connections among the qualities that make up our complex ideas of substances (Essay IV.1.6, IV.3, IV.6).

> Let the *Idea* to which we give the name *Man*, be, as it commonly is, a
> Body of the ordinary shape, with Sense, voluntary Motion, and Rea-
> son join'd to it . . . we cannot with certainty affirm, That *all Men sleep
> by intervals;* That *no Man can be nourished by Wood or Stones;* That *all
> Men will be poisoned by Hemlock:* because these *Ideas* have no connex-
> ion nor repugnancy with this our nominal Essence of *Man*, with this
> abstract *Idea* that Name stands for. We must in these and the like
> appeal to trial in particular Subjects, which can reach but a little way.
> We must content our selves with Probability in the rest: but can have

no general Certainty, whilst our specifick *Idea* of *Man,* contains not that real Constitution, which is the root, wherein all his inseparable Qualities are united, and from whence they flow. (Essay IV.6.15)

The source for our information concerning substances, then, is experience and the collected record of experiences—history. And the proper method for investigating substances is experiment and observation.[8] On this basis we will not attain certain universal knowledge, but we will be able to refine our opinions by weighing probabilities. Judgment is the faculty by which we balance the evidence and regulate our conduct in the absence of certain knowledge (Essay IV.3, IV.12.9, IV.14–IV.16).

> The Understanding Faculties being given to Man, not barely for Speculation, but also for the Conduct of his Life, Man would be at a great loss, if he had nothing to direct him, but what has the Certainty of true *Knowledge.* . . . He that will not eat, till he has Demonstration that it will nourish him; he that will not stir, till he infallibly knows the Business he goes about will succeed, will have little else to do, but sit still and perish. (Essay IV.14.1; see Essay IV.11.10)

We must rely on the judgment of probabilities when our actions depend on the knowledge of substances.

Universal certain knowledge is available to us when our thinking concerns mixed modes and relations. The names of these ideas lead the thoughts only to the ideas in the mind, with no reference to any external existence (Essay III.5.12). The thing the name refers to is the complex idea itself, and it can be completely defined by listing the simple ideas of which it is composed.[9] All the properties of a given mixed mode or relation can then be deduced from the definition of it and its relation to other ideas. For example, from the definition of a triangle it can be demonstrated that the sum of its angles is equal to two right angles. In the same manner, the necessary truth of the proposition *"No Government allows absolute Liberty"* can be proved from the definitions of government and

---

8. "History" is used here as in the expression "natural history." Locke's views on scientific method are closely related to those of his colleagues in the Royal Society. See Gibson, *Theory,* pp. 260–65; Woolhouse, *Locke,* p. 86; Yolton, *Compass,* pp. 7–11, 41, 53–75.

9. Names of simple ideas cannot be defined, but one can learn their meaning by being shown a thing that produces the impression corresponding to that idea; e.g., "red." Names of substances can be taught both by showing and by defining. Confusion concerning an idea that a word refers to is least likely to occur with simple ideas and most likely to occur with mixed modes, because they are arbitrarily created. Although this difficulty with mixed modes has caused much needless argument, it can be remedied if people clearly define their terms. See Essay II.32.21, III.4, III.9–11.

liberty. Again, "the Idea of Property being a right to any thing" and injustice "being the Invasion or Violation of that right," it follows that *"Where there is no Property, there is no Injustice"* (Essay IV.3.18).[10] The knowledge gained by reasoning in this way is universal, eternal, and certain (Essay IV.3.31), and it is so precisely because the ideas involved do not refer to external subsistent things.

Demonstrative reasoning of this sort is the method of mathematics, not the method of the natural sciences, and it is the method that affords certain knowledge. Certainty, the perception of the truth of a demonstration, depends upon intuition. Intuition is to the mind what sight is to the eye. We can no more doubt of the agreement or disagreement of two ideas in some circumstances than we can doubt whether we are looking at something black or red. The faculty of intuition, recognizing "self-evident" truths, operates at each step of a demonstration and is the foundation for the certainty of demonstrative knowledge. When there are no further intermediate proofs to be discovered between two ideas in a chain of reasoning, the mind recognizes the agreement of the ideas in the chain by intuition. The improvement of our knowledge depends upon discovering demonstrations by using the faculty of reason to discover proofs linking propositions. By beginning with clear definitions of mixed modes and relations and proceeding to link these ideas with others through chains of reasoning, we can build demonstrative sciences (Essay IV.2, IV.12, IV.14.1–8). Since moral ideas are mixed modes and relations, a demonstrative moral science is possible. It requires that the method of mathematics be applied in the area of ethics (Essay III.11.15–17, IV.3.18–20, IV.4.7–10).[11]

The faculties of the human mind are in fact particularly well suited to the discovery of our duties. Since this sort of knowledge "is most suited to our natural Capacities, and carries in it our greatest interest, *i.e.* the Condition of our eternal Estate . . . I think I

10. See Richard I. Aaron, *John Locke,* 3d ed. (Oxford: Oxford University Press, 1971), pp. 262–63; David L. Perry, "Locke on Mixed Modes, Relations and Knowledge," *Journal of the History of Philosophy* 5 (July 1967): 219–36; Woolhouse, *Locke,* pp. 134–35; idem, *Locke's Philosophy of Science and Knowledge: A Consideration of Some Aspects of "An Essay Concerning Human Understanding"* (Oxford: Basil Blackwell, 1971), for the controversy over whether propositions of this sort can be "instructive" rather than merely "trifling." Locke himself attacks the logic of the Schools as leading to trifling propositions such as "Right is Right" (Essay IV.8.3).

11. See Yolton's important discussion, *Compass,* pp. 92–103. Locke attacked the formal logic of the Schoolmen, attempting to replace it with a less formal method of demonstration: "Demonstration meant primarily for Locke just the uncovering of conceptual connections" (p. 92).

may conclude, that *Morality* is *the proper Science, and Business of Man-kind in general*" (Essay IV.12.11). Reasoning from our knowledge of the existence of God and of ourselves as his workmanship, we can discover our obligations under the law of nature. The divine law is accessible through revelation, but is also accessible as the law of nature to all men at all times by the "light of reason" (Essay I.3.6, 13, II.28.8). To be guided in our conduct by the law of nature is to be guided by reason (2T.6). And reason is adequate as a guide because knowledge of our rights and duties is derived from the category of ideas that can be perfectly known.

Thus the understanding, as Locke describes it, operates in two very different ways depending on whether its subject is substances or mixed modes and relations. In the first case it attempts to combine ideas so as to copy the combinations of qualities existing in things subsisting by themselves. Its efforts in this regard are always inadequate, and reasoning on the basis of these inadequate ideas can never produce universal certain knowledge. Instead, men have the faculty of judgment that allows them to estimate probabilities on the basis of experience and to act accordingly. In the second case, mixed modes and relations, the understanding creates complex ideas without supposing any existing thing corresponding to a particular idea. Using these ideas as building blocks, the faculty of reason can produce demonstrations providing us with certain knowledge.

That portion of political understanding that involves moral principles belongs to this second case. There is also a portion of political life that can be understood only by considering man as substance, by asking what his capacities are and how he is likely to behave rather than how he ought to behave. There is a distinction between empirical and normative political science that roughly corresponds to the fundamental distinction of Locke's *Essay*.

The *Essay* and the *Two Treatises*

The distinction also corresponds to Locke's own division of political studies into "the art of governing" and "the original of societies and the rise and extent of political power." In "Some Thoughts Concerning Education," Locke recommends Grotius and Puffendorf for instruction in the latter part of political studies: "the natural Rights of Men, and the Original and Foundations of Society, and the Duties resulting from thence." This is the *"general Part of Civil-Law,"* to be supplemented by education in history and the particular laws of one's own country. In "Some Thoughts Concerning

Reading and Study for a Gentleman," where the division of political studies is explicitly made, Locke tells us that the "art of governing," like knowledge of substances, is to be acquired from "experience and history" (see Essay IV.12.10). But he recommends his own *Two Treatises,* in addition to Grotius, Puffendorf, and others, for instruction in that aspect of politics concerned with the rise and extent of power and obligation.[12]

Locke's *Second Treatise,* then, is not a discussion of lessons in the art of government drawn from personal experience or from historical examples. Instead, it is the kind of demonstrative normative theory the possibility of which is argued in his *Essay.*[13] It is an analytical argument demonstrating the grounds for and extent of political rights and duties from the premise of all men's equal natural right to preservation. The *Second Treatise* defines relations; relations of ruler and ruled, master and slave, parent and child, conqueror and conquered, and it demonstrates the grounds for the right to rule and the duty to obey and the limits of each in each case; and in each case the argument derives from the natural law.[14] It is a juridical argument, a kind of "grand jurisprudence." Or in terms closer to those of the *Essay,* it is the political or civil portion of ethics. The *Essay* clearly identifies knowledge of our rights and du-

12. John Locke, "Some Thoughts Concerning Education," in *Educational Writings of John Locke,* edited with an introduction by James L. Axtell (Cambridge: Cambridge University Press, 1968), pars. 185–86, pp. 294–95; idem, "Some Thoughts Concerning Reading and Study for a Gentleman," in *Educational Writings,* p. 400. Compare Hobbes's division of the sciences, p. 149.

13. This characterization of the Second Treatise is best supported by tracing Locke's demonstration from its premises. But incidental support can be found in the subtitle of the *Second Treatise,* "An Essay Concerning the True Original, Extent, and End of Civil Government"; at 2T.42 where Locke mentions "the great art of government," but only "bye the bye": and at 1T.57 and 2T.103 where Locke indicates that an argument from historical example "to what should of right be, has no great force." See Nathan Tarcov, "A 'Non-Lockean' Locke and the Character of Liberalism," in *Liberalism Reconsidered,* ed. Douglas MacLean and Claudia Mills (Totowa, N.J.: Rowman and Allanheld, 1983), pp. 130–40. Tarcov remarks, "Thus by Locke's own account the political teaching of the *Second Treatise* . . . is not fundamentally a prudential teaching about interests but a moral or legal (though pertaining to natural law) teaching about rights and duties. Locke's political theory is deontological rather than utilitarian" (p. 131). See also Richard Ashcraft, "Locke's State of Nature: Historical Fact or Moral Fiction?" *American Political Science Review* 62 (1968): 898–915, esp. 898–900; Tully, chap. 1, but esp. pp. 28–30. And see chap. 1, note 19.

14. Contrast Laslett's claim that Locke does not provide the definition and analysis of important concepts in the *Second Treatise* that a reader of the *Essay* would expect to find there; Introduction to *Two Treatises,* pp. 96–97. For a few examples in support of my position note the definitions of political power (2T.3), state of nature (2T.19), state of war (2T.19), liberty (2T.22), slavery (2T.24), and usurpation (2T.197–98) and the distinction between the dissolution of society and the dissolution of government (2T.211–12 ff.).

ties under the natural law with moral argument, mixed modes and relations, and the capacity to reason from them to certain conclusions (Essay I.3.6, 13, II.28.8, IV.12.11; 2T.6). Thus, if Locke argues in the *Second Treatise* from sound premises and if his demonstration is carefully constructed, his conclusions ought to be as certain as the conclusion of a mathematical proof. The *Essay* contains the defense of the method of the *Two Treatises* in its defense of the possibility of demonstrative moral science.

Peter Laslett, editor of the critical edition of the *Two Treatises,* holds an opposing view of the relation between the two works.[15] He identifies the *Second Treatise* as a work of "policy," but he does so without any recognition of Locke's division of political studies into two parts, only one of which could be called "policy." In defense of his position, Laslett cites an entry in Locke's journals that makes the distinction between demonstrative knowledge of the "truths of mathematics and morality" (which Laslett misleadingly paraphrases as "the truths of mathematics") and knowledge of the "history of matter of fact," which is helpful in matters of "polity and prudence."[16] Laslett mistakenly assumes that what Locke says of "polity and prudence" must apply to the *Second Treatise* as a work on politics, and he concludes that empirical science, rather than philosophy, is Locke's model for his political writing.[17] He reaches this conclusion despite his own observation that the *Second Treatise* is a uniquely ahistorical work.[18] And he reaches this conclusion without considering the possibility that the *Second Treatise* might be a work of political morality and consequently belong to demonstrative science. In the same journal entry that Laslett relies on, Locke specifically includes justice, law, and man's duty to be just as subjects for demonstrative moral science, subjects certainly treated in the *Second Treatise.* The journal entry, taken in conjunction with Locke's division of political studies discussed above, seems rather to support the view that the *Second Treatise* is a work of political ethics that illustrates Locke's methodological approach to ethical argument as he describes it in the *Essay.*[19]

15. Laslett, Introduction to *Two Treatises*, pp. 92–105.
16. See 26 June 1681, in Aaron and Gibb, pp. 116–18; printed also in Lord Peter King, *The Life of John Locke with Extracts from His Correspondence, Journals and Common-Place Books*, 2 vols. (London: Henry Colburn and Richard Bentley, 1830), 1:224–28, dated 24 June 1681.
17. Laslett, Introduction to *Two Treatises*, p. 99.
18. Ibid., p. 91.
19. This view of the character of the *Second Treatise* is shared in varying degrees by Dunn, *Political Thought*, pp. 187, 198–99, 199 n. 1; Tarcov, "'Non-Lockean' Locke," pp. 130–40; Tully, pp. 7, 10–11, 28–30; and Yolton, *Compass*, pp. 181–95. See also Gough, pp. 6 n. 1, 18–22.

Laslett, however, considering the *Two Treatises* a work of policy, denies any methodological relation between the two works.[20] He goes further and argues that the *Two Treatises* and the *Essay* are incompatible because "the *Essay* has no room for natural law."[21] With this, Laslett joins an extensive debate among Locke scholars. The central issues in this debate are whether Locke's epistemology provides an adequate explanation for how men can know the natural law and whether it explains how men can know they are obligated to it. In terms of the relation between the *Essay* and the *Two Treatises*, the problem is whether Locke's claims for the possibility of a demonstrative morality undercut rather than support his argument from the natural law in the *Second Treatise*. And this problem is affected in turn by whether Locke's view of the law is taken to be a voluntarist or a rationalist one.

If the natural law is taken to be the expression of the will of the divine lawmaker, how are its dictates known unless they are promulgated to men through revelation or innate ideas? Locke's critics either argue that by attacking the doctrine of innate ideas Locke has left only sense and reflection as the clearly inadequate means by which men might know the natural law, or argue that Locke relies on the concepts of "self-evidence" and "intuition," which cannot be distinguished finally from the concept of "innateness." Locke's attack on innate ideas in the *Essay* is said to contradict his reliance on natural law in the *Two Treatises*.[22]

Alternatively, if the law of nature is taken to be the embodiment of rules of reason that can be known through unaided human reason, Locke still needs to show the source of our obligation to that law. Locke's analogy between demonstrations of mathematical truths and demonstrations of ethical truths is faulted on these grounds. Logical validity is not the same as moral obligation.[23] And if Locke replies that the natural law obliges men insofar as it is the

---

20. This is again surprising, since Laslett's view is that Locke's ultimate purpose in the *Essay* is to help men to know how to conduct themselves and that the *Two Treatises* is the only work he produced on how men should conduct themselves; Introduction to *Two Treatises*, p. 97.

21. Laslett, Introduction to *Two Treatises*, p. 94.

22. Sir James Fitzjames Stephen, *Horae Sabbaticae*, 2d ser. (London: Macmillan, 1892), pp. 150–54; Sir Leslie Stephen, *History of English Thought in the Eighteenth Century*, 2d ed., 2 vols. (London: Smith, Elder, 1881), 1:35–38; C. E. Vaughan, *Studies in the History of Political Philosophy*, 2 vols., ed. G. A. Little (Manchester: Manchester University Press, 1939), 1:163. See also Perry, p. 232.

23. Aaron, p. 264; Gibson, *Theory*, pp. 157–60; W. von Leyden, Introduction to *John Locke: Essays on the Law of Nature* (Oxford: Clarendon Press, 1954), p. 55; Yolton, *Compass*, pp. 168–69. See also J. Kemp, *Reason, Action and Morality* (New York: Humanities Press, 1964), pp. 18–19.

will of God enforced with sanctions in the afterlife, he must show that we can know without revelation that there is an afterlife with divine rewards and punishments.[24] Apparently contradictory treatments of the moral law, as divine command or as the dictates of reason, can be found throughout Locke's works from the early *Essays on the Law of Nature* to *On the Reasonableness of Christianity*. And many of Locke's interpreters focus their efforts on the need to explain the ambivalent and contradictory character of his treatment of these issues.[25]

There are also, however, a number of Locke scholars who have argued that the conflicts between Locke's epistemological claims and his reliance on natural law in the *Second Treatise* have been exaggerated by the attempts to categorize Locke as a "voluntarist" or a "rationalist." His position combines elements of both. As one scholar has written, "Locke agrees with the voluntarist that God's will is the source of obligation, but rejects the inference that the test of the validity of the natural law cannot be reason. He accepts the rationalist tenet that natural laws are discovered by reason, are wise and good by independent criteria, but he denies that this is the source of their binding force."[26] God's will is the source of obligation, but men can know their obligation to God through reason alone. Locke offers proofs for the existence of God and suggests the line of argument by which we might know our subjection to God's authority.[27] Moreover, Locke expressly denies that his attack on innate ideas in the *Essay* amounts to a rejection of natural law; the natural law can be known by "the use and due application of our natural faculties" (Essay I.3.13). Locke would not have found

24. Strauss, *Natural Right,* p. 204; see also Riley, pp. 442–48.

25. W. von Leyden, pp. 56–59, 67, 71–78 argues that Locke was aware of the contradictions and became increasingly rationalist as his thought developed, while Philip Abrams, Introduction to *John Locke: Two Tracts on Government* (Cambridge: Cambridge University Press, 1967), pp. 88–92, 108 n. 12, argues that the rationalist elements were subordinated to the voluntarist ones. Cox, pp. 1–105, Strauss, *Natural Right,* pp. 202–51, and idem, "Locke's Doctrine of Natural Law," *American Political Science Review* 52 (June 1958): 490–501, argue that the contradictions were deliberate and indicate Locke's politic effort to appear within the natural law tradition while adopting Hobbes's radical departure from it; and Dunn, *Political Thought,* pp. 25–26, 195, argues that Locke's religious faith linked the various competing elements in his thought. See also Gough, pp. 9–10, for a similar view.

26. Tully, p. 41. See also John Locke, *On the Reasonableness of Christianity as Delivered in the Scriptures,* edited by George Ewing (Chicago: Henry Regnery, Gateway Editions, 1965). "He [God] gave him [man] reason and with it a law, that cannot be otherwise than what reason should dictate, unless we should think that a reasonable creature should have an unreasonable law" (par. 252).

27. Essay I.4.9, IV.3.18, IV.10, IV.11.13, IV.13.3. See Gough, pp. 10–17; von Leyden, pp. 48–49, 146–59.

his claims for a demonstrative rational morality to be in direct conflict with his view of the natural law obliging men as subjects of God.[28]

In short, Locke would have been surprised by Laslett's remark that there is no room for natural law in the *Essay*. In fact, he responded to this issue in a letter to his friend Tyrrell. He wrote that his division of law in the *Essay* into three parts—divine law, civil law, and the law of opinion or reputation—did not exclude natural law, since natural law is a part of the divine law.[29] Locke maintained the same set of propositions in both the *Essay* and the *Two Treatises:* that there is a natural law that is reasonable; that God has equipped men with natural faculties suited to the task of discovering its contents; and that men are obligated to follow its dictates as they are the workmanship of the Supreme Being whose will it expresses.

This is not to say that Locke's case is persuasive and complete, but only that it is reasonable and serious. Locke's epistemological defense of the possibility of demonstrative moral knowledge in the *Essay* is not in obvious conflict with his reliance on natural law in the *Two Treatises*. There is no obstacle here to the view that the *Second Treatise* is to be read as an example of Lockean moral demonstration in the field of political ethics. Still, there are problems with Locke's epistemological argument itself that require further investigation to examine the extent to which Locke has shown that ethical knowledge of any kind is possible.[30]

28. For elaboration of these views and replies to authors cited in chap. 1, note 25, see Aaron, p. 266; Aarsleff; Gough, pp. 4, 10; Monson; Martin Seliger, "Locke's Natural Law and the Foundation of Politics," *Journal of the History of Ideas* 24 (July–September 1963): 337–54; Raghuveer Singh, "John Locke and the Theory of Natural Law," *Political Studies* 9 (1961): 105–18; Tully, pp. 35–45; Yolton, *Compass*, pp. 160–80; Yolton, "Locke on the Law of Nature."

29. See 4 August 1690, in King 1:366–73. See Essay II.28.8. Laslett cites this letter in defense of his position, remarking that "Locke fails to convince Tyrrell" (Introduction to *Two Treatises*, p. 94), but he does not present Locke's argument to the reader.

30. One further argument is raised in this dispute; that Locke's failure to write a demonstrative ethics implies a failure of his claim for the possibility of such a project. For Locke's quite different explanation see his letters to Molyneux, 20 September 1692 and 30 March 1696 in *The Works of John Locke*, 10th ed., 10 vols. (London: Churchill and Manship, 1801), 9:294–95, 377. And see Locke, *Reasonableness*, pars. 241–43 for Locke's account of the difficulties, including the political obstacles, that have stood in the way of discovering the complete law of nature, and particularly of making known its authoritative character on the basis of reason alone. See also chap. 1, note 57; Aarsleff, p. 264; Gibson, *Theory*, pp. 159–60; Kemp, p. 20; Yolton, *Compass*, pp. 169 ff. Unfortunately, we could not have Locke's comments on the relation between the *Two Treatises* and the *Essay* because he did not acknowledge authorship of the *Two Treatises* during his lifetime.

The Application and the Foundation of Moral Knowledge

In introducing the *Essay*, Locke makes the claim that the understanding, though limited, is sufficient to guide men's conduct. This claim can be supported only by a showing that the dichotomy can be bridged between certain knowledge of abstract moral principles and uncertain opinions concerning particular existences. The knowledge gained through demonstrative moral reasoning must be applicable in practice and the argument itself must be grounded in reality if Locke's claims for demonstrative moral science are to be maintained.

In epistemological terms the questions are, first, whether there is some relation between our knowledge of mixed modes and our knowledge of substances and, second, whether mixed modes are entirely arbitrary or are instead grounded somehow in experience. In political terms the questions are whether normative political theory can serve to guide political practice and whether theory itself has a secure foundation.

The adequacy of Locke's defense of the possibility of demonstrative moral science is called into question by the very basis of the distinction between our understanding of mixed modes and relations, on the one hand, and of substances, on the other. It seems that the understanding is limited in such a way that either it is capable of universal certainty, but only where its thoughts bear no relation to existing things, or its thoughts reflect real existences, but without universal certainty.[31] Throughout the discussion of mixed modes and relations, we have seen that the certainty of the propositions formed from such ideas depend upon their very arbitrariness. But without some relation of our ideas to reality, demonstrations constructed from those ideas could hardly be the source of useful knowledge. They would be mere castles in the air (Essay IV.4, IV.5).

An examination of these issues not only completes the consideration of the possibility of demonstrative, normative political theory, that is, of the method of the *Second Treatise*, but also raises the substantive question of the political consequences of Locke's epis-

---

31. "Where by the way we may take notice, that *universal Propositions*, of whose Truth or Falsehood we can have certain Knowledge, concern not *Existence;* and farther, that all *particular Affirmations or Negations*, that would not be certain if they were made general, are only concerning *Existence;* they declaring only the accidental Union or Separation of *Ideas* in Things existing, which in their abstract Natures, have no known necessary Union or Repugnancy" (Essay IV.9.1).

temology. The doctrine of the *Second Treatise* must take into account the limits of the rational capacities of men in its prescriptions
for their political life. In politics it is the civil law that serves as a
bridge between the realm of mixed modes and relations and that of
substances. As we have seen, there is a *"general Part of Civil-Law*
grounded upon Principles of Reason"* comprising knowledge of
natural rights, the foundations of political authority, and civil duties. The particular part of the civil law involves the application of
these general principles to the particular circumstances of a given
society.[32] The art of legislation involves both knowledge of the
principles of political right and power and the art of governing.
Legislation is the interpretation and application of the natural law
(see 2T.12, 87–89, 135). Because the civil law bridges principle and
practice, the problems raised in general terms by the epistemological duality of the *Essay* are also legislative problems, and it
is as legislative problems that they will be considered here.

First, if principles are to guide practice, our knowledge of mixed
modes and relations must be clearly related to our knowledge of
substances. Abstract moral propositions often include reference to
substances, but our inadequate knowledge of substances results in
species of substances that are necessarily somewhat arbitrary. Consequently, we may know the truth of the abstract proposition "No
man can be held as property, unless he has forfeited his rights as a
man," and we can recognize that truth in law, but the practical
result depends decisively on who is and who is not included in the
species "man." Men may share identical and clear notions of the
relation of property without agreement as to the things that may or
may not be related in this way (Essay II.25.4, II.28.19–20), and
consequently, without agreement as to the institution of slavery.
One commentator who discusses this issue remarks: "I can find no
basis in Locke's account of substances for criticizing someone who
chooses to define the essence of man in such a way as to exclude
Negroes or any other racial group."[33] Locke himself certainly believed that Negroes were men, else he would not have recommended their conversion to Christianity.[34] But on what basis can

32. Locke, "Some Thoughts Concerning Education," in *Educational Writings,*
pars. 185–86, pp. 294–95.
   33. Eugene F. Miller, "Locke on the Meaning of Political Language: The Teaching of the *Essay Concerning Human Understanding,*" *Political Science Reviewer* 9 (Fall
1979): 163–93, esp. 178 n.6.
   34. Instructions to Governor Nicholson of Virginia from the Board of Trade,
13 September 1698, Virginia Colonial Records Project, Virginia State Library, Richmond, Virginia, microfilm, classification no. COS/1359/266–303. See also chap. 2,
note 22 for further comments on Locke's views on slavery.

he defend his idea of the species "man" against any other if, as he tells us, species are man-made and cannot be tested against natural or real essences?

Locke shows both the difficulty of defining species of substances, particularly the human species, and the legislative or political problems that may result from this difficulty in his repeated discussion of changelings and monsters and how they ought to be treated. Because Locke stresses the disagreements that have arisen about the definition of the human species, one could get the impression that there is no basis whatever for choosing one definition over another, and consequently no basis for determining whether certain creatures ought to be baptized or even allowed to live.

A definition certainly cannot be chosen by identifying some essential characteristic of men. The very fact that men disagree in their ideas of the human species is cited by Locke as evidence that ideas of substances are not determined by natural essences (Essay III.3.14). Furthermore, he says, nature produces males without beards and bearded females, creatures with shapes like ours but hairy and without reason, "naturals," and cases of cross-breeding between female humans and mandrils. It is simply impossible to know whether these creatures are essentially different (Essay III.6.22–23, 39). On the basis of what we can know, there is no reason to prefer Aristotle's definition of man as *Animal rationale* to Plato's definition of man as *Animal implume bipes latis unguibus* (Essay III.6.26, III.10.17, 21, III.11.20). When the question is one of the proper signification of a word referring to a substance, Locke merely asks rhetorically, "Who shall be the Judge to determine?" (Essay III.9.13).

In fact, men do identify other members of their species primarily by shape.

> And whatever is talked of other definitions, ingenuous observation puts it past doubt, that the *Idea* in our Minds, of which the Sound *Man* in our Mouths is the Sign, is nothing else but of an Animal of such a certain Form: Since I think I may be confident, that whoever should see a Creature of his own Shape and Make, though it had no more reason all its Life than a *Cat* or a *Parrot*, would call him still a *Man*; or whoever should hear a *Cat* or a *Parrot* discourse, reason, philosophize, would call or think it nothing but a *Cat* or a *Parrot*; and say, the one was a dull irrational *Man*, and the other a very intelligent rational *Parrot*. (Essay II.27.8; see Essay III.6.2–III.11.20)

For this reason, those who do not nourish and preserve monstrous-looking infants are not considered murderers. Yet Locke himself clearly thinks that they ought to be (Essay III.6.26). Nonetheless, at the same time, indeed in the next paragraph, he remarks:

> And I imagine, none of the Definitions of the word *Man,* which we yet have, nor Descriptions of that sort of Animal, are so perfect and exact, as to satisfie a considerate inquisitive Person; much less to obtain a general Consent, and to be that which Men would every where stick by, in the Decision of Cases, and determining of Life and Death, Baptism or no Baptism, in Productions that might happen. (Essay III.6.27; see Essay III.6.26, III.11.20, IV.7.16–18)

Again, if Locke does not ground his own moral judgment in a true idea of the essential defining characteristics of humanity, on what basis does he judge?

Locke explicitly raises this problem of the uncertainty of our knowledge of substances in the context of defending his claim that *"Morality is capable of Demonstration,* as well as Mathematicks."

> Nor let any one object, that the names of Substances are often to be made use of in Morality, as well as those of Modes, from which will arise Obscurity. For as to Substances, when concerned in moral Discourses, their divers Natures are not so much enquir'd into, as supposed; *v.g.* when we say that *Man is subject to Law:* We mean nothing by *Man,* but a corporeal rational Creature: What the real Essence or other Qualities of that Creature are in this Case, is no way considered. And therefore, whether a Child or Changeling be a *Man* in a physical Sense, may amongst the Naturalists be as disputable as it will, it concerns not at all the *moral Man,* as I may call him, which is this immoveable unchangeable *Idea, a corporeal rational Being.* For were there a Monkey, or any other Creature to be found, that had the use of Reason, to such a degree, as to be able to understand general Signs, and to deduce Consequences about general *Ideas,* he would no doubt be subject to Law, and, in that Sense, be a Man, how much soever he differed in Shape from others of that Name. The Names of Substances, if they be used in them, as they should, can no more disturb Moral than they do Mathematical Discourses: Where, if the Mathematicians speak of a *Cube* or *Globe* of *Gold,* or any other Body, he has his clear setled *Idea,* which varies not, though it may, by mistake, be applied to a particular Body, to which it belongs not. (Essay III.11.16)

The imprecision of our ideas of substances does not disturb the truth of moral argument.

Locke's statement indicates the outlines for the solution to the problem we have been considering. With respect to subjection to the law, the question to be asked is not, Is this a Man? but Is this a corporeal rational Being? Is it an intelligent agent "capable of a

Law and Happiness and Misery?" (Essay II.27.26). It is certainly possible to argue reasonably that physical appearance, whether skin color or monstrous shape, is irrelevant to a determination of this question (Essay III.11.20). Similarly, one need not determine whether a changeling is a man to determine whether it ought to be baptized. It is sufficient to consider a changeling a changeling, and then to consider whether it might have an immortal soul. This is a question open to rational consideration, and Locke proceeds to question the assumptions behind the common opinion, the consistency of it, and whether there is a need for a human determination of the question at all (Essay IV.4.11–16).

In short, some qualities are essential not as defining characteristics of species, but with respect to the purpose and meaning of particular moral propositions. And the presence of these qualities in any particular thing can often be determined empirically or the probability estimated by reasoning and observation. If our moral ideas and the propositions built from them are clear in their meaning, their application will be less arbitrary than it at first appeared.

But we cannot eliminate all ambiguity. The problem is one of application, and Locke concedes in the quotation considered here that an idea may "by mistake, be applied to a particular Body, to which it belongs not." Even when the criterion in question is clearly rationality, for example, rather than membership in the species "man," nature may present us with examples of creatures possessing this quality in all degrees. On the one hand, nature does make similar things, and our ideas of substances are certainly not entirely arbitrary because they do group things with similar qualities; we can recognize, for example, that in general reason is a faculty in which men far surpass the beasts (Essay IV.17.1; but see Essay IV.16.12). But on the other hand, nature is not as precise as the boundaries of man-made species; the species are determined by our decision to group certain qualities under a single name and then to recognize certain individuals as possessing those qualities and others as not (Essay III.3.13, III.6.28–29). There are "gray areas" at the boundaries in considering species of substances, and here at some point a determination must be made that is no more than an approximate empirical judgment.

No matter how clear the law, or how clear the meaning of the substances referred to with respect to that law, there will be borderline cases that require the determination of a judge whose authority is accepted by the parties involved. The law prohibits driving automobiles while drunk; a judge may be required to determine whether a newly invented three-wheeled vehicle is an automobile under the law. This is a determination that can reasonably be made, but with reference to the purpose of the law, not with reference to the essential nature of the automobile. Certain penalties apply only to persons who can be considered responsible for their actions at the time of a crime. A judgment must be made on the basis of relevant facts concerning whether a given individual was "responsible." The application of moral principles in practice always involves an element of judgment, but it is not for that reason entirely arbitrary.

The problem of applying principles in practice is not limited to the difficulties caused by the character of our ideas of substances. Analogous difficulties arise with the application of our ideas of mixed modes to particulars.[35] Suppose the idea of a contract is clearly understood by all parties to be an exchange of promises. Suppose also that all parties understand that one has an obligation to honor one's contracts. This knowledge will be useless in regulating human affairs unless there is some agreement on what counts as a contract. How do you know when two people have one?

In this case, unlike the case of substances, there can be no empirical test for judging what belongs in the species "contract." Whether a handshake, a notarized document, or smoking a pipe together constitutes a contract is an entirely arbitrary determination. Locke remarks that a Swiss and an Indian in a state of nature with respect to one another may have a binding contract (2T.14). But they may have the same idea of what a contract means and of the obligation involved without the same idea of what act indicates that a contract has been made. Consequently, with no ill will on either side, a dispute may arise. The example indicates one of the functions of the civil law. Natural law principles are made operable among men by the establishment of an authority accepted by all concerned in matters that must be arbitrarily determined. The civil law embodies the general moral principle that contracts must be kept, but a variety of conventions, the particular part of the civil law, define what a contract is in practice. The variety of practices among human communities in this respect is not an indication that there is no natural law.

But how much variety is acceptable in our ideas of mixed modes and relations themselves? Can one really speak of just and unjust laws if ideas like murder, adultery, theft, and patricide are arbitrary? "For what greater connexion in Nature has the *Idea* of a

35. See 1T.128, lines 15–18.

Man, than the *Idea of a Sheep with Killing,* that this is made a particular Species of Action, signified by the word *Murder,* and the other not?" (Essay III.5.5–6). It seems to make a great deal of difference whether the laws distinguish between killing men and killing sheep, but here Locke implies that there is no natural foundation for such a distinction. The question is no longer the application of moral principles in practice, but our second question, the foundation of the principles themselves.

Throughout the *Essay,* Locke appears to contradict himself on this issue. On the one hand, he speaks of a natural law accessible to unaided human reason, of the possibility of correct moral judgments, and of the difference between virtue and vice (Essay I.3.6, 13, II.2.21, 46–47, II.28.8, 20, II.32.17). In his preface to the fourth edition of the *Essay,* Locke replies to a critic of his work that anyone reading it carefully would know that he believes the nature of right and wrong to be "eternal and unalterable." On the other hand, Locke's critic may be excused for mistaking his meaning and thinking that Locke went about to "make *Vertue Vice* and *Vice Vertue*" (note to Essay II.28.11). It is an understandable error considering Locke's emphasis on the arbitrary character of our ideas of mixed modes and relations, the absence of any patterns in nature for these ideas, the freedom with which men make them, and the variety of moral ideas that are found in the laws and languages of different nations (Essay II.32.5, III.4,17, III.5.5–8, III.6.51, III.9.7).

The problem arises in part because Locke does not systematically discuss how to distinguish between right and wrong moral ideas and propositions in the *Essay.* Instead, he discusses how men do make moral ideas and propositions. Referring to his chapter on moral relations in a letter written in response to Tyrrell's criticisms, Locke wrote that "it was my business there to show, how man came by moral ideas or notions . . . it is not of concernment to my purpose in that chapter whether they be as much as true or no."[36] The *Essay* is an epistemological work that includes consideration of moral knowledge, but it is not itself a treatise on ethics. Locke discusses directly there how it is that men come to have a variety of moral ideas. It is more difficult to discover his view of the grounds for distinguishing among them.

In the broadest terms, the charge is that Locke's nominalism and empiricism yield only relativism. This charge takes several particu-

36. See 4 August 1690 in King 1:366–73, pp. 370–71.

lar forms. Locke's claim is that men may have demonstrative certain knowledge by reasoning from ideas constructed as they see fit. The idiosyncratic character of these ideas leads to a charge of relativism in its least serious form: two men may collect entirely different sets of ideas but each may signify his set by the word "justice." Each, then, seems to have a perfectly adequate idea of a mixed mode. The confusion and misunderstanding that arise when men use the same word for a mixed mode without sharing the same idea, or vice versa, is a verbal confusion more likely to occur with mixed modes than with other sorts of ideas, precisely because these ideas are constructions of the mind and refer to nothing with an external real existence that can be used to illustrate the idea. For this reason, laws and biblical texts, which use many words referring to mixed modes, are open to endless interpretation. And the situation is exacerbated by scholars and lawyers who display their cleverness by complicating the sense of things. A prince who is clearly understood when he speaks directly to his servants can be almost impossible to understand when he speaks to his subjects through the law. The difficulty at this level is one that Locke maintains may be resolved by care in defining the terms of moral discourse and of legislation. It is a problem of clear communication and not a problem of the validity of moral reasoning. If one man calls "justice" what another calls "injustice," their deductions from their shared idea will be the same despite the discrepancy in word usage.

> One thing more we are to take notice of, That where GOD, or any other Law-maker, hath defined any Moral Names, there they have made the Essence of that Species to which that Name belongs; and there it is not safe to apply or use them otherwise: But in other cases 'tis bare impropriety of Speech to apply them contrary to the common usage of the Country. But yet even this too disturbs not the certainty of that Knowledge, which is still to be had by a due contemplation and comparing of those even nick-nam'd *Ideas.* (Essay IV.4.10; see Essay III.9.9, III.10.12, III.32.9–12)

A second and more serious charge arises from the observation that men, constructing their ideas as they see fit, may reason consistently from their ideas and reach conclusions that are true in the sense that they are consistent, yet their conclusions may be useless and without relation to reality. Locke's criterion for knowledge and truth appears to be only the agreement or disagreement between the ideas or propositions in question. But if consistency is the sole criterion, it is difficult to see how one can distinguish real knowledge from the elaborate constructions of a madman or a dreamer (Essay IV.4.1, IV.5.7–8).[37]

The certainty of our reasoning from mixed modes depends on and is inseparable from their abstract character. And Locke maintains that it is precisely because these ideas are abstract constructions that they can also provide knowledge of reality. Because ideas of mixed modes are patterns formed in the mind rather than imperfect copies of existing things, there can be no false representation of reality involved in the idea of a mixed mode. Instead our knowledge of mixed modes gives us knowledge of reality whenever a real event or existing thing corresponds to the pattern in question. Again, the model is mathematics: if it is true of a three-sided closed figure that the sum of its angles is the same as two right angles, the same will be true of any triangular object that does in fact exist. If it is true of murder that it deserves death, it will be true of any action occurring that fits the definition of murder: "And hence it follows, that *moral Knowledge* is as *capable of real Certainty*, as Mathematicks" (Essay IV.4.2–8). The certainty of our knowledge and the truth of our propositions do not themselves depend on whether there is any existing thing to which they correspond.

The problem appears to be due not so much to the abstract character of ideas of mixed modes as to their arbitrary character. In other words, the central problem is not whether knowledge of the general proposition that "murder deserves death" is knowledge that can be usefully applied to real situations. The problem is whether we can be said to make the idea of the mixed mode "murder" correctly or incorrectly. Does it, or should it, mean "the killing of an innocent man" rather than, for example, "the killing of a sheep"? And on what basis can we conclude from its definition and its relation to other ideas that "murder deserves death"?

Locke remarks in introducing his own argument in the *Essay*, "At least, if mine prove a Castle in the Air, I will endeavor it should be all of a piece, and hang together." But he also claims that his is a construction with a firm foundation in principles that are true. In fact, Locke defines madmen as those who reason consistently, but from false first principles (Essay II.11.13). Locke warns his readers of the dangers of accepting false first principles as the foundation for one's knowledge and recommends instead that men begin their thinking by comparing clear and distinct ideas (Essay IV.12.4–8,

---

37. See Gibson, *Theory*, pp. 321–26; Perry; Woolhouse, *Locke*, p. 128; idem, *Locke's Philosophy*, pp. 120–27, 143–49; and Yolton, *Compass*, pp. 196–223 for discussions of Locke's conception of mixed modes and the problem of their relation to reality.

IV.17.12). He says of his principles that he "can only *appeal* to Mens own unprejudiced *Experience,* and Observation, whether they be true, or no" (Essay I.4.25). He suggests that ideas of mixed modes and arguments from them can be tested against experience; that they are not, after all, entirely arbitrary.

Mixed modes are related to experience in a number of ways. First, they are complex ideas composed of simple ideas that reflect experience directly. Moreover, these simple ideas must be combined in a consistent way so that the resulting combination is something that could possibly exist.[38] In addition, the beginning points of our arguments and demonstrations are often our reflections on the relations between observations we make of the world. Mixed modes are made as they are by men who use them in living with other men and in living in the world.

Ideas of mixed modes are arbitrarily made, but in this context the term "arbitrary" does not mean "unreasonable." "Arbitrary" is used here as the opposite of "necessary" or "determined." In naming mixed modes, the mind acts freely, without conforming to natural necessities. But in so doing the mind does not act "without reason . . . it is done by the free choice of the mind, pursuing its own ends" (Essay II.5.6–7).[39] There are reasons why ideas develop as they do; they are useful to men in pursuing their goals. For example, we can recognize that to establish punishments for killing men will serve to preserve the members of the community, while at the same time we can recognize that killing sheep also serves that end. Reflecting on these observations leads to the conclusion that killing men is deserving of punishment (2T.4, 6) while killing sheep is not.[40]

We invent a distinct term, "murder," and hence a distinct idea of a mixed mode, in order to assist in communicating the intention to punish certain actions. Yet societies may not all do this in the same way, and this is another sense in which the creation of mixed modes is arbitrary. For example, some societies may have different ideas

38. See James Gibson, "John Locke's Theory of Mathematical Knowledge and of a Possible Science of Ethics," *Mind* 5 (1896): 38–59, esp. 43, 57.

39. Compare pp. 72–73 below on the meaning of "arbitrary" as it is used in the *Second Treatise.* See Essay IV.20.16 for an additional example of Locke's usage of "arbitrary" as contrary to "necessary."

40. The magistrate may forbid the slaughter of livestock "for some while, in order to the increasing the stock of cattle that had been destroyed by an extraordinary murrain," that is, to better serve the preservation of the community. John Locke, *A Letter Concerning Toleration,* 2d ed. (Indianapolis: Bobbs-Merrill, 1955), p. 40. The value of preservation can be known both from our experience of our own desires and from our relation to God, which can also be known from reflections on our experience. These points are discussed further in the remainder of this chapter.

and terms for stealing horses or camels than for stealing other things, if those animals have some special importance. But the justice of punishing theft, and punishing theft of some things more severely than theft of others, is not affected by such distinctions.

Species are made as they are because certain distinct ideas are useful for facilitating communication in the conduct of our common affairs.

> Mankind have fitted their Notions and Words to the use of common Life, and not to the truth and extent of Things. For 'tis certain, that in reality, the Relation is the same, betwixt the Begetter, and the Begotten, in the several Races of other Animals, as well as Men: But yet 'tis seldom said, This Bull is the Grandfather of such a Calf. . . . It is very convenient, that by distinct Names, these Relations should be observed, and marked out in Mankind, there being occasion, both in Laws, and other Communications one with another, to mention and take notice of Men, under these Relations: From whence also arise the Obligations of several Duties among Men. . . . And 'tis no wonder Men should have framed no Names for those Things they found no occasion to discourse of. From whence it is easy to imagine, why, as in some Countries, they may not have so much as the Name for a Horse; and in others, . . . they may have not only Names for particular Horses, but also of their several Relations of Kindred one to another. (Essay II.28.2)

As human purposes vary, the complex ideas that can be expressed in a given language will also vary. For the same reason, jargon develops within specialized occupations (Essay II.15.7, II.32.5, III.6.51).

Tully emphasizes the social context of the use of mixed modes in dealing with the problem of the reality of moral knowledge. Mixed modes provide real knowledge because they are "already constitutive of human action and association."[41] But moral language varies from one society to another; there are various social "realities." This is not sufficient to solve the problem of the relative character of moral ideas. There must be some nonarbitrary standpoint from which to judge moral words.[42] Tully's solution is to identify a particular view of man's relation to God as that stand-

41. Tully, p. 26.
42. See Robert R. Albritton, "The Politics of Locke's Philosophy," *Political Studies* 24 (September 1976): 253–67, esp. 259–60. See also 1T.58–59, where Locke attacks custom as a standard for morality, citing the variety of horrible practices found in different cultures. Nature is the appropriate standard: adultery, sodomy, and incest are sinful because they "cross the main intention of Nature, which willeth the increase of Mankind." See also Yolton, *Compass*, pp. 185, 217–23.

point in Locke's work.[43] Alternatively, the standpoint might be found in knowledge of human nature. Mixed modes must be useful to men, and so we can begin with what all men naturally need.[44]

In Locke's view, both our direct experience of human goals and desires and our understanding of our existence as part of divine creation contribute to our understanding of moral laws. The two are related grounds for our knowledge of morality. The relation between them is illustrated in a brief argument that Locke presents in the *First Treatise* for man's property in the creatures of the earth (for the right to kill and eat sheep, for example). God made man with "a strong desire of Preserving his Life," furnished the world with life's necessities, and gave man "Sense and Reason" so that he might use the things of the world to preserve himself. This is God's "design," that men might "live and abide for some time on the Face of the Earth." So, following his "natural inclination" to preservation, man also follows "the Will of his Maker" and therefore has a "right to make use of those Creatures" (1T.86).[45] God gave all men certain desires and purposes and certain faculties by which they might seek the fulfillment of them, and these are the touchstones by which the moral ideas we create and the demonstrations we draw from them can be judged.

To the extent that men pursue different goals, or the same goals under different conditions, their ideas and their discourse will vary. To the extent that there are natural human purposes, ends common to all mankind, and some indication in experience of what they are, ideas of mixed modes and relations, though arbitrary in the sense elaborated here, nonetheless bear some relation to natural standards.

The context for Locke's discussion of moral knowledge is his view of nature as rational and purposive.[46] Locke understands our

43. Tully, pp. 34–35. See also Dunn, *Political Thought*, pp. 96–98.
44. John W. Danford, *Wittgenstein and Political Philosophy: A Reexamination of the Foundations of Social Science* (Chicago: University of Chicago Press, 1978), pp. 63–69. The disagreement between Tully and Danford leads them to opposite conclusions concerning Locke's relation to Hobbes on this point. See Tully, pp. 29–30.
45. See Cox, p. 56; Strauss, *Natural Right*, p. 216, on conflicts between the dictates of natural law and of divine positive law (biblical revelation) on questions such as this, and Yolton's reply, "Locke on the Law of Nature."
46. "That the universe is purposive is a regulative belief in all Locke's [writings]" (Tully, p. 38). See Dunn, *Political Thought*, pp. 87–88, 95; Yolton, *Compass*, p. 17. Richard Ashcraft, "Faith and Knowledge in Locke's Philosophy," in *John Locke: Problems and Perspectives*, ed. John W. Yolton (Cambridge: Cambridge University Press, 1969), pp. 194–223, charges Locke with circular reasoning: with concluding from our perception of an ordered natural world that there is a deity who created it

ideas and our language as functional, and this view is in keeping with his view of nature altogether. There is nothing in nature that is useless, and whatever rational faculties we have, we have because they are useful to us.

> The infinite wise Contriver of us, and all things about us hath fitted our Senses, Faculties, and Organs, to the conveniences of Life, and the Business we have to do here. . . . But were our senses alter'd, and made much quicker and acuter, the appearance and outward Scheme of things . . . would be inconsistent with our Being, or at least well-being in this part of the Universe, which we inhabit. . . . If our Sense of Hearing were but 1000 times quicker than it is, how would a perpetual noise distract us. (Essay II.23.12; see Essay IV.11.8)

> We may, I think, from the Make of an *Oyster,* or *Cockle,* reasonably conclude, that it has not so many, nor so quick senses, as a Man, or several other Animals; nor if it had, would it, in that state and incapacity of transferring it self from one place to another, be better'd by them. What good would Sight and Hearing do to a Creature, that cannot move it self, to, or from the Objects, wherein at a distance it perceives Good or Evil? And would not quickness of Sensation, be an Inconvenience to an Animal, that must lie still where Chance has once placed it; and there receive the afflux of colder or warmer, clean or foul Water, as it happens to come to it? (Essay II.9.13)

Locke's central claim in the *Essay,* that our capacity to reason is sufficient to guide us in the conduct of our lives, is an expression of his view of the natural world as a world where everything has its function. To take a contrary position and postulate innate practical principles as the source of moral knowledge is to imply that our rational faculties are superfluous at best. To take the position of the skeptics that our rational capacities are inadequate because they are limited, or to despair of reason and rely on revelation or miracles, is also to imply an imperfect creation of the natural world. Locke's view of reason is perfectly compatible with his view of nature as rationally constructed. Since our ideas and words are constructed to serve our purposes, there is a natural foundation for these ideas because there are recognizable, universal human ends.

---

and concluding from our knowledge of the deity that his creation must be orderly and harmonious (pp. 202–8). And Spragens argues that ultimately Locke cannot explain how a natural order could be known through sensations, because Locke understands sensations as abstract, discrete, and atomistic in accordance with the corpuscular model of nature (pp. 207–13).

Moral Knowledge and Moral Freedom

Locke maintains that common human ends govern our construction of moral ideas. Certain actions are almost always seen as
virtues or vices because they are recognized as beneficial or harmful to the maintenance of society.

> For God, having, by an inseparable connexion, joined *Virtue* and
> publick Happiness together; and made the Practice thereof, neces-
> sary to the preservation of Society, and visibly *beneficial* to all, with
> whom the Virtuous Man has to do; it is no wonder, that every one
> should, not only allow, but recommend, and magnifie those Rules to
> others, from whose observance of them, he is sure to reap Advan-
> tage to himself. (Essay I.3.6)

> For since nothing can be more natural, than to encourage with Es-
> teem and Reputation that, wherein every one finds his Advantage;
> and to blame and discountenance the contrary: 'tis no Wonder, that
> Esteem and Discredit, Virtue and Vice, should in a great measure
> every-where correspond with the unchangeable Rule of Right and
> Wrong, which the Law of God hath established; there being nothing,
> that so directly, and visibly secures, and advances the general Good
> of Mankind in this World, as Obedience to the Laws, he has set them,
> and nothing that breeds such Mischiefs and Confusion, as the ne-
> glect of them. And therefore Men, without renouncing all Sense and
> Reason, and their own Interest, which they are so constantly true to,
> could not generally mistake, in placing their Commendation and
> Blame on that side, that really deserved it not. (Essay II.28.11)

Interest, duty, and general happiness correspond in such a way
that we can recognize what is right and wrong on the basis of experience. There is a natural foundation for practical principles of
social behavior because "Nature, I confess, has put into Man a desire of Happiness, and an aversion to Misery" (Essay I.3.3) and
because the "Law of God" is meant to secure general happiness.[47]

On the basis, then, of natural inclinations and with a minimum
of rational calculation, even gangs of robbers recognize that they
must "keep Faith and Rules of Equity amongst themselves," since
"Justice and Truth are the common ties of Society" and without
them no society will last (Essay I.3.2). It seems that, because human
purposes correspond to divine purposes for men, men can arrive at

47. See John Locke, MS. c.28 f.3, 26 August 1678, "That vertue is but the name
of such actions as are most conducing to the good of the society and are therefore by
the society recommended to the people seems to me very plain." But see also MS.
c.28 f.1, "Lex Humana," 25 February 1676, "There are virtues and vices antecedent
to and abstract from society."

true moral principles for governing their conduct among themselves by beginning with their natural inclinations. God rewards men for using their faculties to preserve life and pursue happiness, and men are all inclined to do just that (see Essay IV.14.2). Whatever tends to increase human happiness is good.

Our ideas of good and evil are formed according to natural indicators of what will serve our happiness—namely, pleasure and pain. Those things that produce pleasure in us are the things we call "good," and those that produce pain we call "evil." Pleasure and pain are simple ideas associated with both sensation and reflection, and so good and evil, understood in this way, are also simple ideas and not mixed modes or relations. Pleasure and pain are the source of motivation. They prompt us to act and to think (pain more strongly than pleasure), and their promptings direct us away from things dangerous to our preservation and toward things that secure our well-being (Essay II.7.3–4, II.20, II.21.42). To the extent that we reason from moral ideas founded in pleasure and pain, demonstrative ethics has a natural foundation and is not a mere construction.

But Locke also indicates some of the reasons for the insufficiency of this hedonistic standard for morality. First, men can discover on this basis the minimum rules of conduct that are necessary to maintain social life, but there is some question whether anything beyond this minimum can be established in this way. Calculations of social utility might give a society a workable moral code that nonetheless sanctioned infanticide or cannibalism in certain circumstances (Essay I.3.9–10). Second, while men may all recognize the necessity of keeping contracts, for example, they will offer different reasons for the rule. A Christian will say that God requires it, a Hobbist that the public requires it, a heathen philosopher that virtue requires it. The three expect disobedience to be punished eternally, or by the civil authority, or by the condemnation of one's peers, respectively. These various opinions arise "according to the different sorts of Happiness" men consider (Essay I.3.5–6). There are different sorts of pleasures and pains, and men do not always judge them correctly. Often men fear social censure more than civil or divine punishment, for example (Essay II.28.12; see Essay I.3.25). In addition, every rule of morality is broken by some society somewhere, except those necessary to maintain society, and even these are broken between societies.

At bottom, pain and pleasure alone cannot provide the sole foundation for moral knowledge, and they certainly cannot provide the sole foundation for obedience to moral principles.

Nature, I confess, has put into Man a desire of Happiness, and an aversion to Misery: These indeed are innate practical Principles, which (as practical Principles ought) do continue constantly to operate and influence all our Actions, without ceasing . . . but these are Inclinations of the Appetite to good, not Impressions of truth on the Understanding. (Essay I.3.3)

Principles of Actions indeed there are lodged in Men's Appetites, but these are so far from being innate Moral Principles, that if they were left to their full swing, they would carry Men to the overturning of all Morality. Moral Laws are set as a curb and restraint to these exorbitant Desires, which they cannot be but by Rewards and Punishments, that will over-balance the satisfaction any one shall propose to himself in the breach of the Law. (Essay I.3.13)

If men judge of pleasure and pain differently, and if pleasure and pain lead us both toward and away from moral action, then pleasure and pain cannot be the natural foundations by which we can construct our moral ideas and chains of reasoning. The principles of action indicated by our natural inclinations and appetites fall far short of innate, self-evident moral truths.

Locke denies that there are innate moral principles imprinted upon the conscience, and he also denies that there is nothing beyond positive law. Instead, he argues that there is a natural law and that men can come to know their moral obligations under that law through their natural faculties of reason. To know a moral truth means to know it as a command, as a duty, and this requires the idea of law, of a lawmaker, and of reward and punishment (Essay I.3.1, 4, 12–13). Calculations of convenience and social utility are not themselves moral principles; something more than the idea of their usefulness is required to establish these rules of action as moral duties. It is one thing to know that certain rules of behavior are conducive to social harmony and that it is useful to preach that men ought to conform their actions to these rules. It is quite another thing to know that you yourself have a duty to practice what you preach.[48]

Moral good and evil are thus distinguished from simple good and evil in the following way:

Good and evil, as hath been shewn . . . are nothing but Pleasure or Pain, or that which occasions, or procures Pleasure or Pain to us.

48. See Locke, *Reasonableness*, pars. 241–42. "The law of nature is the law of convenience too, and it is no wonder that those men of parts and studious virtue . . . should, by meditation, light on the right, even from the observable convenience and beauty of it, without making out its obligation from the true principles of the law of nature and foundations of morality" (par. 242).

> *Morally Good and Evil* then, is only the Conformity or Disagreement of our voluntary Actions to some Law, whereby Good or Evil is drawn on us, from the Will and Power of the Law-maker; which Good and Evil, Pleasure and Pain, attending our observance, or breach of the Law, by the Decree of the Law-maker, is that we call *Reward* and *Punishment*. (Essay II.28.5)

Good and evil are simple ideas, but moral good and evil involve the idea of an action, which is a mixed mode, as well as the idea of the relation of the action to a rule, which is a particular type of relation—moral relation.[49] And though all mixed modes and relations are ideas composed of simple ideas from sensation or reflection, the composition is a construction fashioned by the understanding (Essay II.28, II.32.17). Moral knowledge and moral action are possible only through the operations of reason in conjunction with the "inclinations of the Appetite to good" (Essay I.3.3).

Full knowledge of our moral duties requires the knowledge that there is a God who rules men and who rewards them as their actions accord with his law, knowledge of the content of that law, and in addition the capacity to govern our conduct according to that knowledge.[50] According to Locke, men can obtain knowledge of God and of their obligation to him by fairly simple reasoned demonstration, beginning with the knowledge of themselves and the knowledge that they must have been created. Knowledge of the law can also be had through rational faculties; revealed scripture is not required. Reasoning from ideas of mixed modes grounded in experience and observation, it is possible to demonstrate that certain rules of behavior serve the preservation and well-being of mankind, which is to say, certain rules serve God's purpose and the preservation of his workmanship (Essay IV.3.18, IV.10, IV.11.14, IV.13.3, IV.18; 2T.2, 6, 7).

Locke's position combines rationalist, theological, and utilitarian elements, and critics of Locke see these elements in unresolved ten-

---

49. Miller notes that good and evil are simple ideas but does not note the distinction between good and evil and moral good and evil; pp. 168, 171.

50. See John Locke, MS. c.28 f.141, "Ethica": "The originall and foundation of all law is dependency. . . . If man were independent he could have noe law but his own will noe end but himself. He would be a god to himself and the satisfaction of his own will the sole measure and end of all his actions." See also John Locke, MS. c.28 f.152, "Of Ethick in General": "To establish morality therefore upon its proper basis and such foundations as may carry an obligation with them we ought first to prove a law which always supposes a lawmaker, one that has a superiority . . . and also a power to reward and punish. . . . The next thing then to show is that there are certain rules, certain dictates which it is his will all men should conform their actions to and that this will of his is sufficiently promulgated and made known to all mankind."

sion with one another.[51] The issue of the relation between the *Essay* and the *Two Treatises* is raised in this context as well. The utilitarian and hedonistic elements of the *Essay* are said to conflict with the argument from natural law in the *Two Treatises*. In Locke's view, what is right and what is useful are related. God governs men according to rational laws whose end is the general happiness of mankind. Consequently what is right is also useful, but it is not right simply because it is useful.[52] Moreover, Locke's discussion of pleasure and pain is not a discussion of a hedonistic ethics but a description of the mechanism of motivation in men. The distinction between the simple ideas of good and evil and the complex ideas of moral good and evil is a significant one. As in my previous discussion of the relation of the *Essay* and the *Two Treatises*, the rationalist criterion of right must be distinguished from the theological ground of obligation, but here both must also be distinguished from the hedonistic psychology of motivation. Reason can tell a man what is right; his relationship to God is the source of his obligation to do what is right; and he will be motivated to do what is right by his expectations of painful or pleasant consequences of his actions.[53]

Locke shows the conjunction of the operations of reason with the inclinations of pleasure and pain most clearly in his discussion of man's capacity to govern the will. Moral action requires not only knowledge of the good and knowledge of God, but also the capacity to direct the will according to that knowledge. Will is the power to prefer one thought or action over another. Freedom is a different power, the power to think or act as we prefer. Once this is understood, it becomes clear that to ask "whether Man's *Will* be free" is as unintelligible as to ask "whether his Sleep be Swift, or his Vertue square" (Essay II.21.14). The question to be asked instead is, What determines the will? (Essay II.21.1–29).

Locke's reply to this question is that the mind, moved by uneasiness, determines the will. Men are so constituted by nature that they are moved by pleasures and pains, desire and uneasiness.

---

51. Aaron, pp. 256–69; Gough, pp. 16–17; Kemp, pp. 24–26; Åke Petzäll, "Ethics and Epistemology in John Locke's *Essay Concerning Human Understanding*," *Götesbörgs Högskolas Årsskrift* 43 (1937): 5–83, esp. 82; Spragens, pp. 203–13; James Stephen, p. 153; Leslie Stephen, 2d ed., pp. 135–44; Strauss, *Natural Right*, pp. 226–30; for the argument that Locke is consistently utilitarian see A. P. Brogan, "John Locke and Utilitarianism," *Ethics* 69 (January 1959): 79–93.
52. See chap. 1, note 48.
53. Seliger, *Liberal Politics*, p. 67; Singh, p. 113; Tully, p. 47; Yolton, *Compass*, pp. 145–47; idem, "Locke on the Law of Nature," p. 491.

> And thus we see that our Allwise Maker, suitable to our constitution and frame, and knowing what it is that determines the *Will*, has put into Man the *uneasiness* of hunger and thirst, and other natural desires, that return at their Seasons, to move and determine their *Wills*, for the preservation of themselves, and the continuation of their Species. (Essay II.21.34)

Apparently God operates through the basic natural fact that there is no motivation without uneasiness. But one need not conclude from the recognition of this fact that men are motivated by pleasures and pains in such a way that they are simply caught up in a chain of natural necessities.

Men are also given the natural capacity to reason, a capacity that gives them a measure of control over their desires. But reason alone has no power to move men. If the mere knowledge and contemplation of a great good that we do not at present enjoy were enough to move men to action, there would be no need for pain and uneasiness to "set us on work" (Essay II.21.34). In addition,

> Were the *will* determin'd by the views of good, as it appears in Contemplation greater or less to the understanding, which is the State of all absent good . . . I do not see how it could ever get loose from the infinite eternal Joys of Heaven, once propos'd and consider'd as possible. (Essay II.21.38)

It would be difficult indeed to explain why men choose evil if knowledge of the good were simply sufficient to determine the will. Furthermore,

> But all absent good does not at any time make a necessary part of our present *happiness*, nor the absence of it make a part of our *misery*. If it did, we should be constantly and infinitely miserable; there being infinite degrees of happiness, which are not in our possession. (Essay II.12.44)

The knowledge that there is a great good capable of producing great happiness will not affect our conduct without the knowledge that that good is essential to our own happiness. We must be able to raise a desire in ourselves for the good in question (Essay II.21.34–44).

Because men are motivated by uneasiness, reason can govern our conduct to the extent that it can effect that uneasiness. According to Locke, reason can both influence what desires we have and allow us to weigh them in relation to each other before we act.

> And thus, by a due consideration and examining any good pro-
> posed, it is in our power, to raise our desires, in a due proportion to
> the value to that good, whereby in its turn, and place, it may come to
> work upon the *will, and be pursued.* (Essay II.21.46)

Men can educate their desires:

> In this we should take pains to suit the relish of our Minds to the true
> intrinsick good or ill, that is in things; and not permit an allow'd or
> supposed possible great and weighty good to slip out of our
> thoughts, without leaving any relish, any desire of its self there, till,
> by a due consideration of its true worth, we have formed appetites in
> our Minds suitable to it, and made ourselves uneasie in the want of it,
> or in the fear of losing it. (Essay II.21.53)

There is a kind of partnership between the operation of the understanding on the one hand and the operation of pleasure and pain
on the other. Pleasure and pain are natural indicators of good and
evil, but they are not sufficient. Reasoning is required to discover
the "true intrinsick good or ill, that is in things." But such a discovery remains ineffective unless it forms expectations of pleasure and
pain that determine the preference of the will.

The capacity to educate our desires is coupled with the capacity
to suspend action and weigh our desires in relation to one another.

> There being in us a great many *uneasinesses* always soliciting, and
> ready to determine the *will,* it is natural, as I have said, that the
> greatest, and most pressing should determine the *will* to the next
> action; and so it does for the most part, but not always. For the mind
> having in most cases, as is evident in Experience, a power to *suspend*
> the execution and satisfaction of any of its desires, and so all, one
> after another, is at liberty to consider the objects of them; examine
> them on all sides, and weigh them with others. In this lies the liberty
> Man has; and from the not using of it right comes all that variety of
> mistakes, errors, and faults which we run into . . . whilst we precipi-
> tate the determination of our *wills,* and engage too soon before due
> *Examination.* To prevent this we have a power to *suspend* the prosecu-
> tion of this or that desire, as every one daily may Experiment in
> himself. This seems to me the source of all liberty; in this seems to
> consist that, which is (as I think improperly) call'd *Free will* . . . and
> when, upon due *Examination,* we have judg'd, we have done our
> duty, all that we can, or ought to do, in pursuit of our happiness; and
> 'tis not a fault, but a perfection of our nature to desire, will, and act
> according to the last result of a fair *Examination.* (Essay II.21.47)[54]

54. Compare Hobbes, p. 127.

Because we have the capacity to govern the will according to reason, we have the duty to do so.[55] We have a responsibility to use our rational capacities, and we can be held accountable for failures of moral judgment. Ill-considered and precipitate action is a misuse of our freedom. The end and use of our liberty is to act only after a fair examination of the consequences of our actions for our happiness (Essay II.21, 47–48, 56, IV.12.11–12, IV.14.2).

Freedom is thus inseparable from the capacity to reason. Understanding would be useless if we could not determine the will according to its judgments, and the freedom to determine the will would be useless without understanding to guide our choice. To subject ourselves to reason in this way is not a limitation of our freedom, but the fulfillment of it. If this were not so, only fools and madmen would be free. Liberty is distinguished from license: it is self-government according to the laws of reason.

Further, that reason cannot operate directly on the will, but instead must raise a desire in us for the greater good, is also not a defect of our nature. We can suspend action, consider the consequences of various possibilities, create a desire in ourselves for the greater good, and act accordingly. We are indeed motivated by pleasure and pain and a calculation of the greatest pleasure, but this is a fact of our nature. And to calculate correctly is the perfection of it (Essay II.21.48–52, 67).

There is nothing wrong in being moved to action by pleasure and pain, so long as one is moved by the right pleasures and pains; and ultimately this means by the expectation of reward and punishment in the afterlife (Essay II.21.70). Men are rewarded in the afterlife to the extent that their conduct on earth accords with the law of nature, the law of reason, the law of God. What this means concretely is that men are rewarded as they exercise their faculties to secure their preservation and happiness in this life without interfering with other men's efforts to do the same (2T.6).[56] Similarly, that all men have the capacity to govern themselves according to the dictates of their reason is an indication that they are meant to submit themselves to self-government, to exercise this freedom. Preservation and freedom are basic elements of the natural law

55. See Tully, p. 37; von Leyden, p. 46.
56. See John Locke, MS. c.28 f.3, 15 July 1678. Locke writes here that men are under obligations that beasts are not because God gave us knowledge of ourselves and we have our faculties for a purpose. Since we have the faculties for preserving society and we cannot subsist without it, we know that God obliges us to act so as to preserve society.

that men can discover through the use of unaided reason. To the extent that our mixed modes and relations are constructed to serve our natural purposes and to suit our natural faculties, they are not divorced from reality and experience.

Conclusion: Reason and Politics

A great deal more would have to be said and demonstrated before Locke's position could be considered a complete and persuasive ethical theory.[57] But to pursue the defense of Locke's position further would lead us far from the task at hand. The concern here is to show the bearing of Locke's view of the capacities and limitations of human reason on the possibility of political theory and on the possibilities for political life. Locke sets out in the *Essay* to show that our rational capacities are sufficient to guide our conduct, but in defending that position he also shows that we are not capable of absolute certainty at every level. There are elements of our ideas and our language that are arbitrary, or conventional, and elements of our knowledge that go no further than judgments of the probable consequences of an action.

There is an ambivalence in Locke's view of the understanding that results from the fundamental division of our ideas into ideas of substances, on the one hand, and ideas of mixed modes and relations on the other. With respect to substances, our ideas are imperfect copies of things with an independent existence in the world, and our knowledge reaches only to probabilities. With respect to mixed modes and relations, our ideas are archetypes or patterns that we create to help us understand our experience, and our knowledge is demonstrable and certain with a mathematical certainty. Because of this duality, Locke's position is open to certain troubling questions: How arbitrary can our ideas be and still afford knowledge of reality? How useful are our demonstrations from ideas of mixed modes as a guide to conduct if the knowledge gained must be applied in terms of our uncertain and imperfect understanding of substances?

In one sense the duality of Locke's position is also its virtue. The

57. Locke's theological claims particularly require further argument. See chap. 1, note 51. But it should be recalled that Locke did not set out to provide a demonstrative ethics in the *Essay* but meant only to argue, among other things, that such a project was possible. Whether anyone ever does derive a complete demonstration of ethics starting from first principles is less important for Locke's purposes than showing that such a demonstration is possible in principle, that ethical questions are proper subjects of rational discourse, and that moral propositions can be subjected to rational criticism.

difficult questions it raises are the kind that are raised in considering any complex theoretical position occupying a middle ground between simpler extreme solutions. Locke makes his case in opposition to both the skeptics and those absolutists who rely on a doctrine of innate knowledge of practical principles. Either of these positions might seem theoretically clear, but neither can explain the complexity of the understanding in the way it guides our actions. If men have innate knowledge of the good, how do you explain error, or men who behave in evil ways despite their knowledge, or the immense variety of social conventions governing behavior? These are phenomena that Locke can explain because he insists that, while certain knowledge of true standards of behavior is possible, it is difficult and requires that we use our rational faculties well. And even then, such knowledge of abstract principle is not sufficient by itself.

There is also a role for judgment when principles are applied in practice, and there are some things that must be determined by convention. When we are considering alternative courses of action or when competing principles are involved, an exercise of judgment is necessary to weigh and balance the probable consequences of the choices and to determine which principle might have precedence. Even when the principle or the rule is clear, a judgment must often be made as to whether it applies to the circumstances in question, whether a given thing or action belongs to the categories included in the rule. In many cases only purely conventional indicators determine what actions are included in a given category or idea, as for example in determining what counts as a contract. There is room in Locke's view for a wide variety of conventions to suit differing circumstances and room for a variety of judgments arising either from differing views of happiness or simply from the necessary uncertainty of human affairs. We cannot know for certain the consequences of our actions before we act. But never do these limitations of our understanding weaken Locke's claim that demonstrative knowledge of the principles themselves is available through reason.

It is this same duality of the understanding that is evident in the character of the civil law. Positive laws can be judged in terms of their consistency with natural law standards. At the same time a wide variety of positive laws is to be expected—all equally legitimate—as men attempt to apply general principles of right in different situations. Locke explains both the possibility of our knowledge of standards and the role of judgment and convention in putting them into practice.

Because he explains both these things, he explains the necessity for politics as neither the skeptics nor the absolutists can explain it. On the one hand, if men could not know anything with certainty, if there were no basis for agreement that some actions are right and others wrong, there would be nothing but force to govern our common life. On the other hand, if all men were governed in their actions by innate principles of right, one would expect to find utopias where no government or force was necessary. Politics is possible because men can discriminate between right and wrong in their common affairs, and it is necessary both because men often fail to do what is right and also because some things must be determined by convention and left to judgment. Those judgments may be reasonable or unreasonable, but they will not be absolutely clear and certain. Locke's view of the extent of the understanding is the basis for his view of government as a common judge among men. It is the basis for framing the political question as the question, Who decides what? And much of Locke's work is organized around precisely this question. What issues must be left to each individual to determine for himself and what questions must be determined by a common authority whose determinations all men are bound to accept? The answers to some questions can be known by all men beyond doubt through unaided reason. The answers to others cannot be known beyond doubt, but nonetheless there must be generally accepted answers to them within any particular society.

In other words, the *Essay* establishes both the possibility of a normative political science and the impossibility of a scientific political practice. It is possible to demonstrate through reasoned argument what men's rights and duties are in relation to each other. This is the kind of argument that belongs to the sphere of ideas of mixed modes and relations. But in applying the demonstrated norms in practice, there can be no comparable certainty. There is room for statesmanship, for judgment, for line drawing where the distinctions around the edges may be arbitrary. Normative political theory can proceed according to the model of mathematics, but the "art of government" remains an art.

This is not to say that theory and practice are divorced from one another. On the contrary, practice is to be guided by principles that can be theoretically demonstrated. And in addition, the theoretical principles themselves must ultimately be submitted to a practical test. Experience is finally the touchstone, and principles are ultimately to be judged by their consequences. No political theory can be right that leads to misery when put into practice. Our theorizing, our reasoning, is meant to serve our natural purposes; it is meant to serve our happiness.

Because of Locke's view of thought and language as functional and of nature as purposive, his assessment of whether an argument is rational depends not only on its consistency, but also always on whether there is a sensible relation of means and ends. And in the case of political argument the ends are indicated by our natural capacities and inclinations. A political prescription must allow for the use of men's rational faculties to govern their actions, for the exercise of their freedom, and it must promise to increase or secure the general happiness and well-being of mankind.

This much we can know on the basis of epistemological argument. We can expect that the *Second Treatise* will be a logical demonstration meant to establish normative political principles, and we can expect that those principles will be defended in terms of their ability to provide for a political life in accord with these common human purposes. The *Essay* contains the argument that normative theory in general is possible. It remains to consider what questions *political* theory in particular must address. We must consider what the specific tasks of the political theorist are before we can consider how, and how well, Locke accomplishes them.

2

Legitimate and Illegitimate Power: The Normative Theory

The Requirements of Political Theory

What must a theory of politics do, what problems must it solve, in order to be judged a success? We can begin to discover Locke's answer to this question by turning to his reasons for condemning Filmer's theory as a failure. The principal failure of Filmer's work is that it provides no measure by which to distinguish legitimate from illegitimate authority or legitimate from illegitimate use of power (see, for example, 1T.9–10, 72, 78–79). The first task of theory is a normative one; to establish a right or title to govern that also permits identification of usurpers and tyrants. The fundamental problem is to identify a standard of legitimate authority that does not dissolve into "might makes right." Locke begins the *Second Treatise* by stating that he means to provide an alternative to Filmer's erroneous theory that will keep us from the conclusion that "all Government in the World is the product only of Force and Violence, and that Men live together by no other Rule but that of Beasts, where the strongest carries it." To leave it at that would be to "lay a Foundation for perpetual Disorder and Mischief, Tumult, Sedition and Rebellion" (2T.1). A theoretical standard of rightful authority is absolutely necessary to the end of political association, "Peace and Tranquillity" (1T.106). It is the responsibility of a political theorist to demonstrate the grounds of that standard.[1]

---

1. The impression that Locke's purpose in the *Second Treatise* is to demonstrate the difference between legitimate and illegitimate government is reinforced by the organization of the book. The introduction is followed by two chapters discussing the fundamental premises of the argument; natural freedom and the natural law of preservation: Chapters 4–9 distinguish political power from other kinds of rule over men and things on the basis of these premises. Chapters 10–14 then discuss

But the standard must also be applicable in the political world as we find it. First, the principle of legitimacy must be one that can justify the existence of legitimate political authority within many coexisting particular communities. Rightful authority must be *political* authority; it must operate at the level of political association, binding men together in groups larger than families but smaller than all mankind. Second, it is not enough to know that there is legitimate authority to govern a particular community; political theory must teach us how to recognize who has it. The task requires a clear means of determining who has the right to the obedience of his fellows. Men must know whom to obey.

The difficulties of establishing an effective practical standard take particular forms for Filmer's divine right theory. Filmer argues that the title to rule descends to Adam's heirs, Adam having received it by divine donation. Locke replies that, on these grounds, Filmer's theory cannot meet the first practical requirement.

> For either this *lordship of Adam over the whole World*, by Right descends to the eldest Son, and then there can be but one Heir . . . or else it by Right descends to all the sons equally, and then every Father of a Family will have it. . . . Take which you will, it destroys the present Governments and Kingdoms, that are now in the World. (1T.142; see also 1T.65, 70–71, 104–5, 148; 2T.113–15)

Filmer's attempts to explain the division of mankind into separate nations after the Flood or at the Tower of Babel founder on this difficulty (1T.143–48).

Second, having argued that certain men have a divine right to govern others, Filmer must show that there is a divine rule to settle who they are. Certainly no positive laws of men can determine the matter, so long as the right is God given.[2] And without a fundamental and clear rule to settle the titles of kings in succession, an

---

legitimate government on the basis of these distinctions. Chapter 15 summarizes and reiterates the distinctions before the discussion of various types of illegitimate government in chapters 16–19 (or in Locke's terms, before the discussion of various circumstances in which legitimate government is dissolved).

2. See 1T.106–7, 119–27. A similar problem would arise for a theorist claiming that the right to rule is based on a natural inequality. He would have to demonstrate a clear rule for recognizing the natural superior. The tendency of Locke's argument is toward the conclusion that succession must be determined by convention.

Various arguments were advanced by English political writers trying to combine divine authority for government power with authority in the people to determine who will wield that power or to resist a tyrant in certain circumstances. See Franklin, pp. 33–52, for a discussion of the efforts of William Bridge, Jeremiah Burroughs, and Philip Hunton in this area.

abstract standard of legitimate rule is meaningless; any claimant who can strengthen his claim with force of arms can command obedience.

> A Man can never be obliged in Conscience to submit to any Power, unless he can be satisfied who is the Person, who has a Right to Exercise that Power over him. If this were not so, there would be no distinction between Pirates and Lawful Princes, he that has Force is without any more ado to be obey'd, and Crowns and Scepters would become the Inheritance only of Violence and Rapine. (1T.81, 121)

Failure to meet the requirement for a clear determination of who rules is a particularly serious failing for those who defend absolute rule.

> The settling of this point being of no smaller moment than the security of Princes, and the peace and welfare of their Estates and Kingdoms, a Reformer of Politicks, one would think, should lay this sure, and be very clear in it. For if this remain disputable, all the rest will be to very little purpose; and the skill used in dressing up Power with all the Splendor and Temptation Absoluteness can add to it, without shewing who has a Right to have it, will serve only to give a greater edge to Man's Natural Ambition, which of it self is but too keen. What can this do but set Men on more eagerly to scramble, and so lay a sure and lasting Foundation of endless Contention and Disorder, instead of that Peace and Tranquillity, which is the business of Government, and the end of humane Society? (1T.106)

In short, Locke charges that Filmer's defense of absolute monarchy amounts, in practice, to a defense of any existing ruler able to maintain his power and consequently is not a distinguishing principle of legitimacy at all. When men are taught that obedience is due to usurpers as well as lawful kings, the distinction between legitimate and illegitimate government collapses and force becomes the rule of right among men (1T.78–79). Filmer fails his own practical test of political theory—maintenance of the peace—and this is quite apart from the argument that the peace that is gained from submission to tyrants is not worth preserving.[3] Locke parts company in the *Two Treatises* with those who teach that absolute obedience to absolute sovereigns will encourage a peacable political order. A doctrine of just resistance must accompany the justification of a duty to obey if the distinction between illegitimate and legitimate authority, and with it civil peace, is to be maintained.

3. This second argument is prominent in the *Second Treatise*. Locke in fact defines the condition of tyranny as a state of war between prince and people. See 2T.19, 199.

The entire problem of establishing criteria for political legitimacy could be stated in terms of the duty of obedience rather than the right to rule, and Locke speaks in these terms at times in his critique of Filmer (1T.119–20). Further, the articulation of the obligations of civil obedience with the doctrine of Christian liberty is the problem of Locke's early tracts and continues as a theme of his later religious writings.[4] The central issue could be understood as the need to demonstrate both the grounds for and the extent of the claims of an earthly authority to bind the conscience to obedience. Throughout, the justification for a given power is also the justification for the limitations on that power. In other words, there is a duty to obey under certain conditions for the same reason that there is a right to resist when the conditions are not met. A theory of political legitimacy that establishes a right to rule within a given community and designates clearly who rules also establishes the grounds for the individual's obligations both to the community of which he is a part and to its government.

> Men too might as often and as innocently change their Governours, as they do their Physicians, if the Person cannot be known, who has a right to direct me, and whose Prescriptions I am bound to follow. To settle therefore Mens Consciences under an Obligation to Obedience, 'tis necessary that they know not only that there is a Power somewhere in the World, but the Person who by Right is vested with this Power over them. (1T.81)

While Locke argues that Filmer has failed to provide such a theory, Filmer in turn confronts consent theorists with charges that parallel Locke's perfectly: their standard for legitimate authority undermines the integrity of existing political communities and threatens the peace. Whereas Locke shows that Filmer's theory of inheritance of authority from Adam justifies either one world community or an infinite number, Filmer asks whether all mankind must consent to form one government, if the power to choose governors belongs to the whole people. And if particular groups can create their own commonwealths, "a gap is opened for every petty factious multitude to raise a new commonwealth, and to make more commonweals than there be families in the world."[5]

---

4. See especially "An Magistratus Civilis possit res adiaphoras in divini cultus ritus asciscere easque populo imponere? Affirmatur" and "Question: Whether the Civil Magistrate may lawfully impose and determine the use of indifferent things in reference to Religious Worship," in *John Locke: Two Tracts on Government*, ed. Philip Abrams (Cambridge: Cambridge University Press, 1967), and *Letter Concerning Toleration*.

5. Filmer, "Patriarcha," II.5.

With respect to determining who has the right to govern, consent theories fare no better. The near impossibility of unanimous consent of the multitude meeting to choose their rulers cannot be overcome by a positive agreement among men that the majority rules, since only a law of nature could establish a right in the majority to overrule the natural right of each member of the minority to choose his governor. This argument is identical in form to Locke's claim that only divine dictates can determine who rules if the right to rule rests on divine grant. The practical problem of obtaining consent can be solved no better by a plan for election by proxy with tacit consent of the others. In this case any conqueror or usurper with sufficient strength can claim "election," and such claims to power shatter the peace. Finally, the problem of tyranny poses a threat to the peace at least as serious as that of usurpation. If the people retain their right to withdraw their consent and their obedience when they judge that a legitimate ruler has overstepped the bounds of his authority, there will be continual rebellion.[6]

Through the mutual criticisms there is a common understanding of the criteria by which political doctrines are to be judged. A successful political theory must establish a criterion for legitimate government that is a practicable standard. The task requires an explanation for the integrity of independent political communities and clear practical guidance for determining who should be obeyed and when. Finally, a theory that can meet these requirements will lay the foundation for peace. These are the elements of the stated purpose of the *Second Treatise;* they are the tests by which Locke judges his opponent; they are the challenges put forth by Filmer. It is on these grounds that Locke's efforts are to be judged.

Legitimate and Illegitimate Power: The *First Treatise*

The problem of defining legitimate political power appears in the *Two Treatises* as the problem of defining political power simply. "Legitimate political power" is a redundant expression. Political power that is not legitimate is not called political power, but is called despotic power instead. In other words, normative standards are included in the concepts that form the basic component parts of Locke's argument.[7] He does not proceed by describing empirical

6. Filmer, "Anarchy," pp. 285–87; idem, "Observations on Aristotle," pp. 211, 217–18, 225–26; idem, "Observations on Milton," p. 256; idem, "Patriarcha," I.1–2, II.6–7.

7. Similarly, the same action in one case would be called prerogative and in another tyranny or usurpation; 2T.157–58, 216, 222. In contrast, Locke uses the

conditions and then applying value judgments on the basis of extrinsic criteria. Locke's procedure, as is to be expected from the author of the *Essay Concerning Human Understanding,* is to derive key definitions from fundamental premises, distinguish each defined category clearly from the others, and then draw his conclusions from the implications of the relationships among the categories he has established. Locke's characteristic procedure explains his characteristic rhetoric. For example, when he speaks of the "Subject, or rather Slave of an Absolute Prince" (2T.91), he is not simply indulging in rhetorical flourishes or expressing the degree of his personal revulsion at such subjection but is employing terms with mathematical precision. It is particularly important, then, to understand the distinctions among Locke's conceptual categories, both in order to follow his argument and, if Locke's claims for his method are correct, to understand the nature of political power.

In his *First Treatise,* Locke attributes Filmer's failure to understand political power to his failure to provide definitions that distinguish between paternal power (either as power over children or as power over family property) and political power. Filmer fails to identify absolute monarchy as illegitimate because he does not distinguish properly between fathers and kings (1T.7–9; 2T.169). This is Locke's initial charge, and he devotes much of the *First Treatise* to the distinction between paternal power from begetting, dominion over things, and political rule over men.

Filmer shares Locke's view of the issue: the viability of the distinction in kind between a family and a commonwealth would threaten the argument for absolute monarchy as patriarchal monarchy and support the claim of man's natural freedom. Filmer denies that the distinction can be maintained: both associations serve the end of preservation; the authority of fathers in early communities included the marks of sovereignty, such as the power of life and death; the power of government originally arose from the rights of fatherhood. We are all born subject to paternal and hence to political authority.[8]

In the *Second Treatise,* the question of the distinction between

---

word "slavery" when referring both to justified and unjustified slavery. See 2T.17, 24, 172, 222.

8. Filmer, "Anarchy," p. 304; idem, "Observations on Aristotle," p. 189; idem, "Patriarcha," II.1–4. Some contemporary critics of the liberal state also reject the radical distinction between the family and the political community, criticizing liberalism for its emphasis on the individual at the expense of communal ties. But the criticism is no longer thought to necessitate support for authoritarian politics.

political authority and other kinds of authority remains critical. Locke's first step in the effort to establish a criterion of legitimacy other than force and violence is to define political power so as to "shew the difference betwixt a Ruler of a Common-wealth, a Father of a Family, and a Captain of a Galley" (2T.2). However, the central issue here is no longer the distinction between a king and a father, political and paternal power, but that between a commonwealth and an absolute, arbitrary ruler, between political and despotic power.

In fact, as we shall see, Locke's refutation of Filmer in the *First Treatise* turns not on the difference between paternal and political power, but on the difference between economic and political power; the difference between ownership and rule. And if the relation of the despot to his slave can be considered one of ownership, the central issue of the *Second Treatise* also appears as the relation of property and politics. Property has two important distinguishing characteristics: it is for the benefit of the proprietor, and it is transferable by agreement. Because it can be transferred, it can be inherited, whereas rule of any kind over men cannot. This proposition permits Locke to refute Filmer. Locke's positive argument in the *Second Treatise* also turns on what kinds of rights and powers are transferable and by what means, rather than on the traditional catalog of powers considered to be marks of sovereignty.[9]

We begin with the distinctions established in the *First Treatise*. Locke's first concern is to show that the grant of dominion over the creatures of the earth to Adam (Gen. 1:28) cannot be the source of an absolute power over men. First, the argument clarifies the difference between a ruler and an owner in the extent of their power. Adam had dominion over the beasts ("the fear of you and the dread of you, says God, shall be upon every beast"), while Noah and his sons had "utmost property" in them; the right to "destroy any thing by using it." It is "the difference between *having Dominion,* which a Shepherd may have, and having full Property as an Owner." The latter seems to be absolute power, though even "utmost property" is limited by the requirement of use, for God is the ultimate proprietor, and man's property in God's creatures is the *"Liberty of using them"* (1T.39). Although Noah's property in the beasts may be absolute, it does not follow that it is arbitrary (see 2T.139).

Second, even if Adam had been made sole proprietor of the earth, that ownership could afford no basis for his sovereignty over men. Property cannot be the source of a claim to political power. To claim a right to the obedience of another in exchange for providing him with life's necessities is no different from putting a knife to his throat and offering him a choice between death and slavery. The principle would amount to nothing more than "might makes right." And even if a claim to obedience could arise in this way, its foundation would be not property but the consent to obey given in exchange for saving a man's life (1T.41–43; see 2T.176, 186–87).[10] Furthermore, God has provided for the preservation of all men and for the increase of the species, and by a title of charity, a man in need has a right to the surplus of another's goods (1T.42; see 2T.183).[11] Throughout the *Two Treatises,* property ownership is clearly separated from claims to political rule. The only direct political implication of property rights is that those whose property is to be taken through taxation have a right to be represented in that decision; their consent is required (2T.139–40, 193–95).

Having distinguished ownership from rule and shown that the latter cannot arise from the former, Locke proceeds to distinguish the rule of a father over his children from the rule of an absolute sovereign. Again, they are first differentiated on the basis of their extent; the power of a father does not reach to the life of a child.[12] More important here is Locke's argument that paternal power, like property ownership, cannot be the source of supreme political authority. The right of parents (mothers included) to be honored by their children arises as a consequence of the act of generation; it is a natural right joined to a natural relation. It belongs to all parents and cannot be abridged by political authority (1T.63–66). The problem this presents for Filmer's position is that the rights of fatherhood cannot be the source of supreme political authority where there are many fathers (and mothers) and only one supreme authority. Locke's challenge here rests on this difficulty with supremacy and not on a basic distinction between the character of familial and political authority relationships.[13]

Political and paternal power are, in fact, the same in the crucial respect for the argument of the *First Treatise;* neither is transferable by compact and hence cannot be passed down as an inheritance by the possessor of it. The governing principle is as follows: "Now in all Inheritance, if the Heir succeed not to the reason, upon which his Father's Right was founded, he cannot succed to the Right

10. Compare Hobbes, p. 228.
11. See Seliger, *Liberal Politics,* p. 175; Tully, pp. 131–32, 137–38.
12. See 1T.51–59; see also chap. 2, note 17.
13. See 1T, chap. 6.

which followeth from it" (1T.85). In the first instance, "reason" has the sense of "origin" or "foundation," so that if paternal power arises from begetting, no one can wield that power over anyone who is not his natural child. Likewise, if rule arises either from divine grant or from consent, no one can assume a position of authority without that divine grant or that consent (1T.74, 94–96; see also 1T.98, 103).

On the basis of this principle of succession, Filmer's contention that monarchs derive their authority by descent from Adam is defeated. Whatever authority Adam had to rule men, whether by paternity or by divine grant, died with him. The current possessor of political or paternal power cannot determine who shall succeed to it, and neither can a conqueror or pretender claim authority without establishing his right based on the reason for that authority. Reason, not might, makes right.

Suppose for the moment we accept Locke's argument that neither political power nor paternal power can be passed down by inheritance unless the heir succeeds to the reason for the right. If the same condition applies to the inheritance of property, has Locke unsettled the justification for that form of inheritance as well? Insofar as the foundation of property rights is God's grant of the earth and its creatures to all mankind, one might expect all property to revert to the common upon the death of the proprietor. Insofar as a man begins a property in anything through his own labor, certainly no one can succeed to this title to it. One would expect that the owner would have a right to will it, as his creation, to whomever he wishes. What then is the grounds for the child's particular claim?

Locke bases the natural right of a child to inherit both on the child's dependence upon his parents for subsistence and on the parents' concomitant obligation to preserve their children, whom they have begotten in accordance with their natural desire to continue themselves in their posterity (1T.88). Every child has the same claim regardless of order of birth or gender.[14] Locke asserts without argument that this claim extends beyond the age of dependence and beyond mere subsistence. He in fact establishes a hierarchy of inheritance rights. The father may will his goods to whomever he pleases. The children inherit if he has left no will. If he dies without children, his father inherits. If there are no kin-

---

14. Locke argues against primogeniture. See also 1T.93. There is nothing here to suggest that only sons inherit.

dred, the property reverts to the common. Property here is understood as family property.[15]

> Men are not Proprietors of what they have merely for themselves, their Children have a Title to part of it, and have their Kind of Right joyn'd with their Parents, in the Possession which comes to be wholly theirs, when death having put an end to their Parents use of it, hath taken them from their Possessions, and this we call Inheritance. (1 T.88; see 1 T.87, 90)

There are three problems here. First, no reason is given for the priority of the father's prerogative in determining who shall inherit over the children's natural right to inherit. Second, no reason is given for the claims of an independent and comfortably settled child. Third, and most important, inheritance in the case of property is not apparently based on the principle that governs the disposition of paternal or political authority, that is, the need for the successor's title to be grounded in the same reason that gave title to the original possessor. Here it seems that children have an independent claim to their parents' goods that derives from their status as children. Why do they not have a similar claim to inherit their parents' authority?

In developing the distinction between property and political power with respect to inheritance, Locke refers to the reason for a right in a second sense; the end or purpose of the right, rather than its origin. Government is for the preservation of right and property from the injury of others and is for the benefit of the governed. Property, originating from man's right to use inferior creatures for his subsistence and destroy them if need be, is for the benefit of the proprietor. Rule or dominion has "another original and a different end" from property in the creatures of the earth. A child's dependence on his parents for subsistence gives him a right to inherit their property for his own benefit. But if his father had any political power, it "was vested in him, for the good and behoof of others, and therefore the Son cannot Claim or Inherit it by a Title, which is founded wholly on his own private good and advantage" (1 T.93; see 1 T.91–93, 97). A claim to property or rule must accord with the purpose, end, or reason for property or rule.

If Locke's refutation of Filmer relies on the principle that an heir must essentially receive his inheritance from its original source, or for the same reason in this sense that his predecessor

---

15. Tully stresses this point at pp. 133–35 but does not mention the father's right to choose his heir.

had it, then the justification for the inheritance of estates is shaken. But if his principle is that claims to power may be based on the ends of power, Locke's case encounters other difficulties with respect to both paternal and political power.

That there is a possibility of conflict between claims based on the original and claims based on the end of right or power is familiar in the theory of liberal democracy. The conflict arises whenever the people consent to a form of government or to government action that does not protect the lives, liberties, and property of the subjects. The problem of majority incursions on minority rights is a form of this problem. Without a clear articulation of the relation between claims based on the origin of power, consent, and claims based on its ends, protection of life, liberty, and property, we cannot identify legitimate authority. We also cannot know what it means for a man to succeed to the reason for a right.

Locke addresses the relation between the origins and ends of paternal power when he shows that Adam could not have willed to his eldest son his paternal authority to rule the others. Since what can be transferred by compact can be acquired by inheritance, to make his case Locke must demonstrate that paternal power cannot be alienated or transferred by compact. To the extent that a father's right to be honored by his child derives from its origin in the unalterable natural fact of paternity, the right can be neither transferred nor forfeited. To the extent that the father's right follows his fulfillment of the duty of nurturing the child, the end of paternal power, it can be forfeited if he fails to perform that duty and can be earned by a foster father who does perform the duty, who does fulfill the condition of the right in this sense.

In the case where a foster father assumes the duties and, with them, the rights of the father, the effect appears to be the same as it would be in the case where the father chose to transfer his authority to another. But Locke must deny the possibility of the voluntary transfer of paternal authority. Locke tells us that if paternal power is by right of nature, it cannot be taken without a man's consent (1T.148); but the argument here requires that it cannot be given even with his consent. For Locke to show that Adam's paternal power could not be inherited, he must claim either that paternal power is an inalienable natural right—a reasonable conclusion if one emphasizes its origin—or that paternal power is not a natural right at all—a reasonable conclusion if the right accrues to the role of the guardian. The argument of the *First Treatise* emphasizes the first possibility, but Locke explicitly refers the reader to the *Second Treatise* for a fuller treatment of the issue, and there the second possibility is supported.[16] In either case Locke's argument against inheritance of paternal power from Adam holds.

Applying this analysis to political power yields the following conclusion. The political ruler, like the father, cannot transfer his authority, whether that authority is based on its purpose or its source. Whether the right to rule belongs only to the one who cares for his subjects or only to the one who has divine right or the consent of the people, no one can acquire it as a gift from its current possessor. Thus, without explicitly ordained rules of succession, no ruler currently on earth can claim any title on the basis of descent from Adam. That it was beyond Adam's power to determine his successor is critical to Locke's refutation of Filmer.

But the analysis leaves a serious problem. To the extent that the right to rule is based on the ends of political power, a good usurper would be justified in deposing a tyrant who, by his tyrannical actions, had forfeited his right. The usurper's position is analogous to that of the foster father. However, to the extent that the right to rule is based on the origin of political power, no challenge could be raised against a tyrant king who had legitimately succeeded to the throne.

Locke's argument in the *First Treatise* does not adequately resolve the conflict, but it does provide a provisional basis for understanding political legitimacy through the distinction between ownership and rule. That political authority cannot be transferred is tied, through the concept of property, to limitations on that authority. Locke establishes here that there is no property in office, and he does so without reference to the idea of an office as a trust derived from the consent of the people. It is the right of a proprietor to transfer his right at will or to destroy or otherwise use for his own benefit that in which he has a property right. These rights do not belong to the ruler of a son or subject. Both paternal and political power, unlike property, are not transferable and exist for the benefit of others.[17] This is the basis for the distinction Locke establishes between power over a son or subject on the one hand and power over a slave on the other (see 1T.8–9, 154, 156). Power

---

16. See 1T.100–102; 2T.65–69. I believe the discrepancy is due to the need to refute Filmer on his own terms, that is, without grounding the refutation in the premise of natural freedom, which is the major point at issue. Locke refutes Filmer by demonstrating the inconsistencies, contradictions, and dangerous or impractical implications of his position.

17. This is why paternal power does not extend to life and death. A power of life and death in the father cannot serve the benefit of the child, whereas that power is necessary for the end of political power, the benefit of the community. See 2T.65.

over a slave is the power of full property, and Locke repeatedly compares it to the relation between man and beast.

The fact that a ruler's power is not his to give away, that there is no property in office, is linked with the limitation that he cannot use his subjects as property. Locke makes the connection by arguing that there is always a reason for power over men or things, and there can be no legitimate power where there is not a reason for it. The difficulties that arise with his argument result from the ambiguity of the term "reason for" and the apparent inconsistencies that result from Locke's usage of it to mean either "grounds for" or "purpose of." It remains, then, in looking at the *Second Treatise*, to discover whether the ambiguity and inconsistencies persist once the constraints of the need to refute Filmer's argument are removed; whether an argument from the "original" and from the "end" of civil government yield consistent conclusions as to its "extent."

Legitimate and Illegitimate Power: The *Second Treatise*

Since it is Locke's stated purpose to establish a rule, other than force, by which one might recognize legitimate authority, one might expect that what that rule is would not be at all difficult to discern. And the problem is not that Locke says too little or conceals his views, but that he says too much. We are given several criteria for legitimacy, or for distinguishing absolute monarchy or despotism from political power, without clear guidance as to their relative weights or their relation more generally. And on their relation hinges the character of Locke's doctrine, theoretically and practically.

The difficulty appears with Locke's initial statement of the definition of political power:

> *Political Power* then I take to be *a Right* of making Laws with Penalties of Death, and consequently all less penalties, for the Regulating and Preserving of Property, and of employing the force of the Community, in the Execution of such Laws, and in defence of the Commonwealth from Foreign Injury, and all this only for the Publick Good. (2T.3)

Characteristically, Locke does not begin, as we might, by defining power simply, distinguishing political power, and then introducing normative considerations such as its proper use. Rather, he defines political power as if he were defining a concept like justice, assuming that the thing to be defined is understood to be something good. Political power *is* a right. You have this power only if you ought to have it. It is a right to act domestically only by making and enforcing laws. You have this power only if you use the methods that ought to be used. It is a right to act "only for the Publick Good." You have this power only if you use it for the purposes for which it ought to be used. There are three criteria here for recognizing political power, two formal and one substantive: legitimate authority, legitimate means, and legitimate ends. Much of the *Second Treatise* is devoted to cases where one or two, but not all, of these standards are met: where laws are made and enforced for the public good, but by somebody without the right to make them (usurpation), where force is employed domestically for the public good, but not in execution of the law (prerogative), and so forth.

The task is to clarify the relationships among these criteria, in order to "understand Political Power right": "To understand Political Power right, and derive it from its Original, we must consider what State all Men are naturally in" (2T.4). There are two characteristics of man's natural state: that all men are free and equal, and that there is a natural law that commands the preservation of all mankind. These are the two premises of Locke's argument. Behind them lies the assumption that nature is the standard of right. Any power that does not serve preservation and in some way accord with the natural freedom and equality of man will be shown to be illegitimate.

From his premises, Locke derives not only the definition of political power, but the definitions of paternal power, despotic power, and property right as well.[18] As in the *First Treatise*, the exploration of the meaning of political power proceeds by comparison with these other sorts of rule, but in this case the comparison with despotic power is particularly important. By following Locke's argument from its premises and by making this comparison, we will be able to precisely identify the defining characteristics of legitimate government. The ambiguous relation of these several characteristics will be shown to have its roots in the ambiguous relation of the two characteristics of man's natural state. If freedom or equality has the same status as preservation, the consequences for Locke's political teaching will be quite different than if the first is subordinate to the second.

18. This is the business of chapters 2–9. A restatement of the premise of natural freedom can be found at 2T.4, 22, 27, 44, 54, 87, 95, 104, 119, and 123, that is, in each chapter except chapter 3, which is a continuation of chapter 2. The premise is not restated after chapter 9.

THE FOUNDATIONS IN NATURAL POWER

The refutation of Filmer's argument cleared the way for the first premise of Locke's. Since it was shown that no one living can claim power over another by divine authority, and since men are equal in nature, the natural condition of man is a "State of perfect Freedom" (1T.67; 2T.1, 4). Each is his own master, and whatever any one may do, each has the right to do. There is an *"equal right* that every Man hath, *to his Natural Freedom,* without being subjected to the Will or Authority of any other Man" (2T.54; see 2T.7). This is the liberal premise: men are naturally free and equal. If man's natural condition is a condition of freedom, political power must be a created condition; the right to rule and the duty to obey must originate. This is the direct implication of the liberal premise, and in this sense every liberal must adhere to some form of state of nature doctrine. The state of nature is nothing more than the name for the relation between any men at any time who have not established a common political authority (2T.19).[19] The state of nature may incidentally be an imagined picture of the historical beginnings of mankind or a useful construct for highlighting the basis for and purposes of political life, but essentially it is a logical necessity. Whatever the variety of opinions concerning man's natural sociality, social organization, or individual isolation, whatever the natural condition of man *is,* so long as men are understood to be free and equal it is *not* a political condition, a condition with legitimate political authority. The critical question is, then, How does one man come to have legitimate power over another? How does the *right* to rule originate?

Although the state of nature is not a political condition, it is not without legitimate power, and this is because it is not without law and right. Because the law of nature governs men in the state of nature, Locke's second premise, a man has the right to use his power to fulfill his obligations or duties under that law; the duty to preserve himself and "when his own Preservation comes not in competition . . . to preserve the rest of Mankind" (2T.6). It would be senseless, unreasonable, for the law to command that certain ends be served without the right to use the necessary means to secure those ends: "For the Law of Nature would, as all other Laws that concern Men in this World, be in vain, if there were no body

19. Members of different political communities remain in the state of nature with respect to one another, as do absolute monarchs with respect to their subjects. See 2T.14, 90–94.

that in the State of Nature had a *Power to Execute* that Law." In addition, power, as a means, is limited by its proper end. The executive power of the natural law is not absolute or arbitrary but is reasonable and lawful. It is limited to punishment of violators of the natural law for purposes of reparation and restraint, purposes consistent with the dictates of preservation (2T.6–8). This discussion of natural executive power is typical of Locke's treatment of the relationships between law, duty, right, and power throughout the *Second Treatise.* Where there is law or duty, then and only then there is power or right. Because this is a relation of ends to means, the justification for the power and for its limitation are the same.[20]

One man's right to rule another originates from this natural executive power only by compact (political power) or by forfeiture (despotic power).[21] This is a direct consequence of the premise of natural freedom. You may voluntarily relinquish your powers and rights or you may lose them, but no man can claim power over you on any other basis. Despotic power, or slavery, arises when one man forfeits his right of preservation by violating the rights of another, by putting himself in a state of war with another. The aggressor may be killed lawfully by any man exercising his natural executive power. Slavery is merely the condition in which the death sentence has not yet been carried out by the master, but could be at will. It is a continued state of war (2T.16, 23, 24, 117).

Locke's discussion of slavery in chapter 4 is the culmination of the discussion of the natural executive power. An argument that begins with the premise of natural equality and freedom quickly leads to a justification of slavery. The argument is as follows: "All men being equal and independent, no one ought to harm another in his Life, Health, Liberty or Possessions" (2T.6). If someone tries, he may be destroyed, "for *by the Fundamental Law of Nature, Man being to be preserved,* as much as possible, when all cannot be preserv'd, the safety of the Innocent is to be preferred" (2T.16). Men being in a *"State of perfect Equality . . .* what any one may do in Pros-

---

20. Locke often uses "right" and "power," and "right" and "law," interchangeably. For examples see 2T.6, 163. For examples of this argument with respect to paternal power see 2T.56, 58, 65; with respect to conjugal rights see 2T.78, 83; with respect to political power see 2T.87, 135, 149, 159, 163; and with respect to property rights see 2T.31.

21. In addition to executive power, parental authority is a legitimate form of authority that exists in the state of nature. But according to Locke, it cannot be the source of authority relationships among naturally equal adults, since it is a temporary authority exercised for the period of natural inequality between adults and children. See 2T.52–76.

ecution of that Law, every one must needs have a Right to do" (2T.7). Consequently, any man may lawfully enslave or destroy a man who makes war on him or on anybody else.

This is the only condition that justifies the absolute and arbitrary power of one man over another in Locke's teaching.[22] Why? Why is it that slavery (identified with absolute and arbitrary power at 2T.23) cannot arise by consent? This is an important question for two reasons: First, since political power arises only from consent, but absolute and arbitrary power cannot, then political power cannot be absolute and arbitrary (2T.135). What appears to be a rather technical issue is in fact the grounds for the argument that legitimate government must be limited government. Second, the answer to this question will serve to clarify further the status of natural rights. Although some commentators have seen Locke's separation of the political from the economic as a means of establishing individual rights to property, Locke was at least equally concerned to establish that men have a property in their rights; to establish what it means to *have* a right. The rights of life, liberty, and estate are property rights in the general sense (2T.87, 123, 173). Property is that which cannot be taken without the consent of the proprietor (2T.138). How, then, do you explain that some rights cannot be given *with* the consent of the proprietor? To ask why slavery cannot originate in consent is to ask what it means to have an inalienable right.

There are three things you can do with something that is yours, or more exactly, with your right to that thing: (1) You can agree to

22. See Seliger, "Locke, Liberalism, and Nationalism," p. 28, for the argument that Locke defended the enslavement of African blacks and American Indians, since they could be considered captives in unjust wars. Locke's participation in drafting the Fundamental Constitutions of Carolina has lent credence to this view. See Laslett, *Two Treatises*, note to 2T.24, lines 1–9, pp. 325–26. Laslett cites the Letter to Governor Nicholson and also Sir Leslie Stephen, *History of English Thought in the Eighteenth Century*, 3d ed., 2 vols. (New York: Peter Smith, 1902), 2: 139, in support of this view. Neither source in fact supports it; both are misused by Laslett. Even if Locke considered the white man a just conqueror in America or Africa, his argument would not justify the institution of slavery as it was found in America. The children of slaves are born as free as any other man by any reading of Locke's teaching. See Polin, p. 280. Furthermore, the legitimate condition of slavery as a continuation of the state of war and an exercise of the natural executive power can be ended at any time if the slave offers peace, reparations, and the security of the innocent for the future. Locke's argument concerning executive power and the duties of the natural law would lead one to conclude that a sincere offer of this sort could not be rightfully refused. In this respect even despotic power is not absolute or arbitrary when it is a legitimate exercise of natural executive power. See 2T.8, 20, 24. The question to be asked of Locke's position is, How closely did his practice in supporting the institution of slavery in the colonies correspond with his theory, which can in no way support that institution?

transfer your right, for example, through a sale or a will. (2) You can retain your right but entrust the management of your property to another. (3) You can forfeit your right [23] According to Locke, with property in things you are entitled to do any of the three. However, with property in rights, with your natural right to preservation, you can do the second and third but not the first. Similarly, with the right to the obedience of others, the right to rule, you can do the second and third but not the first.[24]

This seems a strange position. One would think that the right to transfer by compact, the first, and the right to entrust by compact, the second, would both depend directly on ownership and would be inseparable. The first is an unconditional transfer or one where the conditions are met at once. The second is like a rental or a loan, a transfer with a continuing condition and the right to repossess only if that condition is not met.[25] In other words, it is difficult to see how one could have the power to rent but not to sell. If you are not in fact the owner but are yourself a renter, it is possible to sever the connection between the first and second possibility while leaving the second tied to the third. A renter can sublet so long as all conditions are met, but he may not sell. And he certainly forfeits his rights as renter if he does not meet the conditions attached to the property—that is, if he does not pay the rent.

This seems to be a fair analogy to the position of the Lockean ruler; with no property in office, he holds his power as a trust. He may delegate authority to subordinate officers, but he may not transfer it (2T.141). And he forfeits it through breach of trust. But can the same analogy be made in describing individual natural rights? This would lead us to conclude that individuals hold their natural rights in trust. If so, what are we to make of the fact that Locke includes those rights in the term "property"?

Locke suggests two lines of argument here. Either approach would be sufficient to establish that slavery cannot originate in consent. First, the character of the "having" that is involved when one says that a man "has" a right is qualified. Men have the right to dispose of themselves and their property only by God's permission. In fact all property, including property in one's person, can be viewed as a trust from God. Locke first makes the point in the *First*

---

23. With property and with natural executive power, it is also possible to disown your claim. See 2T.49, 88.

24. In discussing the *First Treatise* above, this situation was considered with regard to paternal power.

25. See 2T.194. A trust is not identical to a rental, of course, since the trustee and the beneficiary are not the same person.

Treatise when considering what it means for a man to have a property right in the creatures of the earth.

> For however, in respect to one another, Men may be allowed to have a propriety in their distinct portions of the Creatures; yet in respect of God the Maker of Heaven and Earth who is sole Lord and Proprietor of the whole World, Mans Propriety in the Creatures is nothing but that *Liberty to use them,* which God has permitted. (1T.39; see 1T.154–60)

Similarly, although each man may be his own master in respect to other men, that is not the case in his relation to God.

> For Men being all the Workmanship of one Omnipotent and infinitely wise Maker; All the Servants of one Sovereign Master, sent into the World by his order and about his business, they are his Property whose Workmanship they are, made to last during his, not one anothers Pleasure. (2T.6)

Our right to our persons, our freedom to regulate our lives as we see fit, does not include the right to destroy ourselves. Since no man has the right to destroy himself, he cannot give that right to another; he cannot consent to his own enslavement (2T.23, 149). The power over our lives is ours to use only so long as we use it in accordance with its intended purpose, that is, in accordance with the natural law of preservation. To willfully enslave oneself would be as great a violation of God's law and his trust as to threaten the preservation of another man. Slavery can arise through forfeiture, the consequence of a breach of trust, for the same reason that it cannot arise through consent.

The same conclusion is supported by a second line of argument that does not depend directly on man's relation to God. Instead, the conclusion can be reached through consideration of what the right is that men have in nature.

> The *Natural Liberty* of Man is to be free from any Superior Power on Earth, and not to be under the Will or Legislative Authority of Man, but to have only the Law of Nature for his Rule. . . . *Freedom of Nature* is to be under no other restraint but the Law of Nature. (2T.22)

"Reason, which is that Law" limits man's freedom (2T.1, 6, 8). To be ruled by reason is the privilege of human life. Locke consistently finds its opposite in the rule of force, which is the rule among beasts (2T.1, 11, 16, 172, 181). It is the human capacity to reason that makes possible man's rule over the beasts (1T.30). And it is only when a man abandons the moral rule of the human community, open to all who reason, and substitutes the rule of force that he descends to the level of the beasts and can justly be ruled as if he were a beast—as a slave. The slave, subject to the arbitrary will of his master, is ruled by force. To consent to place oneself in that position would be to renounce one's humanity, to relinquish the natural freedom to be master of one's life in accordance with the dictates of reason (2T.172).

In accordance with the dictates of reason means in accordance with the natural law of preservation. Man's natural freedom is the right to act to secure for himself a comfortable life so long as he does not interfere with the right of others to do the same. Nature is directed toward the preservation of life, and this is the standard for reasonable and rightful action. Even man's dominion over the creatures does not include the right to wantonly destroy them, but only "where some nobler use, than its bare Preservation calls for it" (2T.6). There is no rightful power in nature that is absolute or arbitrary.

> This Freedom from Absolute, Arbitrary Power, is so necessary to and closely joyned with a Man's Preservation, that he cannot part with it, but by what forfeits his Preservation and Life together. (2T.23)

As reasonable creatures, men cannot be supposed to consent to a condition that renders their continued preservation uncertain (2T.131, 137, 164). Like property in things (and unlike rule), property in life and liberty is for the benefit of the proprietor. But unlike property in things, to alienate or transfer these natural rights can never be a means of securing that benefit. To consent to slavery would be unreasonable and unnatural.

Again, slavery cannot arise through consent because no man has the right to the arbitrary use of force to destroy life, his own or any other. Not having that right, he cannot agree to give it to another. The right that each man has is a right to govern himself by the light of reason to secure his preservation. It is a right that is inalienable, both because to have that right defines a man's humanity and because it is the necessary means to the natural end of preservation.

If despotic power is incompatible with freedom, reason, and preservation, why is it that political power is not? If we can answer this question, we will know Locke's criteria for legitimate government. The rhetorical function in Locke's argument of despotic power, which is the state of war continued, is identical to the rhetorical function in Hobbes's argument of the state of nature: it is the condition to be avoided at all costs, the worst case; it is the condition that men seek to avoid in forming governments, the negative standard by which governments are to be judged. By identifying the state of nature as the worst case, Hobbes teaches obedience to civil government. By identifying the state of war as the worst case, Locke justifies resistance. This is the rhetorical reason for distinguishing the state of nature from the state of war. Locke is not concerned to show that men may be naturally peaceful. Rather, he is concerned to show that the condition of men under governments may be warlike: "*Force without Right, upon a Man's Person, makes a State of War,* both where there is, and is not, a common Judge" (2T.19). The dangers of war that men face when all are in the state of nature are like the "mischiefs" of "*Pole-Cats, or Foxes.*" But the danger is far greater where all are in society with the exception of the ruler, who remains in a state of nature with his subjects. The subjects of such an absolute monarch may expect to be "devoured by *Lions*" (2T.93; see 2T.13, 91). Locke repeatedly identifies slavery and the state of war with absolute monarchy and tyranny (2T.17, 20, 91, 149, 222, 226–27, 232, 239). The subjects of an absolute monarch, like slaves, share the status of beasts; they resemble herds of cattle (1T.156; 2T.93, 163). Comparing slavery or despotic power with political power, then, is tantamount to comparing illegitimate with legitimate government.[26]

ABSOLUTE, ARBITRARY POWER AND POLITICAL POWER

Slavery has been characterized as absolute and arbitrary power. Each of these terms has two related meanings in Locke's usage, one substantive and one formal. Absolute power signifies (1) the power of life and death (its substantive usage) and (2) the highest authority, the final arbiter, the power that must be obeyed (its formal usage). Absolute authority is sovereign authority, and one of the chief marks of sovereignty is the power of life and death (see, for example, 1T.64, 68, 129; 2T.17, 90, 93, 139). Arbitrary power means both (1) power that is not used for the legitimate purpose of securing preservation and (2) power that is exercised at will rather than in accordance with stated rules or laws—its substantive and formal usages respectively (2T.23, 135–39, 214, 221). That these two usages may run counter to one another appears in the case of prerogative, which is not arbitrary in the first sense but is arbitrary

---

26. "The right of resistance is an instance of the right of war exercised by a civil society against an enemy with whom it is in the state of nature. For practical purposes it is even the instance for the sake of which the general discussions of the state of nature, the state of war, and civil society are provided." Nathan Tarcov, "Locke's *Second Treatise* and the 'Best Fence against Rebellion,'" *Review of Politics* 43 (April 1981): 12.

in the second (2T.160–61). Yet Locke refers to prerogative power as discretionary rather than arbitrary. The latter is a pejorative term because it applies to actions that are not reasonable. This thought unifies the use of the term as a synonym for willful with the use of the term to describe actions that are not causally related as means to proper ends. Legitimate authority must be governed by a rational principle, and arbitrary authority is not. The two terms, absolute and arbitrary, often appear in conjunction with one another, and with all four of their specific meanings taken together, the phrase describes unlimited authority.[27]

In what respects, then, is political power not absolute or arbitrary? How exactly is it limited? Locke's treatment of political power will be tested against these characteristics of despotic power in each of their significations in turn in order to determine the distinguishing characteristics of legitimate power. The first possibility, that political and despotic power can be distinguished with respect to the power of life and death, must be rejected. The civil authority may punish criminals with death and order soldiers to march up to the cannon's mouth (2T.3, 139). In fact, the power of life and death belongs only to the slavemaster and the legitimate ruler. Locke draws the reader's attention to this by explicitly contrasting the power of the ruler with that of the father, husband, and property owner on this basis.[28] As we have seen, Locke argues that because the right to life is an inalienable natural right, no man can consent to be a slave. Nonetheless, the political power of life and death originates only in consent. Locke must show that to consent to submit to a political authority that can take or risk your life is consistent with the right to life.[29] Locke's theory of consent, based as it is on the premise of natural freedom, is a thread running through the consideration of each of the three remaining possible grounds for distinguishing political from despotic power.

In forming political society, men resign their natural executive power to the community. A public authority is established to punish violators of the natural law "amongst the Members of that Society, (which is the *power of making Laws*)." Each man retains his

27. It is easy to see why the two terms might be used together and that each use does not correspond exclusively to one of the specific meanings I have isolated. For example, absolute in the first sense, the power to take a life, would be identical to arbitrary in the first sense, the use of power contrary to the natural law of preservation in some circumstances.

28. See 2T.65, 72–73, 83, 86. As we have seen, Locke argues in the *First Treatise* that no man can acquire the power of life and death over another by virtue of his ownership of property. See 1T.41–43.

29. See Filmer, "Anarchy," p. 285.

right to life, but the legislative determines and specifies what shall constitute the conditions for its forfeiture. In addition, the public authority punishes violations of the natural law between members of the society and nonmembers "(which is the *power of War and Peace*)" (2T.88–89). Each man retains his right to life, but each equally incurs an obligation to risk or sacrifice his life in order to fulfill "the *first and fundamental natural law . . . the preservation of the Society,* and (as far as will consist with the publick good) of every person in it."[30] Locke argues here that in yielding your private right of judging to a public judge, you also agree to execute those judgments if need be. This is no more than is required of a man for effective use of his natural executive power in the state of nature. In joining civil society, by consent, each man incurs an obligation to submit to the public judgment and thereby puts an end to the continual controversies that result when each has an equal right to judge and to execute his judgments (2T.21, 88–89, 123, 127–31, 134).

Locke characterizes political authority as a judge or umpire in this first full statement of the origin of political power and when he first explicitly contrasts political power with absolute monarchy. Civil society exists only where there is a common judge among all members of the society. One of those members cannot himself be that judge. An absolute monarch, on the other hand, is the final arbiter, the highest authority, absolute in the second sense of the term. For this reason, absolute monarchy is inconsistent with civil society. Membership in a community and obligation to its judgments follow from the same act of consent. The absolute monarch, owing no obedience, remains in a state of nature with respect to his subjects. Political power is apparently not absolute in the second sense of the term even though it is absolute in the first. Those who exercise political power have the power of life and death, but no officeholder is himself the sovereign authority (2T.13, 90–93, 96–97).

Men have a common judge when they live under the same set of standing rules and when they can appeal for a decision under those rules to a recognized authority should controversies arise between them. The peaceful resolution of controversies requires both a common law and a common judge to execute that law. Locke's terminology here can be confusing to the modern reader. Locke does

---

30. See 2T.134. This civil duty is in striking contrast to the natural duty to "when his own preservation comes not in competition . . . *preserve the rest of Mankind*" (2T.6). This is a problem to which we will return. See chap. 3, esp. pp. 128–36.

not distinguish the executive from the judicial power but uses the terms interchangeably when speaking of the process that applies the force of the community in particular cases according to the general rule. This is a process that requires judgment. Making the rule, the legislative function, is also an act of judgment. It may be recalled that the legislative arises out of the natural executive power to judge and punish breaches of the natural law. Positive law merely sets down "what punishment shall belong to the several transgressions which [the Commonwealth] thinks worthy of it" (2T.8; see 2T.135). When positive law is understood as a particularization or articulation of natural law, the legislative, as well as the executive and judicial powers as we understand them, are included in the conception of political power itself as a judge.[31] All three are required in order to apply the general principle to the particular case for the purpose of resolving disputes.

How is it possible for there to be a common judge, thus understood, between ruler and ruled? This seems to be a necessary condition for establishing political, rather than despotic, power. First, an avenue for an appeal must be open to the subjects even against the actions of the government. This requires both that executive officers be responsible for their actions and that the legislative and executive functions be placed in separate hands. Otherwise there is no authority that can serve as an impartial judge (2T.91, 205–7). Second, the same rules that apply to the subjects must also apply to the rulers. This requires both that the laws be made by collective bodies of men who periodically return to their status as subjects and that the legislative and executive functions be separated. Otherwise legislators might exempt themselves from the laws they make (2T.94, 143). In other words, political power is characterized by the rule of law. The law is to be obeyed by all members of the society (2T.93–94, 202).

Locke's position that political society requires a common judge between rulers and ruled and that the law serves as that judge seems identical to the claim that the law is itself the sovereign power, that which is by right to be obeyed. For example, the executive can claim obedience not to his own private commands, but only

as the publick Person vested with the Power of the Law, and so is to be consider'd as the Image, Phantom, or Representative of the Commonwealth . . . and thus he has no Will, no Power, but that of the

31. See 2T.19–20, 87–89, 91, 93. Laslett notes that Locke "talks of the Legislative where the Judiciary might be expected." *Two Treatises*, note to 2T.89, lines 14–21, p. 369. Note also Locke's discussion of the biblical "Judges" as generals. See 1T.158; 2T.109.

Law. But when he quits this Representation, this publick Will, and acts by his own private Will, he degrades himself, and is . . . without Power . . . that has any right to *Obedience;* the Members owing no *Obedience* but to the publick Will of the Society. (2T.151; see also 2T.202)

Locke makes his case, however, without reference to the concept of sovereignty. In fact he abandons that concept in the *Second Treatise.* Although the term is used repeatedly in the refutation of Filmer in the *First Treatise,* it appears rarely in the *Second Treatise,* most prominently in passages directly refuting Filmer, and never as a part of a description of legitimate political power (2T.4, 6, 61, 69, 83, 108, 115). Abandoning the term, Locke effectively distinguishes the elements that are joined in the concept of sovereignty; authority that can claim obedience and a set of powers, including the power to make laws with penalties of death, that are understood as concomitants of that authority.

This is a major point of difference between Locke and Filmer.[32] Filmer's theoretical ground is that the power to make laws is an attribute of sovereignty. Laws are an instrument of the sovereign will, and they have the compulsive force necessary to their being laws only as expressions of that will. The sovereignty of the king is incompatible with his subjection to the laws. Were the king to be subjected to the law, he would also be subjected to whomever could make and enforce that law. He would no longer be the sovereign, or highest, authority. The law itself, as an abstraction, cannot be sovereign. It has no will; it can only be the expression of someone's will. And that someone must therefore necessarily be above the law. Similarly, sovereignty, as the highest authority, cannot be divided. Mixed government or the separation of powers is strictly speaking impossible. In a case of conflict one element or the other finally decides, and the deciding element is sovereign.[33]

Locke strongly emphasizes Filmer's position that the king is above the law when he summarizes his argument in the *First Treatise* (1T.8). Yet on this point Locke does not directly attack Filmer's case as it is presented in "Patriarcha," perhaps because Filmer relies so heavily on the evidence of English constitutional history and legal practice.[34] Locke does, however, challenge the conceptual basis of Filmer's position.

32. Contrast Laslett, *Two Treatises,* note to 2T.88, lines 18–27, where Laslett states that Locke shared Filmer's traditional analysis of sovereignty.

33. Filmer's theory of sovereignty drew primarily on Jean Bodin. See Filmer, "Necessity of the Absolute Power of Kings," and Introduction, note 3.

34. It is possible that Locke countered Filmer's argument from legal history in the portion of the *Two Treatises* that was lost. I think this is unlikely. Locke is making

When dealing with the claims of public authorities to obedience, Locke uses a terminology of supremacy and subordination. He describes a chain of entrusted or delegated powers where the persons authorized to exercise those powers are supreme over their delegates and subordinate to those from whom they receive their power. While the government lasts, the legislative remains supreme, "for what can give laws to another, must needs be superior to him" (2T.150; see 2T.132). But it does not follow from this that the legislator has a sovereign power, for two reasons. First, as we have seen, if the law is to rule as a common judge for all members of the society, the legislative and executive functions must be placed in separate hands and the legislative in a collective body. This allows both legislators and executive officers to be subordinated to the law. Second, the chain of authority originates in the people who retain the supreme power to alter their legislative should it violate its trust. And for legislators to place themselves above or beyond the law would be a violation. The principle here is that what is given in a fiduciary relationship may be taken away (2T.149–52).

That a trust is the form of compact, or mutual consent, that founds political society is crucial to Locke's understanding of legitimacy and, consequently, to the contrast between political and despotic power. To create political authority, the right to life is neither forfeited (as in the case of slavery) nor alienated (which is impossible). The powers each man has to secure that right in the state of nature are entrusted to a common authority to make that security effective for all. The position of the political authorities in relation to the people resembles the position of men in relation to God in the state of nature. Political authorities, holding their power as

---

a general theoretical case meant to have a stronger foundation than English constitutional practice: "an Argument from what has been, to what should of right be, has no great force" (2T.103). See 1T.57. See also Filmer, "The Freeholder's Grand Inquest Touching Our Soveraigne Lord the King and His Parliament," in *"Patriarcha" and Other Works,* pp. 127–84.

According to Pocock, Locke was exceptional among his contemporaries in omitting historical legal argument from his reply to Filmer. He argues that Locke's nonhistorical approach was an important shift because Filmer's arguments could not be adequately met on the basis of the current Whig interpretation of English history. J. G. A. Pocock, *The Ancient Constitution and the Feudal Law* (Cambridge: Cambridge University Press, 1957), pp. 46, 187–88, 234–38. Ashcraft disagrees, arguing that Locke was not unique in adopting a natural law approach rather than a historical one, and that it was Filmer's "Patriarcha," not Locke's *Two Treatises,* "which acted as a catalyst forcing the ideological battle onto the terrain of natural law" (*Revolutionary Politics,* pp. 189–90). See also Quentin Skinner, "History and Ideology in the English Revolution," *Historical Journal* 8 (1965): 151–78, on the importance of a particular account of English history for Whig ideology.

trustees, may not alienate it. As trustees, it is not theirs to give away (2T.141). They may, however, forfeit their power, and furthermore, it is the people who judge whether they have forfeited it,[35]

> for who shall be Judge whether his Trustee or Deputy acts well, and according to the Trust reposed in him, but he who deputes him. (2T.240)

> And this Judgement they cannot part with, it being out of a Man's power so to submit himself to another, as to give him a liberty to destroy him . . . since he cannot take away his own Life, neither can he give another power to take it. (2T.168)

For the same reason that slavery cannot arise from consent, the form of consent that begins political power is a trust (2T.149).

From this second point of view, Locke's description of the subordination of the powers of the commonwealth looks like a description of the case where the people are sovereign. The people may alter the constitution of all government authorities if need be. But having delegated their powers, they do not exercise any essential political powers, and they do owe obedience to the authorities they have empowered. To call the people sovereign because they retain the right of resistance is to obscure the situation. So long as political power operates, all members of the society owe obedience to the law as the expression of the public will that is supreme over the private will of each. Locke succeeds in describing political power that includes the effective exercise of all powers thought to be "marks of sovereignty" without establishing an absolute authority in any man over his fellows. This is the effect of abandoning the concept of sovereignty as the grounds of the argument. To repeat, political power, like despotic power, is absolute in that it includes the power of life and death; but unlike despotic power, it is not absolute in that government includes no final judge who is himself beyond judgment.

Political power, then, is limited in two senses—through the supremacy of the law and through the supremacy of the people— and both of these limitations derive from the principle of consent. The law rules all members of the community because to consent to be a part of a political community means to obligate yourself to its laws. The people are supreme because all authority originates in their common consent.

Filmer explicitly denies that the source of a ruler's authority has

---

35. If it were a contract relationship, a third party would be needed to judge between them. See Filmer, "Patriarcha," II.17.

any bearing on the question of his subordination to the laws. This is a question that can be determined solely on the basis of the characteristics of sovereign power.[36] The contrast between the analysis based on the concept of sovereignty with its concomitant powers and Locke's analysis can be seen by comparing Filmer's position with Locke's on several particular issues.

Filmer uses the king's power to summon Parliament as evidence to support his general argument that the king is not limited by positive laws.[37] Locke is at pains to show that the powers of the executive in convoking, proroguing, and dissolving the legislative body do not make him superior to the legislative (2T.153–58). One cannot infer sovereign authority from the possession of particular powers, even the power of war and peace, the example Locke uses to make this point in the *First Treatise* (1T.129–33).

Filmer argues that the king must be above the laws in order to exercise prerogative powers that correct deficiencies in the laws—the power of pardon, for example. These prerogatives are for the good of the people and therefore do not reduce the people to a slavish condition.[38] Locke recognizes the need for executive prerogatives of this sort but insists on the right of the people to limit those powers should they be abused. Were the king to be the final judge of the use of his prerogatives, the absolute authority, the people would indeed be reduced to slavery (2T.163–64).

According to Locke's historical account, laws and collective legislatures arose primarily to restrain princes who had abused their prerogatives (2T.94, 107–12, 162–66). Filmer, on the other hand, maintains that laws arose as a more efficient instrument of monarchical authority so that the people might know the sovereign's will without the need for him to personally judge each case.[39] Locke does quote Hooker in a note to the effect that the laws permit everyone "to see their Duty beforehand and know the Penalties," and he remarks that standing rules allow everyone to "know what is his" (2T.94, 111, 136), but there is surprisingly little discussion of the value of standing rules over extemporaneous decrees in reducing conflict and facilitating the ordinary conduct of business in the society in general. Locke explains that controversies abound in the state of nature where the law is unwritten and each may apply it as he sees fit, but this is not a sufficient reason to conclude that stand-

36. Filmer, "Patriarcha," III.8.
37. Filmer, "Patriarcha," III.14.
38. Filmer, "Anarchy," pp. 292–93; idem, "Observations on Milton," p. 258; idem, "Patriarcha," III.6–9.
39. Filmer, "Patriarcha," III.4–6.

ing, established laws are necessary in society. One might only conclude from this that men must agree that some third party will be
the acknowledged judge of the natural laws (2T.124, 136). Locke
may have given little emphasis to arguments that defend rule by
standing laws on grounds of their usefulness for effective government because such arguments were also used in defense of absolute
monarchy.[40]

In stressing the need for government by stated, standing rules,
Locke emphasizes that such laws function to restrain the power of
government. Rule by standing laws that apply equally to all is primarily a security against arbitrariness.[41] Standing rules ensure that
people may be punished for certain stated reasons and upon showing cause, not "at pleasure."[42] The government must be satisfied
with punishing only the guilty.[43] Political power is not arbitrary in
the formal sense, not willful, because rulers are bound to rule according to the laws they make. This criterion of legitimacy is to be
distinguished from the criterion that the law itself must rule so that
no political authority is absolute in the formal sense, the final
judge. The first criterion could be called "rule by law," the second,
"rule of law." While the rule of law presupposes also the rule by
law, the reverse is not the case. Without the collective legislatures
and appeal against government officers that is necessary for the
rule of law, a prince might be bound to rule by his laws or face the
legitimate resistance of the people. Even without a right of re-

---

40. Locke and Filmer use the same quotation from James I on this issue. Filmer
uses it to show that the king, though above the law, ought to rule by the law. Locke
uses it to show that the king must make "the Laws the Bounds of his Power, and the
Good of the Publick, the end of his Government," else he is acting as a tyrant,
without right. See 2T.200; Filmer, "Patriarcha," III.6. See also idem, "Anarchy," p.
292.

41. For the connection between standing laws and equality under the law, see
2T.142, where Locke writes, "They are to govern by *promulgated establish'd Laws*, not
to be varied in particular Cases, but to have one Rule for Rich and Poor, for the
Favourite at Court, and the Country Man at Plough."

42. See 2T.136–37. This distinction appears with respect to legislative-executive
relations when 2T.152 is compared with 2T.153. It resembles the difference between the American president's power to remove officers wholly subordinate to him
at will and the power of impeachment, where legislators act on behalf of the people
as judges of executive officers for constitutional violations. Unlike the American
constitutional system, Locke's executive, as executive, has no independent constitutional grant of power. Locke may be suggesting that the legislative may remove any
executive officer at pleasure, but where the supreme executive also has a share in
the legislative, executive officers may be removed only for maladministration and
upon showing cause. But the two passages are ambiguous.

43. See Laslett, *Two Treatises*, note on title page, p. 170.

sistance, an absolute prince who is himself above the law might be obliged in principle to rule by the laws he makes.[44]

The protection against arbitrariness provided by standing laws preserves the natural freedom of men in that they remain free from subjection to the will of any other man.

> *Freedom of Men under Government,* is, to have a standing Rule to live by, common to every one of that Society, and made by the Legislative Power erected in it; A Liberty to follow my own Will in all things, where the Rule prescribes not; and not to be subject to the inconstant, uncertain, unknown, Arbitrary Will of another Man. As *Freedom of Nature* is to be under no other restraint but the Law of Nature. (2T.22)

This passage occurs as Locke introduces the subject of slavery. Slavery is contrasted with freedom from the arbitrary will of another. The point is also emphasized in Locke's discussion of paternal power (2T.54, 57–59). As soon as a child is capable of guiding his own will by the law, he is freed from subjection to the will of another. Subjection to the public will expressed in the form of a law is apparently compatible with freedom, whereas subjection to the private will of an individual altered at pleasure is not.

Is there comfort in the thought that the public will derived from the consent of the people stands behind the law? Locke does use the argument that the consent of each member makes the commands of the government, as his representative, identical to his own judgments when he justifies the duty of men to risk their lives to execute those judgments, but this is not a central Lockean argument (2T.88–89, 228). By itself it is a formal, legalistic notion of representation that has a rather hollow ring.

And it would certainly not be typically Lockean to argue that legal forms are themselves sufficient to provide legitimate government.

> For wherever violence is used, and injury done, though by hands appointed to administer Justice, it is still violence and injury, however colour'd with the Name, Pretences, or Forms of the Law, the end whereof being to protect and redress the innocent, by an unbiassed

44. This was Filmer's position. See chap. 2, note 40. Filmer's attack on limited monarchy corresponds to a critique of the requirement of rule by law backed up by a right of resistance. His attack on mixed monarchy includes a critique of separation of powers. Filmer also argues that all power of making laws is arbitrary because you cannot make a law according to a law. Locke would of course disagree, since positive law is to be enacted according to natural law. See Filmer, "Anarchy," esp. p. 277.

application of it, to all who are under it; wherever that is not *bona fide* done, *War is made* upon the Sufferers. (2T.20)

The processes of the law, the actions of your deputy, must in fact serve the ends for which power was entrusted. Men consent to government for certain reasons, to fulfill particular purposes. Political action must be reasonably related as means to those ends or it ceases it be political and is instead despotic. Political power, then, is also unlike despotic power in that it is not arbitrary in the substantive sense; it is power to act only to meet legitimate political purposes.

The exact substantive limits on political power are determined by the purpose of the trust.[45] Locke states that men form governments for two reasons: "to preserve their Lives, Liberties and Fortunes; and by *stated Rules* of Right and Property to secure their Peace and Quiet" (2T.137). The preceding discussion depicted political power as if it were entrusted for the second reason, in order to

> avoid, and remedy those inconveniences of the State of Nature, which necessarily follow from every Man's being Judge in his own Case, by setting up a known Authority, to which every one of that Society may Appeal upon any Injury received, or Controversie that may arise, and which every one of the Society ought to obey. (2T.90; see 2T.21)

But

> The great and *chief end* . . . of Mens uniting into Commonwealths, and putting themselves under Government, *is the Preservation of their Property.* (2T.124; see 2T.21)

It is to *this* end that men establish settled, known laws, known and disinterested judges, and a power to execute their judgments. Considering preservation as the end of government and law as the means requires reconsideration of the analysis above, in which legitimate government was characterized by the supremacy of the law (2T.123–31, 134–42).

That analysis yielded a picture of Locke's political position as one that includes all the basic elements of the liberal idea of the rule of law and constitutional government. All government power arises from a positive grant from the people. Government functions are separated, to be exercised by different personnel. Each

---

45. Locke uses this argument in distinguishing the sphere of political authority from the sphere of religious authority. See Locke. *Letter Concerning Toleration*, pp. 17–19.

officeholder is subject to the laws constituting his office as well as to all other laws. Laws are made by collective bodies, meeting periodically, and all lawmakers are subject to the laws they make. They are lawmakers, but not rulers. The personal ruler is replaced by an institutional system that ensures no man is above the law. And all of this serves as security against abuses of government power.

But these legal structures and practices, with the limitations they provide, must give way in certain circumstances if they are understood as mere means, particularly when the end is understood as the fulfillment of the dictates of a higher law. No positive law can be valid against the antecedent and paramount natural law that commands the preservation of mankind or the society (2T.12, 134–35, 159, 168). In other words, for government action to be directed toward its legitimate end, nonarbitrary in the substantive sense, it may have to dispense with the boundaries set by law and thus act arbitrarily in the formal sense. Does Locke's argument for lawful government as a government of and by laws mean nothing more than government, however constructed and conducted, in accord with the natural law (see, e.g., 2T.165)? Or does Locke's support for the supremacy of law and the institutional apparatus of the liberal state survive despite the recognition of limited exceptions in cases of necessity?

PREROGATIVE AND PATRIARCHY

At first glance, Locke's discussion of executive prerogative appears to be the greatest threat to the claim that his criteria for legitimate government require that all members of the society be subject to the laws of that society: "This Power to act according to discretion, for the publick good without the prescription of the Law, and sometimes even against it, *is* that which is called *Prerogative*" (2T.160). In all "well-framed" governments where the legislative and executive powers are separated, this power belongs to the executive, since the executive is always in being and has the capability to act should the need arise.[46] Locke argues that the people retain the right to limit executive prerogatives by establishing specific positive laws in areas that might otherwise be left to executive discretion (2T.164). Law and discretion are understood as on the same continuum. But government entirely by standing laws is an impossibility. The question before us then is, Is there any limitation on executive power in those cases where discretion is a necessity?

---

46. See 2T.143–44, 159. This includes governments where the executive shares in the legislative power and governments where he does not.

There are three inadequacies to government by law: (1) The legislature cannot anticipate every situation that might arise requiring immediate action. The executive must be able to act in these cases until the legislature can. (2) Certain government functions cannot be properly served by antecedent rules; for example, foreign affairs or assembling the legislature. These functions must be left to the discretion of the executive (2T.88, 145–48, 156). (3) A rigid application of the law to every case can be harmful and unjust. The executive has the right to consider mitigating circumstances and to suspend or disregard the law, for example, the pardon power (2T.159–60).

In cases of the first type, executive action is justified only if the legislature is not sitting, and only temporarily, until it is. In cases of the third type, the executive's power is a negative one. He may suspend the law in particular cases, but he may not issue a general decree. In all cases the legislative may remove the executive power from any particular officer who has abused it. Where the chief executive shares in the legislative power, only subordinate executive officers are effectively subject to removal in this way (2T.152–53).[47] Only if the legislature is not assembled, that is, in the case where the prerogative power in question is the power of convening the legislature, does the question of abuse of prerogative necessarily require the extraconstitutional appeal to the people (2T.155, 167–68).

In general, executive prerogatives can be justified by their tendency to promote a benefit or prevent harm that would not have been promoted or prevented had the power of the government been limited to the strict letter of the law. The right of the executive to act in these instances is not different in principle from the right of any citizen who, "having the power in his hands, has by the common Law of Nature, a right to make use of it for the good of the Society" (2T.159). For example, anyone may break into a person's home to save a child from a fire and may even have a duty to do so. The executive, having greater power at his disposal, is more likely to be in a situation where he is capable of fulfilling his duty under the natural law in a comparable manner. In other words, even the broadest prerogatives do not raise the prince above the people as a matter of his rights of office.

Locke's discussion of prerogative could thus be interpreted as follows: In every political community the legislative power is su-

47. See chap. 2, note 42. For judicial removal or censure of executive officers, see 2T.205–7.

preme. In well-ordered commonwealths, the executive function is separated from the legislative and placed in separate hands. The executive is permitted certain prerogative powers in recognition of the inadequacy of standing rules to govern every situation, but these prerogatives are not unlimited. Executive prerogative may be limited only to cases where the law cannot provide, and even in these exceptional circumstances the power is limited by its temporary quality, by impeachment powers, as applicable only to particular cases, as a suspending rather than an initiating power, or by the nature of the executive trust.

The private will of the executive is not exalted or given any political status by his prerogative powers. Those powers are entrusted to him to use for the public good. They do not belong to him by right of office (2T.162–68): "It is impossible that any body in the society should ever have the power to do the People harm" (2T.166). This is what distinguishes legitimate prerogative from slavery to an absolute prince. It can appear that Locke interprets prerogative powers as narrowly as possible in order to consistently protect as far as possible the rule of law and the rights of the subject, with the idea of a political trust as the ultimate foundation for the limits on all political authorities.

A more serious threat to the liberal vision of the rule of law emerges from consideration of Locke's historical, rather than his theoretical, point of departure.[48] Early political communities were ruled by father-kings, and their government was "almost all *Prerogative*" (2T.162). And a good prince "cannot have too much *Prerogative*" (2T.164). Laws apparently were introduced as an unfortunate necessity to limit the prerogatives of rulers after the people had experienced their abuse. But in principle, discretionary government may be justified not only in emergencies where law cannot reach the end of government, but also where that end may be reached just as well or better without the law.

A complex set of laws is least likely to be necessary in early, simple societies that are either extended families or groups of families united for mutual protection. These groups are united by common interests as well as by affection, and there is little domestic conflict. There are no parties or partisans, and, most important, the rulers are not likely to develop interests distinct from the common interest. In these circumstances either the demonstrated effective-

---

48. In general, Locke's theoretical discussion of government powers begins with the legislative and gradually builds a strengthened executive out of it. See 2T, chaps. 10–14. The historical discussion moves in the opposite direction.

ness of one man as a general or confidence in the trustworthiness of the father leads men to give their tacit consent to entrust their protection to one man's leadership in war and to submit the few domestic disputes that arise to his judgment for resolution.

If these early patriarchies are legitimate governments, then government without a separation of legislative and executive functions, without standing rules, and without a common judge between ruler and subjects—without either rule of or rule by law—is legitimate government. It looks as if the claim that absolute monarchy is inconsistent with civil society must be revised or, alternatively, that these early patriarchal governments cannot be considered true civil governments.[49]

The power of the ruler in these early forms of society is nothing more than his own executive power, the others permitting him alone the exercise of this power that they each have by nature or joining their strength to his in the exercise of his judgments. There is no collective resignation of the power of each individual to the community, which then authorizes some person or persons to declare and execute the public will. And these early patriarchs ruled "without any express Limitation or Restraint, but what the Nature of the thing, and the End of Government required" (2T.110).

Further, political power is a right of making laws, and the ad hoc judgments of a single man can be considered laws only if the term is used in the broadest sense as any action that annexes a penalty to a transgression of the natural law (2T.88, 135). But Locke tends to speak of lawmaking when a general rule is established and of the executive power of the law of nature when the action pertains to a particular case. And ad hoc judgments certainly cannot fulfill the requirement that governments operate by *standing* laws (2T.124, 136–37). If this requirement applies to all legitimate governments, and if the requirement that executive and legislative powers be separated in order to have an effective common judge between rulers and subjects also applies to all legitimate governments, then neither absolute monarchies nor early kingships are governments. It seems that both father-kings and absolute monarchs remain in a state of nature with their subjects, though the first is peaceful and the second warlike.

In both cases there is personal rule according to private judgment. We have arrived at a ruler who is not a lawmaker, whereas before we arrived at lawmakers who were not rulers. This looks like

49. The latter position is argued in Ashcraft, "Locke's State of Nature," pp. 912–13.

despotism, albeit benevolent despotism so long as the ruler is good and wise. We can rephrase the question under consideration as whether benevolent despotism is a contradiction in terms in Locke's view. Is benevolence sufficient justification for authority?

Benevolence is not the only characteristic distinguishing the rule of the first kings from that of absolute monarchs. These early kingships are true governments because they originate in the consent of the people and are limited by it. The tacit acquiescence to or active participation in enforcing the judgments of a single man is sufficient to "in effect make him the Law-maker, and Governour over all" (2T.105; see 2T.74 and cf. 2T.88, 94, 127). Evidently Locke does here speak of lawmaking in the general sense, and these early father-kings are indeed governors.

Locke's primary reason for discussing this early stage of civil society is to show that governments originate in every case in consent in the form of a trust. Despite the fact that the earliest governments resembled patriarchal monarchies, and thus it could appear that political authority derives from paternity, governments arise only by consent because among men there is no "natural superiority or subjection" (2T.102; see 2T.74–76, 102–12). The consent of the people and government in the interests of the people are the sufficient criteria, then, for legitimate government.

These early monarchical governments are not benevolent despotisms or absolute monarchies so long as the people can reclaim the right to form a government to their liking if malevolence sets in. The right of resistance is a concomitant of the government's foundation in consent. These are limited governments, and that is the minimum condition for legitimate government.

The separation of powers and the balance of powers that are necessary to subject all members of the society to its laws become requirements for legitimate government only at a later stage in the historical development of societies.

> But though the *Golden Age* (before vain Ambition, and *amor sceleratus habendi,* evil Concupiscence, had corrupted Mens minds into a Mistake of true Power and Honor) had more Virtue, and consequently better Governours, as well as less vicious Subjects; and there was then no *stretching Prerogative* on the one side to oppress the People; *nor* consequently on the other any *Dispute about Priviledge,* to lessen or restrain the Power of the Magistrate; and so no contest betwixt Rulers and People about Governours or Government: Yet, when Ambition and Luxury, in future Ages would retain and increase the Power, without doing the Business, for which it was given, and aided by Flattery, taught Princes to have distinct and separate interests

from their People, Men found it necessary to examine more carefully *the Original* and Rights of *Government;* and to find out ways to
restrain the Exorbitances, and *prevent the Abuses* of that Power which
they having intrusted in another's hands only for their own good,
they found was made use of to hurt them. (2T.111; see 2T.107, 110)

This Golden Age is the age before the invention of money. Though
"government is hardly to be avoided amongst Men that live together" (2T.105), kings are "little more than *Generals of their Armies*"
(2T.108) before money gives men reason to acquire more than they
can use, thus fostering ambition and luxury, making possible vastly
unequal possessions in land, and increasing controversy over property. Locke is apparently ambivalent toward economic development. Life among the American Indians is both poorer and better
governed for lack of it (2T.41, 48–49, 108). In simple, frugal societies the people, though poor, are less likely to be exploited by
those in power (2T.47–51, 105–12).[50]

Once the Golden Age has passed—which is to say, for all practical purposes—legal restrictions and an institutional balance are
necessary to bring rulers within the bounds of the society (2T.94).
Mixed government and standing laws are necessary in practice to
maintain limited government where princes might come "to have
distinct and separate interests from their people." But in principle,
at any historical period the laws could legitimately give way to the
discretion of a good and wise prince. The expansion of prerogative
with the consent of the people in the reign of such a prince is as
legitimate as is its limitation by the people when faced with princes
of a different sort (2T.163, 165). Prerogative and simple early
monarchies are justified on the basis of the same two principles:
consent and the good of the community.

TWO INTERPRETATIONS

We have in fact found four normative conditions for characterizing
legitimate government and some support in Locke's argument for
two interpretations of the relations among them. Political power is
not absolute or arbitrary in that those who rule must base their
right to rule on the consent of the people; political power must be
exercised only for the sake of the preservation of the society and its
members; political power must be exercised by known, standing
laws; and no member of the society can be exempt from subjection

---

50. The association of simplicity, poverty, virtue, and good government is more
often considered "Rousseauean" than "Lockean," but the thought is clearly present
in the *Two Treatises.*

to its laws. The first three of these conditions correspond directly to the origin, end, and means of political power contained in Locke's initial definition of political power:

> *Political Power* then I take to be *a Right* of making Laws with Penalties of Death, and consequently all less penalties, for the Regulating and Preserving of Property, and of employing the force of the Community in the Execution of such Laws, and in defence of the Commonwealth from Foreign Injury, and all this only for the Publick Good. (2T.3)

Further, each of these four conditions is directly derived from one of the two premises of Locke's argument. Political power originates in consent because all men are free and equal in nature. Political power serves the public good because the natural law commands preservation. The last two conditions, the formal conditions of rule by and of the laws, derive, like the first, from the premise of natural freedom. Legitimate power cannot include submission to the absolute, arbitrary will of another man.

We began by noting that Locke seemed to say too much, and that the character of his thought depends upon the relation of the several criteria he develops. That relation in turn depends upon the relation between his two fundamental premises. Locke gives some support both to the argument that the formal criteria, based on the premise of natural freedom, are subordinate and instrumental to preservation and to the argument that they are necessary conditions with an independent status. By juxtaposing these alternative arguments and evaluating the strength of the supporting evidence from Locke's position as it was elaborated above, we can determine the place of the law, the integrity of the formal standards, in the liberal state as Locke understands it. In the process we should see the full range of theoretical positions that are possible when one begins with the thought that all men have an equal right in nature to be preserved.

There is a range of liberal political theories that might arise on the basis of the twofold premise of an equal natural right to preservation. That political power must be exercised only for the sake of the preservation of the society and its members is a matter of principle accepted by all, and certainly by Locke. Each of the remaining three criteria for legitimate government can be considered either necessary in principle, necessary because in practice the end cannot otherwise be achieved, or merely recommended as most likely to secure that end. The range of theoretical possibilities is produced by the variety of combinations of the three normative criteria with these three alternative judgments as to their status.

The first interpretation begins with the premise that preservation is the natural end of all human life and consequently is the end of government. All power is both justified and limited by the extent to which it is a means to that end. Freedom is to be secured and an impartial process of judging controversies established insofar as these are the necessary securities for, or "fences" to, our preservation (2T.17, 23, 93, 123–26, 136). An authorized process of dispute resolution, a common judge, is necessary because without it the natural desire of each for a comfortable life is not likely to be satisfied. The natural law, in this view, is not so much a moral imperative as it is a general statement of the natural tendency of human actions, not unlike the law of gravity in relation to the actions of inanimate bodies. Men desire preservation, and so we call it good.[51]

Thus understood, the premise of the natural law of preservation carries with it also a particular understanding of freedom and reason. We get a distinctive answer to the original question: How is it that political power is compatible with man's natural condition as a free and rational being, and therefore is a fit object for consent, and slavery is not? Obviously, political power is legitimate, first, because it serves preservation as nature dictates. It is reasonable to submit to such a power on the same grounds, since reasonable action is action that is an appropriate means to a given end.[52] In this case the end is the satisfaction of the primary human desire for preservation, and the creation of a political authority capable of resolving disputes can reasonably be expected to increase the chances that that desire will be satisfied. In submitting to such an authority, one does relinquish some of the freedom available in the state of nature, with freedom here understood as the absence of external impediments to the pursuit of one's wishes (2T.57, 123). But freedom, after all, is to be valued as a "fence" to preservation, and to forgo some of it to secure the rest and to fulfill the primary wish for security and a comfortable life is to show a sense of priorities in accord with the natural law.

To emphasize the primacy of preservation leads to an interpretation of Locke's doctrine as theoretically almost indistinguishable from Hobbes's. The distinction is to be found on the practical level in Locke's claim that slavery can never in fact serve preservation,

---

51. It should be noted that evidence for this view of the natural law is not to be found in the *Second Treatise*. See 1T.86, 88, and Essay II.20.

52. And see 2T.26, to this end in particular.

that the right of resistance is not more dangerous than absolute monarchy, that the "pole-cats" and "foxes" of the state of nature cannot compare to the "lion" of a monarch with absolute authority (2T.93). While Locke is more pessimistic than Hobbes about the security promised by authority, he is more optimistic in another respect. Men are fortunate that there is so little conflict between their interests and their rights; that their preservation can best be served by the maintenance of certain freedoms.

Curiously, this characterization of Locke's position is compatible with two quite different interpretations of his view of the authority of the state. The first stresses Locke's theory of prerogative powers and sees him as gradually modifying the statement of legislative supremacy with exceptions that reveal his preference for the rule of "godlike" princes (2T.42, 166). His recommendations for formal limitations on the exercise of political powers are prudent ones for ordinary times and ordinary rulers, but they may be disregarded if that should be necessary or useful for the protection or prosperity of the community. The second stresses the role of the state as the protector of the greatest possible individual freedom for the pursuit of a comfortable and secure life, because such freedom is the indispensable means to security and prosperity. Hence, limitations on the sphere of state action are of considerable importance. (It would be possible to hold both of these positions simultaneously by applying the first only to foreign affairs and the second to domestic affairs.) Those who interpret Locke in either fashion may share a common ground in criticizing Lockeanism as morally insufficient because based on the individual pursuit of selfish satisfactions—mere preservation.[53]

But there are problems with the interpretation that begins with the premise of preservation, and not surprisingly, they derive from insufficient attention to Locke's arguments from the natural freedom of men. On the basis of this interpretation it would be difficult to explain why Locke describes a man's natural power as twofold, a power to seek his preservation as he sees fit and a power to punish other men for breaches of the natural law even when he himself is not their victim. The executive power of the law of nature is not a simple right of self-defense included in the general right to act to preserve yourself. The natural executive power, as Locke understands it, is the logical consequence of a situation where each has a duty to respect the rights of his equals. This is extremely important for Locke's description of the rise of political power and its char-

---

53. See Macpherson, pp. 194–262; and Strauss, *Natural Right*, pp. 202–51.

acter as the realization in a particular community of the moral condition of the entire human community (2T.7–8, 16–18, 87–88, 128–31, 171).

Moreover, it would be difficult to explain why absolute monarchy would be considered inconsistent with civil society rather than simply the worst form of government, least likely to protect the lives, liberties, and property of its subjects. In general, any requirement for legitimacy derived from the premise that government authority must originate in the consent of the governed would be weakened, resting only on a defense in terms of practical possibilities. For example, Locke argues that the legislative may not delegate its lawmaking power and, on similar grounds, that the people are entitled to resist anyone who usurps political authority (2T.141, 212). But if preservation is the end of government and this is the primary principle, is not a good usurper to be preferred to an ineffectual but rightful ruler? This is one aspect of the problem that appeared at the close of our discussion of the *First Treatise*. If the "reason for" political power is its purpose or end, there seems to be no justification for resisting any government that fulfills that end. In fact, one might suppose that the man who could best fulfill it, the best protector, would have a right to the power necessary to do the job. But this is not Locke's view. By interpreting Locke as if preservation were clearly his foremost principle and related to all others as the end is to the means, one quickly reaches clearly non-Lockean conclusions.

Serious consideration of the foundation of the requirement of consent in the premise of natural freedom is the basis for the second line of interpretation. Because freedom is the natural human condition, all legitimate government derives from the consent of the people. Each man has an equal right with every other to pursue a comfortable life under the natural law. No man can claim a right to rule another, and legitimate government cannot violate this condition of man's humanity. It is essential that there be no rightful subjection to the private will of another man. The establishment of an impartial judge common to all members of the society with authority from consent to execute his judgments enforces the natural law of preservation as a moral law. Its purpose is "to protect and redress the innocent" in a manner that respects the natural equality of rights (2T.20). The natural law of preservation is a matter of interest, but it is also a matter of right, and the violation of another's rights is both a threat to his preservation and an insult to his humanity (2T.91, 172).

When the legitimacy of political power is compared with the illegitimate character of slavery from this perspective, the concepts of reason and freedom receive striking reinterpretations. Certainly, political power is legitimate in that it consists with preservation, since each man's right to preservation is secured in accord with the natural law. The natural law is a rule of reason that governs men as the only creatures capable of reason.[54] Political authority, unlike slavery, is an appropriate form of government for rational creatures because it operates according to general rules of reason. The rule between slaves and their masters, like the rule among beasts, is the rule of force. It is force without right operating to impose the will of one man on another, whereas political rule is force with right operating to guide the will of each according to the same general principles (2T.19, 87–88). Because political power rules men as rational, it rules men as free creatures. Freedom is freedom under law, a freedom that replicates the natural condition of man as subject to no superior will but bound to guide his own according to the natural law.

These relationships among law, liberty, reason, and will are most clearly developed in Locke's discussion of paternal power (2T.57–63). A child is not free but is subject to his parents because, and only so long as, he cannot understand the law that governs him.

> The *Freedom* then of Man and Liberty of acting according to his own Will, is *grounded on* his having *Reason,* which is able to instruct him in that Law he is to govern himself by, and make him know how far he is left to the freedom of his own will. To turn him loose to an unrestrain'd Liberty, before he has Reason to guide him is not the allowing him the priviledge of his Nature, to be free; but to thrust him out amongst Brutes, and abandon him to a state as wretched, and as much beneath that of a Man as theirs. (2T.63)

Whereas the first interpretation finds freedom in the extent to which men can pursue the objects of their will unimpeded and in a manner indicated by the rational calculation of the best means to do so, this interpretation sees freedom as an alternative to willfullness, arbitrariness, government "at pleasure." The first view permits no distinction between liberty and license; the second finds liberty in a subjection to reasonable laws.[55]

---

54. The natural law understood as a desire for preservation would not distinguish men from beasts.

55. Locke connects the two ideas as follows: to be free from the restraint of the actions of others is to be free in the sense that you are subject only to rational laws, laws that are required to prevent interference with your actions. Locke suggests that Filmer's position is that of the first interpretation. This difference is closely related to their differences regarding sovereignty. If freedom is to follow your own will and law is the expression of the sovereign's will, then liberty and law are contrary to one another. Locke's understanding of the law is not voluntaristic in this way. See 2T.6, 22, 57.

On the basis of this interpretation, Locke's political thought appears more satisfying than Hobbes's morally and psychologically. Unlike the slave, a free man, as a rational creature, is "Master of his own Life," with a right to the means of preserving it and a right to "judge of, or to defend his right." Free men are capable of property.[56] For this reason men are capable of creating contractual obligations through consent. These obligations are not evaluated solely on the basis of the individual's desire for preservation. In contrast to Hobbes, there is no right in the soldier to avoid his service or the condemned man his punishment. And no obligation to obedience can arise in exchange for protection of life when the conqueror's sword is at your throat (1T.42; 2T.176, 186). Furthermore, compacts are binding even in the state of nature (2T.14). A human life is a life as a free man capable of incurring moral obligations, and each is obliged under the natural law to respect the equal status of others in this regard. Certainly this is not a political morality of humility that demands the sacrifice of one's interests or the suppression of all desire. And neither is it a political morality where honor and virtue are the avenues for the satisfaction of pride. But Locke does accommodate pride, rather than submerging it with the overpowering fear of violent death, by justifying only a politics in which no man is above the rest.[57]

In considering the political consequences that might be drawn from this fundamental understanding of Locke's position, this second interpretation, like the first, permits several variations. What the variations share is the recognition that political power is not private power based on unequal private right but an arrangement that creates an authorized public power to maintain the status of each as equal with the rest in their fundamental rights.

The requirement that political power respect the natural equality of men may be adequately met by founding the government in the consent of the people as a trust where the people retain a right of resistance. This is certainly Locke's minimal condition. That political authority must derive from the consent of the governed is a matter of principle in Locke's doctrine. This conclusion escapes the

56. Slaves are not, and hence are not members of civil society, since civil society exists for the sake of protecting property. This would be another way of stating why there can be no civil society between an absolute monarch and his subjects. The same conclusion was reached by viewing the establishment of a common judge as the end of civil society. See 2T.85, 91, 172.

57. See 2T.123. Compare Hobbes, p. 211, and see Leo Strauss, *The Political Philosophy of Thomas Hobbes: Its Basis and Its Genesis*, trans. Elsa M. Sinclair (Oxford: Clarendon Press, 1936; reprint ed., Chicago: University of Chicago Press, 1952).

difficulties presented by its alternative, that consent is necessary on practical grounds, without raising interpretive difficulties itself. On this basis, absolute monarchy is illegitimate because it recognizes no right in the people to alter their government, whereas early patriarchies are legitimate governments based on consent even though they also are not ruled by standing laws. Limited government is sufficient in principle to meet the requirement that government accord with natural freedom.

Other variations of liberal theory might find that the consent of the people—with its corollary, the right of resistance—is not sufficient to assure that no man's will is elevated above the rest. The rule by standing laws and the subjection of all members of the society to them could be seen as necessary, in practice or in principle, to fully satisfy the requirements of a politics that conforms to man's natural right.[58] Only mixed and balanced government would meet the requirement for legitimate government. To interpret Locke in this way would mean emphasizing his support for republican institutions and legislative supremacy and interpreting the doctrine of prerogative as the narrowest possible concession to unavoidable deficiencies in the law.

With respect to the rule by standing laws, Locke's continual repetition of this requirement, its inclusion in the definition of political power,[59] and the analysis of freedom as the equivalent of subjection to general laws produces the impression that legitimate government in principle must rule by established laws. But a stronger case can be made by arguing that standing laws become necessary in practice as the condition without which subjection to a ruler will mean subjection to his arbitrary, personal rule.[60] This occurs whenever the ruler may come to have an interest distinct from that of the people, which in Locke's view is less likely in that Golden Age of societies ruled by father-kings than thereafter. Where the will of the ruler serves the good of the society, where all live under the

---

58. Some of the institutional arrangements required to establish the rule of law can be seen as a first line of defense to forestall revolution. See 2T.207. James Madison argues in *The Federalist Papers*, nos. 49–50, pp. 313–19, that the separation of powers is an alternative to direct appeals to the people. Filmer questions the value of a freedom to choose your government if it cannot be exercised without constant rebellion. Filmer, "Observations on Milton," p. 256.

59. Though rule by law may be distinguished from rule by standing law. See 2T.3 and p. 86 above.

60. See John Locke, MS. c.28 f.8, 20 July 1670, where Locke comments on a society described in a travel book where justice is well administered through a complicated sort of hearing before judges, though there are no written laws at all.

natural law enforced by a good and wise prince, rule without positive laws may be legitimate.[61]

Once rule by standing laws becomes necessary, institutions also become necessary to ensure that rulers will not place themselves above the laws. The rule of law requires a separation of legislative and executive power, collective legislatures that disband periodically, and an avenue of appeal against actions of executive officers. These institutions provide security that those holding political power will behave as officers of the law, with a public charge and not a private power. Though Locke states that these institutions are required for rulers to be considered members of civil society (2T.13, 91, 94), these are characteristics of "well-order'd" governments and not requirements for legitimacy (2T.10, 143, 159).[62] Locke's theory can accommodate a wide variety of forms of legitimate government.

Locke does, however, argue that representation is required as a matter of principle in any legitimate government, or at least in any government that wishes to collect taxes.

> 'Tis true, Governments cannot be supported without great Charge, and 'tis fit every one who enjoys his share of the Protection, should pay out of his Estate his proportion for the maintenance of it. But still it must be with his own Consent, i.e., the Consent of the Majority, giving it either by themselves, or their Representatives chosen by them. For if any one shall claim a *Power to lay* and levy *Taxes* on the People, by his own Authority, and without such consent of the people, he thereby invades the *Fundamental Law of Property*, and subverts the end of Government. For what property have I in that which another may by right take, when he pleases to himself? (2T.140; see also 2T.192)

The power of government to preserve property includes the power to regulate it, but not to take it for the use of the governors. One safeguard against such exploitation is collective legislatures that are not always sitting. But where there is no such legislature, a representative body must be created for the purpose of consenting to tax collection (2T.138–40, 142). Thus every legitimate government

---

61. To have a government that serves the public good and not the private interest of the ruler *is* to protect the right of preservation for each with no unequal subjection to another's will. It is nonarbitrary government in both the formal and the substantive sense and fulfills the condition of Locke's two premises at once; preservation and freedom. See 2T.199–200.

62. At 2T.205–6, Locke suggests that the lack of personal responsibility of the king is a wise institutional addition. A veto power for the chief executive is also alluded to (a share in the legislative) but not explicitly mentioned. See 2T.151. The institutional arrangements listed here are more strongly endorsed.

sufficiently advanced to collect taxes must include, as a minimal condition, some form of representative assembly. It seems that the argument here would apply equally to life and liberty, to property in the general sense. Men have a property in their rights, and they create government to protect those rights. It is a short step from this beginning to the conclusion that legitimate government must include a representative body for broader, or even general, legislative purposes. "For what property have I in that which another may by right take, when he pleases to himself?"[63]

Legitimate government must accord in principle with preservation and with equality of right, or freedom. In fact, all legitimate power or right accords with these two premises. Parental power is justified by the parents' obligation under the natural law to provide for their children's preservation and is limited and temporary owing to respect for the child's eventual status as an equal. Despotic power, when it is legitimate, is so because the slave has forfeited his freedom and right to preservation by threatening the life and liberty of another. Property right arises out of a combination of the right of preservation and the fact that each is master of himself and proprietor of his person (2T.26–27, 31, 44).

Throughout, Locke's arguments from the two premises, or from the elements of the single twofold premise of an equal natural right to preservation, proceed in tandem. This is the source of the interpretive difficulties and of the apparent ambiguity and ambivalence of Locke's thought. It is the source of the duality in the argument of the *First Treatise* as well. There as here, the "original" and "end" of civil government did not always seem to lead to the same conclusion regarding its "extent." But Locke's is a dual standard. One element cannot be elevated above the other, and there is no need to choose between them. Both preservation and freedom

63. Locke uses the example of military discipline to advance his argument and so calls attention to the question of the authority of the state to take your life. Historically, taxes were imposed primarily for the purpose of raising armies. To argue that taxes cannot be imposed without consent may be tantamount to arguing that wars may not be fought without consent. Once Parliaments were called for the purpose of consenting to the king's requests for taxes, it was difficult to limit their activities. They could refuse consent to win concessions on other matters.

It seems as difficult to distinguish life and liberty from estate when the issue is the need to consent before your property can be taken as it would be to distinguish life and liberty from property when the issue is the requirement that they can be forfeit only on a finding of a violation by due process of law. In other words, there is a large opening wedge here toward a requirement for a representative body for many purposes.

For a discussion of the problem of taxation and representation in the *Second Treatise* see John Dunn, "Consent in the Political Theory of John Locke," *Historical Journal* 10 (1967): 153–82, esp. 169–73.

are necessary conditions for legitimacy, while neither alone is sufficient.

There are a variety of ways of meeting that dual standard, and the variations necessarily become more complex as societies become more complex, prosperous, and divided. With the complexity and increased occasion for conflict, laws and formal institutions are introduced as means of restraining abuses of power. They embody and express the authorizing consent of the people and provide limiting checks on public authority. They help to identify in practice who is to be obeyed and how far.

If Locke's dual standard of legitimacy is to be practicable, it must provide sufficient guidance to determine precisely this: Who is to be obeyed, and how far? We turn now to a consideration of the grounds for obedience and for resistance in order to determine whether Locke has fulfilled the practical requirements of political theory.

3

Legitimate and Illegitimate Power:
Practical Tests of the Normative Theory

Introduction

Locke writes that in the "Community of Nature" "every one as he is *bound to preserve himself,* and not to quit his Station wilfully; so by the like reason when his own Preservation comes not in competition, ought he, as much as he can, *to preserve the rest of Mankind*" (2T.6). This is the dictate of the law of nature in the state of nature. But in forming political communities, men incur new obligations (2T.97); obligations consistent with "the *first and fundamental natural Law,* . . . *the preservation of the Society,* and (as far as will consist with the publick good) of every person in it" (2T.134). There are two significant differences between these two statements of the substance of the natural law. First, the priority of the individual has been replaced by the priority of the community. Second, the relevant community has shifted from all of humankind to a particular society. How are these shifts to be explained?

Liberal political thought in general is identified with the dual emphasis of Locke's first statement: the emphasis on individualism, on the one hand, and our common humanity on the other. For this reason, liberalism bears a complex relation to nationalism. It has been faulted precisely for its inability to provide secure foundations for the priority of the national community. The charge is made that a liberal community cannot sustain itself because it cannot justify the claims of the public good against individual self-interested claims, and because it fails to secure the loyalty to the community that is necessary to overcome strong individual ties of loyalty or conscience.

These charges represent contemporary versions of the challenges with which Filmer confronted consent theorists.[1] According to Filmer, these theorists failed to justify the legitimate exercise of authority in distinct political communities, communities that retain their integrity over time from one generation to the next. And they failed to explain and justify the individual's obligation to a particular ruler or government. When any individual or group can claim at any time a right to sever its connection with either the society or the government, the result is the death of the society through disintegration or anarchic rebellion.

In addition to the problems of the relation of the individual to society and government, modern critics of liberalism raise a second group of issues concerning the relations of society and government to one another. Liberalism's individualistic premises are problematic when the political issue is that of the claims of the national community or the people as such against conquering or colonial governments or oppressive indigenous ones. An individual right of resistance is not the same as a national right of self-determination. Claims of the latter sort depend upon an understanding of the constitution of a people or a political society that can explain how such an entity can have rights in relation to governments. And the question arises again in this context whether a political community retains its integrity over time even, for example, under conditions of conquest or tyranny.

In responding to Filmer's charges, Locke also confronts this second group of issues. Having explained what a political community is and its relation to government, Locke proceeds to consider the situations in which societies and governments are altered: conquest, usurpation, tyranny, and rebellion. The investigation of the bonds of society, the bonds of government, and the criteria for when those bonds are dissolved is required to resolve both the question of individual obligations and the question of the rights of the community vis-à-vis government.

These are issues that are hardly to be distinguished from what were identified earlier as the practical requirements of political theory. Having established standards for legitimate government, Locke must show that they provide clear guidance for justifying authority within political communities, determining who rules, and judging the extent of each individual's obligations to the group and to its duly authorized rulers. Locke's ability to provide this guidance is one test of the success of his political theory. Whether this guidance

1. See pp. 55–56.

is conducive to peace among and within political communities is the other.

Obligation

THE BONDS OF SOCIETY AND GOVERNMENT

Political society is constituted, according to Locke, by two distinct factors: the decision of a group of men to act as one body for the sake of their preservation, and the presence of a common authority capable of judging and executing their common law.

> Whereby it is easie to discern who are, and who are not in *Political Society* together. Those who are united into one Body, and have a common establish'd Law and Judicature to appeal to, with Authority to decide Controversies between them, and punish Offenders, *are in Civil Society* one with another. (2T.87)

As with the elements of the definition of political power, Locke emphasizes now one factor, now the other, obscuring rather than clarifying their relation. In this case the relation between the two factors, the unity of the group and authority within it, determines whether political society can exist independent of government in any sense.[2]

Each factor is described as constitutive of political society, and neither is described as sufficient in itself to constitute it. A common authority, with its two elements of law and judicature, distinguishes civil society from the state of nature:

> Where-ever any persons are, who have not such an Authority to Appeal to, for the decision of any difference between them, there those persons are still *in the state of Nature*. (2T.90; see also 2T.19)

And the decision to join together to form a group makes the same distinction:

> That which makes the Community, and brings Men out of the loose State of Nature, into *one Politick Society*, is the Agreement which every one has with the rest to incorporate, and act as one Body, and so be one distinct Commonwealth. (2T.211; see also 2T.95)

---

2. Our question in chapter 2 was whether there could be government without law. Here we consider whether there can be society without government, with government understood as a "common establish'd Law and Judicature . . . with Authority," as cited above. Locke sometimes speaks of the legislative as if it were synonymous with government. See, for example, 2T.212.

Political societies are distinguished from other types of associations, as well as from the state of nature, on the basis of these factors, but only by their combination. No single factor is a sufficient defining characteristic. For example, because all men are subject to the same law, the natural law, all mankind is a community distinct from other species (2T.128; see also 2T.6, 171). But lacking a judge on earth to execute that law, it is not a political community. Men may also establish a common judge between them and clearly not form a political society thereby, as when a contract designates an arbitrator to settle disputes arising under it.[3] Even where men are subject to a common law and have an effective common judge, they may not be members of the same society, as is the case between a member of a given society and a resident alien (2T.122). Similarly, consent to unite with others for the sake of the preservation of all is not sufficient to create a political society. A planter in the West Indies making war and peace along with family, neighbors, slaves, and mercenaries is not the leader of a political community (1T.131–32). Theirs is only a temporary union for defense from outsiders with no common binding domestic authority. An association in which members are not permanently obligated by their own consent to a common authority for the sake of the protection of themselves and their property may be a marriage, a family, a church, an army, or a business partnership, but it is not a political society.[4]

It appears, then, that both the decision to form a unit and subjection to a common authority are required, and that each has equal status as constitutive of political society. But Locke at times emphasizes a common authority as the distinguishing characteristic of civil society, and when he does the unity of the society seems to

3. Locke wrote a contract with his publisher that designated a third party as arbitrator should disputes arise. Maurice Cranston, *John Locke: A Biography* (London: Longmans, Green, 1957), p. 319.

4. It is easy to get a distorted view of Locke's general understanding of human relations if one focuses exclusively on political relations. Political society is "individualistic" in origin, requiring the consent of each member. The individual's obligations in society are not like obligations of filial loyalty, but are like contract relations. But Locke stresses in other contexts the importance of bonds other than a common law and individual consent in cementing social relations. See, for example, Essay III.10.13 and III.11.1, where a common language, not law, is called the bond of society. And see Essay II.28.10–12 for the importance of the "Law of Opinion or Reputation," or social norms, in governing behavior. Locke's work on education clearly shows his view that the family is a crucial social institution. In other words, for a people to be a people as a cultural and historical community is not the same as for a people to form a political community. In fact, Locke describes the former as a precursor of the latter in discussing the historical origins of nations. See 2T.106–10; Seliger, "Locke, Liberalism, and Nationalism," pp. 19–27.

depend on, and almost to be identified with, the subjection of each to the same government.

> Civil Society being a State of Peace, amongst those who are of it, from whom the State of War is excluded by the Umpirage, which they have provided in their Legislative, for the ending all Differences that may arise amongst any of them, 'tis in their *Legislative,* that the Members of a Commonwealth are united, and combined together into one coherent living Body. This *is the Soul that gives Form, Life, and Unity* to the Commonwealth: From hence the several Members have their mutual Influence, Sympathy, and Connexion. (2T.212)

Laws, "by their execution," are the "bonds of the Society" (2T.219). Since life is "but an ill condition" in the state of nature, men are "quickly driven into Society," which is to say, to "take Sanctuary under the establish'd Laws of Government" (2T.127). When a man joins himself to an existing "Government," he "authorizes the Society, or which is all one, the Legislative thereof to make Laws for him." (2T.89). Although the mutual agreement to form one community or the individual decision to join an existing community is the *origin* of political communities, or how they come about, or "that which makes the Community" (2T.211), to be members of the same society *is* to have one government. It seems that political society cannot exist without government.

But this is clearly not a satisfactory final conclusion as to Locke's understanding of the relation between society and government. If government powers are a trust from the people, the people as such must exist independent of and prior to government. Locke's doctrine of resistance depends on this understanding of their relation and on the correct distinction between the dissolution of government and the dissolution of society (2T.211, 240, 243). When Locke emphasizes the decision of each to join with others into a community for their mutual protection as the distinguishing characteristic of civil society, the society does seem to take priority over government both temporally and theoretically. Its temporal priority is evident in that the creation of the government is the act of the society.

> For the *Essence and Union of the Society* consisting in having one Will, the Legislative, when once established by the Majority, has the declaring, and as it were keeping of that Will. The *Constitution of the Legislative* is the first and fundamental Act of Society, whereby provision is made for the *Continuation of their Union,* under the Direction

of Persons, and Bonds of Laws made by persons authorized thereun-
to, by the Consent and Appointment of the People. (2T.212)[5]

The theoretical priority of the society appears in the understanding of government as the *means* for its maintenance. Government is
an instrument of the society for the preservation of the society.
Although political society originates in consent and is maintained
by the actions of a common authority, it is defined by its *end*, the
preservation of the whole. Only when men can no longer "maintain and support themselves, as *one intire* and *independent Body*," is
their society dissolved (2T.211).

Locke's position on the question of the relation between society
and government seems ambivalent at best. His thought is open to
misinterpretation or the charge of self-contradiction on this question for two reasons. First, the formation of a political community
by unanimous consent of the members obligates each member to
abide by the decisions of a majority of that community. Thus every
society begins as a perfect democracy (2T.132). The same act of
consent that forms the society also forms this democratic government (2T.99). In this sense, then, political society cannot exist without government, that is, without political obligation and rightful
power. This is why the terms community and government can be
used interchangeably and still correctly in certain contexts: "When
any number of men have so *consented to make one Community* or Government, they are thereby presently incorporated, and make *one
Body Politick* wherein the *Majority* have a Right to act and conclude
the rest" (2T.95).

The majority of the community has in its hands both the ordinary
legislative and executive political powers and the right to constitute a
government for the community. In exercising the latter, the former
are entrusted to representatives of the community (2T.95–99, chap.
10). When the term "government" is used in the somewhat re-
stricted sense to apply to the designated forms according to which
representatives exercise the legislative and executive powers of the
community as a trust, then Locke's position is that the community
can exist independent of government, create government as its
agent, and resist the illegitimate exercise of power by its agent.
When the term "government" is used in a broader sense to include
the basic political democracy of every political community, then
Locke can be said to take the position that society cannot exist without government. With this understanding in mind, Locke's appar-

5. The passage is the continuation of the passage quoted on p. 103 above.

ently contradictory statements on the subject become clear in their meaning.

The second problem with Locke's position is not so much terminological as practical. Locke maintains that society can exist without a designated form of government long enough for the majority to create a government, at least when it is initially formed or at the moment of resistance when government must be reinstated in opposition to tyranny, usurpation, or conquest. That a political community can act as a unit to play the role of creator in this way is a theoretical necessity for Locke's position, and his theory is consistent here. When the designated government dissolves, the people do not immediately return to a condition of anarchy or to the state of nature. Instead, the legislative power returns to the community. The individual remains obligated to the community so long as the community is capable of acting through the decisions of a majority of its members (2T.220, 243). But is this capability a theoretical fiction rather than a practical possibility?

Locke's own argument seems to undermine any claims for the independent viability of political society in its basic democratic form. Locke emphasizes that an established legislative and impartial execution of the law are indispensable means to the preservation of the society.[6] Without such a common authority or umpire, any controversy among members of the society would produce a continued state of war. Government is the "bar to the state of war" because an appeal to the law prevents an act of war from initiating a spiraling cycle of revenge (2T.20–21, 212). In practice, no society can exist for long without an operating government.[7] Society can no more continue without government than the body can continue without a soul; without a soul, the body soon disintegrates and dies.[8] When an established government has forfeited its authority, the people may be capable of resisting illegitimate government actions, but can the majority act as a government to maintain the bonds of the society? Locke so emphasizes the importance of a

6. See 2T.123–27, 220.

7. "Government is hardly to be avoided amongst Men that live together" (2T.105). "For Laws not being made for themselves, but to be by their execution the Bonds of the Society, to keep every part of the Body Politick in its due place and function, when that totally ceases, the *Government* visibly *ceases*, and the People become a confused Multitude, without Order or Connexion" (2T.219).

8. See 2T.96, 212. Locke abandons the metaphor of soul and body, for obvious reasons, in order to make the point that government (soul) also cannot continue without society (body). If government is like a house or the frame of a house, society is like the building materials (2T.175, 211). Government gives shape, motion, and direction to the body politic.

common authority capable of acting to resolve disputes among individuals as the barrier to chaos that it is difficult to see how, in a situation where the established government no longer has authority, justice could be administered sufficiently well by the majority or its new agents to prevent the total dissolution of the society.

This problem arises only because of the peculiar two-stage relationship between government and society that Locke describes. Individuals form a society, obligating themselves to the majority of the group, which in turn obligates the community to a particular government established by it. The problem also indicates the fundamental issue to which this two-stage theory is a response. Locke's treatment of the relation between society and government is part of his effort to solve the overriding problem of justifying both the authority of government and resistance to tyranny or usurpation.

This was the central problem for English political theory in the seventeenth century. In the 1640s, 1660s, and 1680s, it took the form of justifying both the independence of the king in a mixed constitution and resistance to the king.[9] In the 1640s, arguments for resistance tended to elevate Parliament as supreme within the government, since Parliament, as the representative of the people, was viewed as the proper organ for expressing the people's right of resistance. On the other hand, arguments for the monarch's independence from Parliament tended to become justifications for monarchical absolutism. To escape this dilemma by postulating a right of resistance, but one exercised directly by the people rather than through the authority of Parliament, was to run headlong into the charge that resistance then would mean chaos, and frequent chaos too. A defense of resistance, then, had to be one that not only would be compatible with shared authority in a mixed monarchy in ordinary times, but would also prevent total anarchy in times of trouble. In dealing with these difficulties, publicists and theorists used a variety of distinctions between several kinds of power or sovereignty in order to find some foundation for the obedience of the people and independence of the king in ordinary times that would nonetheless permit some kind of orderly resistance to Charles I, Charles II, or James II. The distinctions used included that between constitutive and ordinary power, real and personal majesty, ownership of sovereignty and usufruct rights, "civitas" and "commonwealth," and the king as "singulis major" but "universis minor."[10]

---

9. The discussion that follows is drawn from Franklin.

10. Franklin, pp. 23, 64–76. Locke takes pains to explain his use of the term "commonwealth" at 2T.133.

Locke's distinction between political society and the government it creates corresponds to these distinctions. While Locke does not speak in terms of two abstract types of power or juridical categories, his discussion of the relation between political society and government confronts the same problems that these distinctions were meant to address. And while political society does not possess special "constituent" power distinct from the "ordinary" power of government, the effect of Locke's line of argument is much as if it did. Typically, Locke avoids arbitrarily creating abstract categories of right or power and then trying to delineate their precise content, specify who can exercise them, and so forth. Instead he makes his case both for obedience and for resistance with one argument: there is always a reason for, or end of, any power or right that explains both its necessity and its limit. Although there is no "constitutive power" or "real majesty," political society is the juridical unit with the right to constitute a government by delegating its political power to be exercised by the society's trustees for the preservation of the society. The right to delegate power, that is, to form a government, is one that the community cannot lose, and it is a right that cannot itself be transferred. The government may not alter its own form or abdicate its authority but instead is subject to the *"first and fundamental positive Law"* of the community that established its form and authority (2T.134).

On the other hand, the community is not free to alter its government so long as that government exercises its power in accordance with its trust (2T.134, 198, 220, 243). The government has all the authority necessary to rule—all "ordinary" power. Unless and until the government acts contrary to the purposes for which it was empowered, all members of the society owe it obedience.

This is Locke's constitutionalism: the people are supreme but at the same time subordinate; and the same can be said for the government. These relationships are the consequence of founding all political obligation in consent. The people as a whole are the source of the government's power; the form of government and designation of who rules are directed by a fundamental positive law of the community; and political power reverts to the people as a body only on the default of the government.

The default of the entire government occurs when either the legislature or the executive forfeits its authority. This principle was the innovation that resolved the problem of justifying both the independence of the king and a right of resistance without at the same time establishing a doctrine of parliamentary supremacy. Where the executive shares in the legislative power, the executive

and the legislative assembly are coequal branches, and the cooperation of both is required to exercise the legislative power of government. Should the king abuse and therefore forfeit his authority,
the legislative power of government dissolves in its entirety. The
Parliament retains no authority to repair the defect or continue to
govern. Instead, the society as a whole may exercise its right to
constitute a new government.

George Lawson introduced this resolution of the problem with
his *Politica Sacra et Civilis* in 1660, and according to Julian Franklin,
Locke borrowed it for use in 1681 and 1688.[11] Lawson held that
the people, not their Parliament, had the right to resist Charles I.
But the radicalism of his position made it unattractive to the dominant opposition to Charles I. Their accusation was that the doctrine
of popular resistance eliminated all barriers to anarchy.

The anarchy problem has two facets: Can the community sustain itself when the government has dissolved? And does the community have the power to dissolve the government at will? Locke's
theoretical responses to these problems are clear. Because of the
dual levels of obligation between the individual and the community
and between the community and its government, the community
remains as a political unit when its government is dissolved, and the
community remains obligated to its government until its government dissolves. These relationships of obligation make possible a
doctrine of resistance that is not an invitation to anarchy. But we
have already seen that, as a practical matter, Locke casts doubt on
the viability of a community as a political unit in the absence of an
established government. And there is a serious practical difficulty
with the second facet of the problem as well. If the community is
judge of when the government has dissolved, does it not in practice
have the power to dissolve the government at will?

Locke's defense of his theory of obligation in the face of these
difficulties and the difficulties raised by Filmer's challenges to consent theorists is the subject of the remainder of this chapter. In
chapter 2 we discussed what I have called Locke's constitutionalism
as his alternative to Filmer's theory of sovereignty. Locke substitutes the dual supremacy of the people, on the one hand, and the
law, on the other, for Filmer's assertion of the sovereignty of a
single will. The earlier discussion stressed the way Locke's theory
provides for certain limitations on government power. Rulers are
constrained to govern according to their trust both by a popular

11. Franklin, pp. 88–89.

right of resistance and by their obligation, as members of the community, to its laws. But the theory also explains the grounds for the obligation of each member to the community and to the government established by it. The consent of each individual to membership in the community creates a binding obligation to the authorities empowered by the community and governing within the sphere of their entrusted powers. Obligation and resistance are two sides of the same coin.

The purpose of Locke's discussion of society and government is to establish the relationships of right and obligation between them and between each of them and the individual. The subject is essential to his examination of sovereignty, is the grounds for his constitutionalism, and is the basis for his resolution of the problem of rebellion and resistance. Perhaps modern commentators on his work would have focused clearly on these issues had he argued in terms like "constituent" and "ordinary" power, for example. Instead, they have discussed Locke's consideration of society and government primarily with a view to settling whether his political thought rests on a view of humanity as naturally selfish or as naturally social.[12] The question whether society can exist without government is taken to be identical to the question whether the state of nature is or is not peaceful in character. A good deal of the discussion is distorted by forgetting that Locke speaks here of political society only, not of the various other forms of human association. Moreover, according to Locke, the formation of political society is coeval with the formation of political obligation and authority— with government in the broad sense. Locke's initial premise is neither natural selfishness nor natural sociality, but natural freedom. His efforts are directed toward explaining how obligations arise out of the condition of natural freedom that are consistent with natural freedom.

Locke's psychological premises become important for modern commentators because of the historical developments linking liberal politics and capitalist economics. It can be argued that both are based on the same premises regarding human behavior: both the individualism of Locke's politics of consent and the assertion of competitive economic interests are said to assume self-interested individual actors. The political arrangements of the liberal state appear as rules for regulating the competition among them, con-

12. See Cox, pp. 73–105; Macpherson, pp. 241–47; Seliger, *Liberal Politics*, pp. 99–100; Strauss, *Natural Right*, pp. 224–34.

trolling the conflict. The premise for such rules is a hardheaded suspicion of human motives, including the motives of those in power.

On the other hand, the political assumptions can appear optimistic and out of harmony with the economic and social ones. The liberal expectation that the rules of the game will remain neutral and that they will be respected seems naive and softheaded in a social system where men are encouraged to pursue their individual economic interests to the utmost. The system is said to work only until it is put to the test by a serious clash of economic interests among classes. These sorts of issues inform much of the scholarly commentary on Locke as well as on the relation between Hobbes and Locke. Do the Hobbesian psychological assumptions that sit so comfortably with capitalist economics necessitate a Hobbesian sovereign, and is Locke's sovereign a substantial departure or only a set of refinements?

Locke's views on society and government, on the need for government and the nature of sovereign power, are all relevant to this set of issues. But Locke's views were not formulated in terms of these issues. Locke was in the midst of and looking over his shoulder at a period of civil war, constitutional crisis, and political revolution. He was not primarily looking forward to a period of economic revolution. Locke used the distinction between society and government in the context of his contemporary debate over the problems of political right and power. Recognition of the context allows us to recover the meaning of the distinction in Locke's thought. It also allows us to recover Locke's analysis of society and government for consideration in our own discussion of the problems of political right and power and of the viability of liberal consent theory as a response to them. Locke used the distinction between society and government in his treatment of the relations of obligation between the individual, his community, and its government, and he used it to argue that a theory of consent could form the basis both for legitimate and stable governments and for a practicable political response to illegitimate ones.

THE THEORY OF OBLIGATION DEFENDED

Beginning as he does with the premise of natural freedom, Locke argues that all political obligation to the community and to its government arises from the consent of free individuals. This thought provides the basis for Locke's solution to the two practical problems immediately raised by the confrontation with Filmer that structures the *Two Treatises:* how to justify the simultaneous existence of several political communities that remain unified over time and over territory, and how to determine who rules within those communities. Locke had to defend his solutions and his doctrine of consent against Filmer's sharp criticisms of consent theories as both theoretically inconsistent and grounded in practical impossibilities.[13]

Filmer takes the principle of indefeasible individual natural right to mean that all obligation must arise out of unanimous consent and that all obligation lasts only until the individual retracts the consent he has given. His criticisms of consent theories are in fact criticisms of the practical impossibility of unanimity and retractability as the bases for political life and criticisms of any theoretical departure from unanimity and retractability as inconsistent with the premise of natural freedom.

Locke dismisses one of Filmer's criticisms with a single sentence. The formation of a political community does not require the unanimous consent of all mankind because "it injures not the Freedom of the rest; they are left as they were in the Liberty of the State of Nature" (2T.95). This point parallels one of the important arguments concerning property, though in the case of property it takes considerably more argumentation. Private property can emerge from the natural situation of mankind's common possession of the earth without "any express Compact of the Commoners" on condition that it does not prejudice the rights of the others (2T.25; see 2T.27, 31, 33, 50). The two arguments together allow for the creation of political communities and for individual landownership.

But these are not sufficient to establish territorial nations, unless a nation is understood as a community consisting exclusively of individual landowners who happen to have contiguous plots. Apart from the obvious impracticability of such a conception, Locke certainly does not connect landownership and membership in civil society in this way.[14] Communities as such can claim territories for the use of their members; for example, nomadic tribes settled in cities and claimed the surrounding lands. These claims are also limited, as individual claims are, since anything more than the people "do or can make use of" remains part of the common (2T.45).

13. See James Daly, *Sir Robert Filmer and English Political Thought* (Toronto: University of Toronto Press, 1979). Daly credits Filmer with forcing the development of stronger versions of consent theory in response to his critique, particularly those of Edward Gee and James Tyrrell, p. 103. See pp. 84–86 for a discussion of Filmer's problems with the element of consent in his own theory. Filmer maintained that, if the sovereign dies without heirs, heads of families designate a new king by consent.
14. See chap. 3, note 32.

But why do such claims supersede the claims of any other community or individual to a given territory? Locke's response is that *"Labour . . . puts the difference of value* on every thing" (2T.40). Locke makes this case with regard to individual claims to land, but the argument applies at least as strongly to the claims of a single community over those of mankind in general. To understand the justification for territorial nations, we must first follow out Locke's argument concerning individual property.

The issue here is the relative claim of any individual proprietor as against the claims of other men, and Locke argues that the individual's contribution in labor creates the greatest part of what he enjoys as proprietor. The question of the character of the labor under consideration must be raised. Is the greatest contribution to the improvement of man's estate a product of individual labor or a social product? Locke's examples bring the question forcefully to mind.

> Bread, Wine and Cloth, are things of daily use, and great plenty, yet notwithstanding, Acorns, Water, and Leaves, or Skins, must be our Bread, Drink and Clothing did not *labour* furnish us with these more useful Commodities. (2T.42)

> 'Tis *Labour* then which *puts the greatest part of Value upon Land. . . .* For 'tis not barely the Plough-man's Pains, the Reaper's and Thresher's Toil, and the Baker's Sweat, is to be counted into the *Bread* we eat; the Labour of those who broke the Oxen, who digged and wrought the Iron and Stones, who felled and framed the Timber imployed about the Plough, Mill, and Oven, or any other Utensils. . . . 'Twould be a strange *Catalogue of things that Industry provided and made use of, about every Loaf of Bread.* (2T.43)

The production of a loaf of bread involves not only cooperation of many arts in a society where labor is divided, but also the invention of breadmaking. Each individual depends decisively on learning such things from the previous generation. Men do not provide for themselves out of simply their own labor; it could easily be argued that the greatest contribution to an individual's well-being and to the productivity of the earth is made by the society as a functioning group. Since the argument assumes that the greatest property right belongs to the factor contributing the greatest value, this might give the community a stronger claim than the individual to landownership, though the individual's labor is the sine qua non of the production of any particular thing.

The point can be clearly made by a critical reading of the concluding paragraph of this portion of Locke's argument:

From all which it is evident, that though the things of Nature are given in common, yet Man (by being Master of himself, and *Proprietor of his own Person,* and the actions or *Labour* of it) had still in himself *the great Foundation of Property;* and that which made up the great part of what he applied to the Support or Comfort of his being, when Invention and Arts had improved the Conveniences of Life, was perfectly his own, and did not belong in common to others. (2T.44)

The "Inventions and Arts," however, are not perfectly his own and do belong in common with others.[15]

What Locke has in fact succeeded in showing is that particular societies have a claim to the land and its products that is stronger than the claim of all mankind in general, to whom God gave it in common. This is not the same as showing that individual men have a greater claim than the societies of which they are a part.[16] It is, however, sufficient for the resolution of the particular problem raised by the confrontation with Filmer.[17] Locke is arguing, against Filmer, that this great common can be divided without the consent of all the commoners. This is part of his argument that particular societies are possible on the basis of the premise that all men are born free, and that the supposition of a divine donation of the earth to Adam and his heirs forever is unnecessary and inadequate. The right of a community to settle in a given territory and claim jurisdiction within its boundaries is established by the need to appropriate in order to make use of God's gift, the fact that use limits appropriation so that there is enough left for others, and the argument that the value of what is produced results primarily from the labor of the community.

But Locke tells us that territorial boundaries are settled between nations by mutual agreement, leagues, or treaties; in other words, by consent (2T.38, 45). Again, the case parallels that of individual property rights. Consent settles property claims between communities as it does between individuals of the same community. Men merely recognize through consent the property rights begun by labor and industry (2T.30–45). The consent of all mankind is not necessary to begin property right, but only to reduce conflict over

15. See 2T.101 for an additional reference to the development of arts in civil society.

16. Locke recognizes that the community can set land aside for common use where this arrangement contributes more to the common good than individual landownership would. See 2T.35.

17. I do not mean to suggest that Locke's sole purpose in the discussion of property is to counter Filmer's criticism concerning the integrity of territorial nations, but perhaps his argument is more successful in this respect than in some others.

claims to discrete portions of the earth. The creation of a political community itself, whether settled or nomadic, requires only the consent of each individual wishing to be a member. It is easy to see that many distinct communities could come into being on this basis. There is no necessity for the unanimous consent of all mankind.

But the unity and continuity of political communities are at the mercy of any dissatisfied subgroup wishing to form a new community if only the consent of the prospective members and not the consent of all is required. In other words, once the principle of unanimity is abandoned, the unrestricted right of individuals to form groups would in fact prejudice the rights of others by rendering all groups unstable. But the right of consent is not unrestricted: men are not free to alter their allegiance at will. Consent freely given cannot be freely retracted. Consent need be neither unanimous nor retractable to remain consistent with natural freedom.

Natural freedom is so far from being inconsistent with obligations incurred through consent that it *is* the right to be obligated only on the basis of one's own consent.[18] When an individual agrees to become a member of a political community, he gives up some of the liberty of the natural state and takes on the obligation to abide by the will of the community.

> This *original Compact*, whereby he with others incorporates into *one Society*, would signifie nothing, and be no Compact, if he be left free, and under no other ties, than he was in before in the State of Nature. For what appearance would there be of any Compact? What new Engagement if he were no farther tied by any Decrees of the Society, than he himself thought fit, and did actually consent to? This would be as great a liberty, as he himself had before his Compact, or any one else in the State of Nature hath, who may submit himself and consent to any acts of it if he thinks fit. (2T.97)

The compact that is the result of the mutual consent of the parties is a binding compact. To hold otherwise is not to uphold a doctrine consistent with natural freedom, but to misunderstand the meaning of consent in a manner that renders the concept self-contradictory and hence unreasonable. That obligations arise from the mutual consent of the parties that form a compact is inconsistent with a right of the parties to break the compact at will. Consent, because it is the grounds for obligation, can indeed be the basis for forming lasting and stable communities.

Having established that membership in a community entails the

18. Slaves are not capable of incurring contractual obligations because they are not free. See 2T.172.

obligation to abide by the will of the community, the question remains: Who rules? Locke replies: "The *Majority* have a Right to act and conclude the rest" (2T.95). Locke defends majority rule as a right, and he must if his theory of consent is to be consistent with his own theoretical requirements. Locke's argument for majority rule is brief:

> For that which acts any Community, being only the consent of the individuals of it, and it being necessary to that which is one body to move one way; it is necessary the Body should move that way whither the greater force carries it, which is the *consent of the majority;* or else it is impossible it should act or continue one Body, *one Community,* which the consent of every individual that united into it, agreed that it should; and so every one is bound by that consent to be concluded by the *majority.* (2T.96)

> For, if *the consent of the majority* shall not in reason, be received, *as the act of the whole,* and conclude every individual; nothing but the consent of every individual can make any thing to be the act of the whole; But such a consent is next impossible ever to be had, if we consider the Infirmities of Health, and Avocations of Business . . . variety of Opinions, and contrariety of Interests, which unavoidably happen in all Collections of Men, the coming into Society upon such terms, would be only like *Cato's* coming into the Theatre, only to go out again . . . which cannot be suppos'd till we can think, that Rational Creatures should desire and constitute Societies only to be dissolved. For where the *majority* cannot conclude the rest, there they cannot act as one Body, and consequently will be immediately dissolved again. (2T.98)

Locke's defense of majority rule has been criticized for failing to meet two objections.[19] First, the charge is made that the defense of majority rule is the simple assertion that, as a practical matter, the majority tends to be strongest and therefore to be the decisive force in a community; Locke's doctrine collapses into "might makes right." Second, as Filmer recognized, any departure from unanimous consent violates the individual's right to consent to his government. Since natural law is the basis for the contention that each individual has this right, only natural law can provide sufficient justification for the right of the majority to overrule the rest. Locke fails to provide a natural law justification.

The first of these objections arises, perhaps, from a confusion brought about by taking literally Locke's use of the metaphor of a physical body moved by the greatest force for a community moved by the majority of its members. Any sort of body must "move that

---

19. See Laslett, *Two Treatises,* notes to 2T.95, 98; pp. 375, 377.

way whither the greater force carries it." And in the case where the "body" is the "Body Politick," Locke states that the "greater force" is "the *consent* of the majority." "*For* that which acts any Community being only the consent of the individuals of it" (2T.96, my emphasis), only the consent of a majority of them can determine the direction the community will take. The majority moves the community because it represents the greatest agreement in a situation where the principle of action is agreement, not force. The majority is a numerical majority that does not necessarily control the greatest physical power or economic power.[20] This is "one man, one vote," not "might makes right."

To interpret Locke's argument for the right of the majority as if it were an argument that the majority has the physical power to rule the community is to contradict the sense of the text and to make this portion of Locke's argument irreconcilable with the major thrust of much of the *Second Treatise*. Locke introduces the metaphor of a physical body to explain why, in any "Body Politick," the majority "have a *Right* to act and conclude the rest" (2T.95, my emphasis). This is an argument about rights and not simply a factual claim that the majority is stronger than the minority. Locke was certainly well aware that the majority does not always have "might" on its side. And if he meant to say that the majority has a right to rule the community only when it also has the physical power to do so, it would be hard to explain his consideration of situations where the people are oppressed by conquerors, usurpers, or tyrants. These illegitimate rulers may be stronger than a majority of the people, but they remain illegitimate nonetheless, while the people retain a right to resist and to establish a government by majority consent.

But the second objection to Locke's argument remains. The principle of majority rule seems to violate the right of each individual in the minority to consent to his government. How does an argument that begins with the principle that each man's voice counts as one end with the conclusion that some men's voices may be overruled by others? Each individual must agree to his membership in the community; at this level, consent is unanimous. That agreement entails the agreement that the community survive and

20. "It is significant that the 'greater force' which moves a community 'one way' is made by the majority, entirely without reference to the 'force' supplied by the ownership of property. The argument leads straight to the counting of individuals in apportioning political representation." J. R. Pole, *Political Representation in England and the Origins of the American Republic* (Berkeley: University of California Press, 1966; California Paperback, 1971), p. 24. Pole is not correct as to where the argument leads in Locke. See chap. 3, note 23, and accompanying text.

continue to function. This is impossible without some power that has the right to bind all members of the community. Since it is impossible that decisions be made unanimously, "by the Law of Nature and Reason" the acts of the majority pass for the acts of the whole (2T.96). To agree to act to reach a certain end but reject the only possible means to that end is irrational.[21] Majority rule is the only practicable procedure for reaching decisions within the group that is consistent with the principle of consent, and consequently it is the dictate of the law of nature, which is the law of reason.

Locke's argument here is a defense of majority rule as a procedure for reaching decisions within any group. It matters not at all in considering the justice of the procedure whether the group is the entire community or some small select assembly.[22] In other words, this is not an argument for democracy or an argument defending an egalitarian system of representation.[23] Although the initial group is the entire society, the majority of that group may decide that fewer than a majority, even one man and his heirs forever, will rule that community. Locke is not only, or even especially, endorsing direct democracies or simple representative republics. What the majority of the society has the right to decide, in Locke's view, is the answer to the second practical question under consideration here: again, Who rules? Since the majority has the right to bind the whole, the legislative power, the majority may entrust that right by designating a government and a procedure by which the offices of that government shall be filled.[24] Because a positive act

21. Compare Locke's argument with the positions developed by Edward Gee and James Tyrrell in response to Filmer. Gee argued that majority rule is a principle of right reason. Tyrrell argued that consent is initially given for the common good, not only for private ends, and therefore commits the individual to support the continuation of the community. See Daly, pp. 88–91. This is another example of Locke's use of the law of nature and reason to mean the appropriate relation of ends to means.

22. Locke compares the entire commonwealth to a legislative assembly twice in the course of the argument. See 2T.96, 98.

23. Kendall, *Majority Rule*, pp. 112–19, and Pole, p. 21, make these errors. Kendall argues that Locke's position is a defense of unrestricted democracy, but this distorts Locke's view. Natural law limitations apply to democratic government as well as to other forms. Filmer attacks consent theory for its egalitarian tendencies (toward women's suffrage, for example) on the basis of the same error. See Daly, pp. 92–96, for a discussion of this criticism and for Gee and Tyrrell's efforts to respond to it by making the family, rather than the individual, the unit of consent.

24. See 2T, chap. 10, and 2T.198. Laslett suggests that chapter 10 was originally the continuation of the argument for majority rule of chapter 8. See *Two Treatises*, note to 2T.132, p. 399. But see chap. 3, note 45. It is worth noting that Locke does not distinguish republican or representative government from democratic government in his list of forms of government. His categories are the government of many, few, and one—democracy, oligarchy, and monarchy, and mixed forms of these.

determines who rules, Locke escapes the problem with which he confronted Filmer: how to recognize "who Heir" in the absence of a clear divine designation.

Government thus established is representative government only in the sense that the designated government is authorized by consent to speak for the whole and to bind its members. The government thus represents the society in the same way that it could be said that the decision of a majority of a legislative body represents the entire body.[25] Each member is obligated whether or not an act of the society is one that "he himself thought fit, and did actually consent to" (2T.97). Locke is concerned to establish that membership in a society creates duties and that these duties are consistent with a theory of consent based on natural freedom.

But it is not at all clear that an argument for majority rule is necessary to accomplish this task. It seems it would be equally well accomplished if Locke were to argue that the decision to form a government with binding authority must be a unanimous decision of the community. Locke does imply at one point that a rule of unanimity might be preferable in principle to majority rule were it practicable (2T.98). And in the next paragraph he states that the members of society may give up their power "to any number greater than the majority" (2T.99).

If the defense of majority rule is not a defense of democratic or elective forms of government, and if it is not necessary to establish the basis of citizens' obligations, why does Locke make the argument? Had Locke argued that a unanimous act of the community is required to establish a government as well as to establish a community, the two stages of the process would collapse into one.[26] There would be no political society with authority distinct from the designated government. When the government dissolved, the society would also dissolve: each individual would be free from any obligation to the others.

For this reason, unanimity as the operating principle for reaching decisions within a group is not a properly political principle. Where unanimous consent is required to reach a decision, each individual actually continues to be governed by his own judgment. There is no obligation to the group, no common authority within

25. At 2T.88 and 2T.140, Locke identifies one's own judgment or consent with that of one's representative or the majority. Through consent, one "owns" the decisions of the authorities.

26. Compare Hobbes, p. 228, and Jean-Jacques Rousseau, *On the Social Contract,* ed. Roger D. Masters, trans. Judith R. Masters (New York: St. Martin's Press, 1978), p. 52.

the group, no political community. A requirement of unanimous consent and the principle of majority rule differ in kind, not in degree.[27] The argument for majority rule establishes that there is a political authority within every existing society, an authority that can act as a common judge among conflicting members, that is inherent in or natural to the society's existence as a group. The community can act as a unit when its government has dissolved, and the individual's obligation to the community remains distinct from his obligation to its government. These are the critical points for the theory of resistance that is the culmination of the *Second Treatise*.

Locke's argument for the right of the majority is the theoretical ground for the distinction between duty to society and to government, the distinction that permits an argument for resistance without anarchy. When the designated government dissolves, men remain obligated to the society acting through majority rule. But the practicability of society acting as a direct democracy was questioned earlier. And here again we find that Locke's theoretical claims for majority right are not matched by empirical or historical claims for practicable majority action. Locke takes up two objections to his contention that consent is the sole origin of political obligation. His responses make it clear that, in practice, the act of consent to become a member of society is rarely if ever distinguished from consent to its existing government and that, consequently, for all practical purposes consent to the government is unanimous.

The first objection is the practical one that there are no examples of free and equal individuals coming together to form a society and establish a government. Locke's reply is to give some examples and to remark that the lack of written histories of such events is really not surprising (2T.100–104). But having concluded his response, Locke goes on to concede to the patriarchalists that most governments probably were governments of one man in the beginning and often that man was the father of a large family (2T.104–12; see 2T.74–76). According to Locke, the father became a political ruler as his children continued to submit to his rule when adults and to join with him in the execution of his judgments. This is a

27. Kendall sees the difference in kind in that the principle of unanimity requires all objections to be considered and answered, whereas majority rule simply gives power to the greater number. *Majority Rule*, pp. 109–10. This is so, and it indicates the defect of unanimity as a political principle. It might be objected that a requirement of unanimity would obligate individuals to the community in that they would be duty-bound to abide by decisions once unanimously agreed upon. But it is difficult to see a principled defense of unanimity that would permit a defense of nonretractable consent.

process that would take place over time as each child came of age and gave his "express or tacit Consent," his "tacit, and scarce avoidable consent" (2T.74–75, 94, 110). It would not be a decision of the community taken at a given moment and determined by majority rule. Nonetheless, the society as such retains the juridical rights to act to choose a new ruler on the death of the father; to join with others and establish a common government; and to limit the prerogatives of the ruler (2T.105, 162). Thus described, the operation of consent at the origins of most political societies is not markedly different from its operation in a mature society, consent "being given separately in their turns, as each comes of Age, and not in a multitude together" (2T.117).

Locke describes the process of consent in existing societies in response to the second objection to his consent theory; the objection that each man is born subject to an existing government and therefore is not free to join with others to establish a new one (2T.113–22). In dealing with this second objection, Locke is also dealing with its reverse: since men are free to join or create societies as they choose, consent theories provide no support for the continuation of societies or governments from one generation to the next. Present and future generations cannot be bound by preceding ones (2T.116).

Locke replies that unless and until an individual consents as an adult to membership in an existing society, he is free to join with other free men to create a new society. If this were not so, it would be impossible to explain the number of legitimate governments in the world. It is clear from the practice of men and governments, according to Locke, that men are understood to be free to join an existing society or to create a new one. And if one adult has this freedom, on what grounds can he deny it to his son when he comes of age? A father's consent cannot bind his son.

Fathers may require, however, that their heirs become members of society, and governments ordinarily require that all landowners be members of the society. This has led people to mistakenly assume that fathers could create political obligations for their sons. To accept an inheritance, a man must also consent to become a member of the society. But a man is certainly free to reject his inheritance and join a society of his choice. And if neither the government nor the father requires it, men may possess land without membership in society and remain free to leave and join a new community whenever they wish (2T.73, 116–18, 191).

But though each individual is free to become a member of any society when he comes of age, his agreement to join an existing society also obligates him to its established government (2T.89, 117, 118). This is theoretically justified because, at any given moment when an individual comes of age and makes the decision to join the society, the government rests on the consent of at least a majority of the society's members.

In fact, an established government is supported by the unanimous consent of the society's members precisely because in practice the condition for membership is recognition of the government's authority. But none of the remaining members of the society after the founding generation dies have participated in any constitutive act establishing the government. In this respect Locke's argument does not entirely eliminate the rule of the dead hand of the past. There is no direct right to choose your governors. Instead, the requirements of natural freedom are met not by participating in the choice of governors, but by consent to membership in a given society. The natural right at the basis of the requirement of consent can best be stated negatively: it is a right to be ruled by no other man without your consent. Consent to membership in a society with an existing legitimate government is sufficient to meet that requirement.[28]

The situation is further complicated by recalling how Locke describes the submission of children to their fathers' authority as the origin of most governments. There never was any collective decision of a founding generation establishing government in most cases. This line of thought supports the conclusion that Locke's distinction between the unanimous consent originating society and the majority rule determining the form of government is not meant as a historical claim that most political communities operated as direct democracies in the beginning. Rather it establishes, first, that "the *Majority* have a Right to act and conclude the rest" in any society at any time when there is no other legitimate government and, second, that any established government derives its authority from the society as a unit (2T.95). From this second proposition it follows that the agreement to join a given society entails subjection to its government. In this way the continuity of government authority is secured in a manner consistent with the requirement that all political authority originate in individual consent.

With the continuity of government authority secure, Locke turns to the security of government jurisdiction over territory. This

---

28. This explains how Locke can maintain without contradiction both that hereditary monarchy is a legitimate form of government (2T.132) and that no man can "by any *Compact* whatsoever, bind *his Children* or Posterity" (2T.116).

involves two issues: the jurisdiction of the government over the territory itself and its jurisdiction over all individuals within its territory. The questions are, If individuals are free to withdraw from a society, does the government of that society retain jurisdiction over their land? and What constitutes sufficient consent to obligate an individual to obey the laws of a given government? (2T.119–22).

In response to the first question, Locke argues that the government cannot lose its jurisdiction over the property belonging to the members of society.

> For it would be a direct Contradiction, for any one, to enter into Society with others for the securing and regulating of Property; And yet to suppose his Land, whose Property is to be regulated by the Laws of the Society, should be exempt from the Jurisdiction of that Government, to which he himself the Proprietor of the Land, is a subject. . . . *Whoever*, therefore, from thenceforth, by Inheritance, Purchase, Permission, or otherways *enjoys any part of the Land*, so annext to, and under the Government *of that Commonwealth, must take it with the Condition* it is under; that is *of submitting to the Government of the Commonwealth*, under whose Jurisdiction it is, as far forth, as any Subject of it. (2T.120)

Men are not born subject to government; but should they choose to join some other society, their inheritance remains under the jurisdiction of the government they were born under. The government's authority over a given territory and over all men within that territory is secure.

To the second question, Locke replies that possession or enjoyment of any part of the dominions of a government constitutes tacit consent to obey the laws of that government. Thus the government can command the obedience of anyone within its boundaries, even if he is only passing through as a traveler (2T.119).[29] The government temporarily has jurisdiction over these men, even though they are not members of the society, because it has jurisdiction over the territory they temporarily inhabit or possess. The government's authority over all men within its territory is secure.

But Locke is careful to note that the tacit consent indicated by mere presence within the territorial boundaries of a nation is not sufficient to make a man a member of the community. Only "positive Engagement, and express Promise and Compact" (2T.122; see

---

29. But see 2T.9, 74. The magistrate has the right to punish a stranger within his territory for violations of the natural law by virtue of his natural executive power. But the stranger can be obligated to obey the civil laws and the magistrate's authority only by his own consent.

2T.121) can make a man a member of a society and a permanent subject of its government. Permanent political obligation can be created only by a deliberate act of consent. Locke's central concern in this discussion, after all, has been to correct the misunderstanding that political obligation and citizenship are determined by the mere accidents of birth and geography.

In making his argument, he has also covered every case where the integrity of the authority of government might be challenged without jeopardizing either the rights of property or the right of each individual to consent to his government. There is no necessary connection between property ownership and membership in society. It is possible to own land and not be a member, and it is possible to be a member and not own land. It is not possible to alter the territorial jurisdiction of a society by secession; it is not possible to be within the territorial bounds of a society and not be bound to obey its government; and there is no right to renounce your membership once consent to membership has been given.

Consent theory as it appears in Locke's work does permit the formation of new communities when free individuals who are as yet uncommitted withdraw from the societies of their birth, or when communities freely join together to form a larger unit. But these are not serious threats to the continued existence of established communities. The serious threats that Locke considers are conquest, usurpation, tyranny, and the resistance to these. But in ordinary times both the ties of obligation to society and government and the territorial integrity of the community are justified and secure on the basis of a theory whose primary principle is that all men are born free.

But there are several ambiguities and contradictions in Locke's account and several possible interpretations of his meaning, none of which resolves all the difficulties. The difficulties arise with the distinction between tacit and express consent that concludes Locke's discussion.[30] His statements that express consent is required to

30. For discussions of these difficulties see John Dunn, "Consent"; idem, *Political Thought*, pp. 131–47; David Hume, "Of the Original Contract," in *Essays: Moral, Political and Literary* (Oxford: Oxford University Press, 1963), pp. 452–73; Carole Pateman, *The Problem of Political Obligation: A Critical Analysis of Liberal Theory* (Chichester: John Wiley, 1979), pp. 15–17, 60–80; Hanna Pitkin, "Obligation and Consent—I and II," *American Political Science Review* 59 (December 1965): 990–99, and 60 (March 1966): 39–52; J. P. Plamenatz, *Consent, Freedom and Political Obligation* (London: Oxford University Press, 1938), esp. pp. 7–8; idem, *Man and Society*, 2 vols. (London: Longmans, Green, 1963), 1:220–41; Riley, pp. 449–52; Seliger, *Liberal Politics*, pp. 224–30, 267–83; A. John Simmons, *Moral Principles and Political Obligations* (Princeton: Princeton University Press, 1979), pp. 57–100; Michael Walzer, *Obligations* (Cambridge: Harvard University Press, 1970), esp. pp. 18, 100–102, 110–11.

make a man a member of society seem to contradict his claims else-where that tacit consent was sufficient to make monarchs of the fathers of families during the early periods of history (2T.74–75, 94, 110). This is a textual problem that has no satisfactory resolution.[31] What was Locke's understanding of the form of consent that is necessary to establish obligations to society and government?

The attempt to answer this question is further complicated by Locke's arguments concerning the relation between territorial jurisdiction and consent. Locke says that only express consent can make a man a member of society, and that ordinarily only members of society are entitled to inherit property (2T.117). But any possession or enjoyment of property within the jurisdiction of a legitimate government constitutes tacit consent to obey the laws of that government during the period of possession or enjoyment. These propositions have been misinterpreted in two conflicting ways. Some authors view inheritance itself as a form of express consent, even as the only form of express consent, and conclude that only proprietors of land can be members of a Lockean society.[32] Others argue that since most people do not give express consent, tacit consent applies to almost everyone and inheritance is one form of it.[33]

The most probable interpretation, I think, is that Locke envisions a situation where men who give their express consent to membership in society "as each comes to be of Age" (2T.117) thereby qualify to receive their inheritance at the appropriate time. Membership is ordinarily a condition of inheritance, but inheritance of land is not itself an act of consent to membership. In the rare situation where a government might allow nonmembers to inherit land, inheritance would constitute an act of tacit consent to obey the laws of the government just like any form of residence within its territories. Tacit consent is meant to apply narrowly to foreigners or resident aliens. Express consent, probably in the

31. One approach would be to view tacit consent as applying only to one peculiar historical situation or only to the establishment of government in the father and not to membership in society. Alternatively, one could view express consent as applying only to foreigners, who might already have political obligations, whereas residence would suffice to establish membership for the native-born. Neither approach withstands careful scrutiny of the text. Dunn makes the strongest case that Locke requires express consent, but he takes no account of Locke's reliance on tacit consent in the historical discussion. *Political Thought*, pp. 131–47; see also Dunn, "Consent," pp. 73–74. Seliger argues that Locke is a tacit-consent theorist by interpreting "express consent" to mean the absence of express dissent. *Liberal Politics*, pp. 224–30, 267–83.

32. Macpherson, pp. 249–50; see also Gauthier, p. 41; Pateman, pp. 71–72, 74. For criticism of Macpherson's position on this question see Dunn, *Political Thought*, pp. 134–36; Seliger, *Liberal Politics*, pp. 270–74.

33. Pitkin, "Obligation—I," p. 995; Riley, p. 451.

form of something like an oath of allegiance, is meant to be the form of consent appropriate to native-born residents upon coming of age (see 2T.62, 151).

I have already alluded to the difficulties with this position. Express consent, although it could be instituted as a practical requirement, had not been required widely as an act of consent to membership in society.[34] We are in danger of placing Locke, not Filmer, in the position of unsettling all the governments that ever were. Moreover, this interpretation does not explain the sufficiency of tacit consent in those early patriarchies. But the alternative position, that Locke relies on tacit consent as the grounds for political obligation, also faces textual, practical, and theoretical problems.

If tacit consent suffices to establish membership, Locke's statements to the contrary must be explained. And as a practical matter, if tacit consent is indicated by continued residence in the country of your birth, you must have had a viable opportunity to leave that country when you came of age in order for your remaining in it to be considered a voluntary action. Most important, it is difficult to view an action as a meaningful expression of consent where a man may have "made no Expressions of it at all" (2T.119). What kind of action counts as consent, if consent can be "tacit" to this extent?

There are only a few examples of tacit consent from which to draw some inferences as to Locke's meaning: residing in a foreign country; accepting money as something of value;[35] and men in the state of nature continuing to accept their fathers' authority after reaching adulthood. These cases share certain elements. By a voluntary action undertaken in order to enjoy certain benefits, a man consents to the necessary conditions for or consequences of those benefits. This consent is tacit in that it is both unstated and implied.[36] There must be some voluntary individual action, that is,

34. See Dunn's discussion of the use of oaths in Locke's time. An oath could be required of any Englishman at any time to publicly declare his preexisting status as an Englishman, but it was not considered to be the act of consent to membership in society. Even Dunn, who argues that Locke requires express consent to membership, acknowledges that Locke would have considered native-born residents remaining in England as English subjects and interprets express consent as a "hypothetical event." Men would express their consent if they were asked. "Consent," p. 168; idem, *Political Thought*, pp. 138–42.

35. "Tacitly agreeing in the use of Money" implies agreement to "disproportionate and unequal Possession of the Earth," since the latter is the consequence of a money economy. See 2T.50.

36. See Simmons for the distinction between acts that are "signs of consent" and acts that "imply consent." His example of the latter is joining a baseball game, which implies consent to be governed by the umpire's decisions (p. 89).

one that is not coerced (1T.42; 2T.176, 186), but it need not be a spoken or written declaration, and its implications need not be fully self-conscious. Those young men who first made their fathers into kings need not have had the self-understanding of good Lockeans.

There is a general dilemma in the effort to specify what constitutes consent. If the criteria are "strong," for example, express consent alone, then consent theory is likely to be morally satisfying but practically problematic. Consent is a meaningful expression of the intentions of a free and rational individual, but one will find few legitimate members of legitimate political communities in the history of the world. If the criteria are "weak," for example, mere residence in one's native country, then consent theory provides a practical criterion that includes almost everybody, but one that blunts the point of the claim that no man is subject to the authority of another without his own consent. Consent comes to mean the necessary implication of a voluntary action, but not a deliberate expression of intent.

Locke probably would have considered ideal the situation where a government institutionalized a mechanism for the expression of consent.[37] But even this would not have solved his problem. Regardless of the answer to the initial question, whether the form of consent to membership in society must be express or may also be tacit, Locke's consent theory must allow for consent to be something less than fully self-conscious and deliberate. After all, Locke is arguing that men have been mistaken about the grounds of their obligation, that they have in fact consented even though they have not understood themselves to have done so. Consent has often been "little taken notice of" (2T.117, 175), and Locke is bringing it to men's attention. Unless Locke were willing to maintain that there have not yet been any legitimate governments, he must maintain that there have been governments based on consent throughout history without a full consciousness in their subjects of the true nature of their origins or of the meaning of consent.

At this point, it is important to distinguish between the individual's act of agreeing to become a member of society and the content of that agreement. Locke is quite clear that the content of the agreement need not be explicitly stated. In his summary chapter distinguishing paternal, political, and despotic power, his definition of political power includes the statement that society and

37. Such a mechanism is provided in "The First Set of the Fundamental Constitutions of South Carolina: As Compiled by John Locke," in *Historical Collections of South Carolina*, ed. B. R. Carroll, 2 vols. (New York: Harper, 1836), 2:362–90, arts. 117, 118.

government are established with "this express or tacit Trust," that political power shall be employed for the good of the people and the preservation of their property (2T.171). Moreover, men "must be understood to give up all the power, necessary to the ends for which they unite," and this is done "by barely agreeing to *unite into one Political Society*, which is *all the Compact that* is or needs be between the Individuals that enter into or make up a *Commonwealth*" (2T.99).

At the very least, consent may be tacit in the sense that the terms of the compact establishing society and of the trust establishing government need not be explicitly stated. Consent must "make sense"; if a man chooses to act to secure a certain benefit, he can be understood to have acceded to the conditions necessary to secure that benefit. His actions have certain necessary implications, regardless of his own understanding of what he has done.[38] To become a member of society and to establish government involves certain rights and obligations, and these can be known as logically necessary implications of the actions of men. The extent of men's obligations follows from the nature of their actions. Each individual who voluntarily agrees to join a society does so in order to enjoy the benefits of society, and in so doing he acquires the obligations necessarily associated with membership. So long as this is so, it becomes relatively unimportant for Locke's general purposes whether that initial agreement is or is not expressly stated.

The distinction between tacit and express consent and the problems associated with it arise in the context of a discussion of a very particular problem. Locke is concerned with the question of what actions can be taken to indicate sufficient consent to oblige a man to obey the laws of any government (2T.119) or to become a permanent member of a society with an established legitimate government (2T.121–22). This is not the same as the question of what forms of consent are sufficient to establish the legitimacy of a government. This second question is a matter of the relation between the people and their government rather than a matter of the relation between the individual and his society. Part of the confusion surrounding this issue arises because Locke's answer to the first question is sometimes brought to bear in discussions of the second. In fact, Locke gives us less than a complete treatment of either

38. Pitkin sees correctly that the extent of men's obligations can be known from the natural law but wrongly concludes that that fact makes consent superfluous. "Obligation—I," p. 996. See Simmons's critique of Pitkin, pp. 84–86. See also Dunn, "Consent," for the best treatment I know of the meaning of consent in Locke's thought.

question. We know, for example, that the transformation of fathers into kings required only that their sons continue to accept as authoritative the fathers' use of their natural executive powers and join them in enforcing their decisions when necessary. We know that these relatively passive conditions are not sufficient to constitute popular consent to the government of a conqueror or a usurper. In those cases representation in a legislative body is the very least that is required (2T.192, 198).[39] We do not know enough to say what Locke's specification might be of the range of actions that qualify as acts of consent in various situations, either where the individual consents to membership in society or where the people consent to establish a government.

What we do know is that consent is understood to be a voluntary, rational act undertaken to secure certain benefits, and that its terms can be inferred from the character of the benefits sought. This is sufficient to serve Locke's general purpose. Political obligation can arise only for the sake of particular benefits and as a consequence of an individual choice. This is the ground for Locke's argument for limited government and a right of resistance. Locke is concerned to show that legitimate governments arise from the consent of free men in order to show that governments can be resisted when they become illegitimate. And because the terms of consent are implicit, we can know the extent of our obligations through an analysis that uncovers those terms. We turn now from the question of how political obligations arise to what exactly those political obligations are.

THE EXTENT OF OBLIGATION

Granting that a man can become obligated to obey the dictates of other men only by his own consent, what is the extent of his obligation? We know that consent does not give unlimited title to rulers, since no man can consent to be a slave (2T.23). There are other limiting conditions on consensual obligation as well. For example, consent must be given freely and not under duress (2T.176, 186); no rational creature can be supposed to consent to a condition that is not beneficial to him; and so on (2T.131, 164). In general, Locke argues that all obligation must be consistent with the dictates of the law of nature and reason.

But this discussion began with two conflicting statements of the requirements of the natural law. In the state of nature, each man is obliged "when his own Preservation comes not in competition . . . *to*

39. See pp. 157–58 below.

preserve the rest of Mankind" (2T.6). In civil society, the law of nature dictates *"the preservation of the Society,* and (as far as will consist with the publick good) of every person in it" (2T.134; see also 2T,171). Might there be a conflict between the preservation of mankind and the preservation of a particular society? And does the priority of the community outweigh the individual's right of preservation? How does the individual's act of consent in joining a society alter his obligations under the natural law? The distinction between the individual's obligations to his society and to its government complicates the responses to these questions.

First, the individual's obligation to the society of which he is a part and his obligation to mankind need not come in conflict. Particular communities are formed to secure the preservation of their members by establishing effective positive laws that interpret and apply the natural law. The formation of such communities clearly serves the general preservation of the human race by securing peace among groups of men and by increasing the productivity of the earth. The defense of nations and allegiance to a national community are not incompatible with a general humanitarian concern. Rather, the natural law obligation to preserve mankind as far as possible is partially fulfilled through the creation and defense of a nation.

But obligation will become conflictual in the situation where the particular society in question has a government unjust either in its domestic laws or in its international conduct. The rules for international conduct are analogous to the rules for conduct between individuals in the state of nature (2T.14, 88, 145–46, 176–81). Unjust war is offensive war; just war is defensive.[40] Should a government deviate from the natural law standards in international affairs or in domestic ones, no member of the community is obligated to follow the government, and not simply because to do so might be harmful to him personally. In these cases the issue is clear, at least in its theoretical principle: no action is authoritative if it violates the general law of the human community.

> The end of Government is the good of Mankind [not "of Society"], and which is *best for Mankind,* that the People should be always exposed to the boundless will of Tyranny, or that the Rulers should be sometimes liable to be oppos'd, when they grow exorbitant in the use

40. But defense should not be confused with passivity. Presumably nations, being in the state of nature, are governed by the rules that apply to individuals in the state of nature and may punish aggressors, come to the aid of their victims, and strike first if necessary to ward off attack. See 2T.7–12, 14, 17–19.

of their Power, and imploy it for the destruction, and not the preservation of the Properties of their People? (2T.229)

For the People having given to their Governours no Power to do an
unjust thing, such as is to make an unjust War, (for they never had
such a Power in themselves:) They ought not to be charged as guilty
of the Violence and Unjustice that is committed in an Unjust war,
any farther, than they actually abet it; no more, than they are to be
thought guilty of any Violence or Oppression their Governours
should use upon the People themselves, or any part of their Fellow
Subjects, they having impowered them no more to the one, than to
the other. (2T.179)

Governors, not society as such, are accountable for their unjust actions. Moral responsibility for unjust actions is individual responsibility. For this reason too, when participants in a unjust attack are
taken captive, they can be enslaved.[41] Individuals can be held responsible for their unjust actions in collaborating with an unjust
government, but the people itself is always guiltless.

This conclusion is not affected by the individual's obligation to
his society as a unit distinct from its government. Even if the majority of the society should support the actions of an unjust government (or become directly tyrannical in the case of pure democracy),
no member of the minority would be obligated to follow the group
or its government. Just as the prince loses his public character, descends to the level of the beasts, and becomes an enemy rather than
a member of society, so the majority of the society becomes an aggregate of criminal individuals and no longer even part of, let
alone authoritative representatives of, "the people" as soon as they
act to destroy rights and property that ought to be secured to each
member of the society equally. This is only to say that Locke does
not ever take the absurd position that there is a moral duty to com-
mit injustice. There is no obligation to preserve a society whose
actions are inconsistent with the natural law dictate to preserve
mankind. In fact, this line of argument suggests that such actions
dissolve the society just as unjust government actions dissolve a
government. Again, the people as a people are guiltless.

But the individual's distinct obligation to his society appears as
distinct in the case where the society as such opposes the unjust

---

41. In this case there is no protection for prisoners of war as representatives of
their nations. Rules protecting prisoners of war consider them as social actors. The
premise of conscientious objection is the opposite; that the soldier's actions are a
matter of individual responsibility. The Lockean model of warfare is between an
aggregate of hostile *individuals* and a *society* defending itself. Compare Rousseau, pp.
50–51.

actions of its government. The right of the people to resist an oppressive government also involves the duty on the part of each
member of the society to join a resistance aimed at preserving the
society from the aggression of its rulers. The individual then is
obliged to disobey his government in order to preserve his society;
the duty to revolt is justified on exactly the same grounds as the
duty of the soldier.[42] In both cases the obligation goes beyond the
natural obligation to act so as to preserve mankind, which might
require joining others in a just cause. This natural duty is limited to
situations where it may be fulfilled without risk to one's own life.
The duty of a man to defend his society against external or internal
aggression as a member of the society is based on his consent to
membership in it, not simply on the justice of its cause, and is unlimited. How is the duty to a society acting against its government
as a matter of national self-preservation articulated with an individual right of self-defense?

The theoretical justification for the individual's obligation to a
just society is less clear than the justification for his right to disobey
an unjust one. In consenting to membership in a community, the
individual leaves a situation where his own preservation takes precedence over any other obligation and enters one where his obligation to the community supersedes his own preservation. Locke
leaves no doubt that it is "justly Death to disobey" military orders
necessary to the preservation of the society even if a man is ordered
to "march up to the mouth of a Cannon, or stand in a Breach,
where he is almost sure to perish" (2T.139). What is it about the act
of consent that justifies this level of obligation?[43]

In joining a society, you relinquish your private judgment of
how best to secure your preservation to the society in all cases
where the society, with its authorized public judge, can provide that
security. Your engagement includes the duty to participate in the
execution of the public judgments. In the formal sense these judgments are your own, since you have agreed that the public authority speaks for you in matters of security (2T.88, 227). Although this
agreement may cost you your life, it is not an agreement that forfeits your right to life. There is a distinction between slavery and
political power even though both the slavemaster and the political
ruler have the power of life and death. In the first case that power
is absolute and arbitrary, and the slave has forfeited his right to life.

42. See Pitkin, "Obligation—I," pp. 41–42, and Walzer, p. 3, for the claim that
Locke does not adequately provide for a duty to resist.

43. Locke nowhere systematically treats the question of a soldier's duty. Compare Locke's position on military duty with Hobbes's, pp. 268–70.

In the second case the members of society retain the right to life so long as their lives are placed in jeopardy only for the sake of preserving the society and with their own consent (2T.88–89, 138–40, 171).[44]

The agreement to submit to government to this extent seems reasonable when we recall that there is never a guarantee against violent death, that the right to life in the state of nature must also be defended, and that self-defense relying on individual judgment and strength involves greater and more frequent risks than collective defense. The case also can be made without the specter of the state of nature. To risk your life to preserve the community against an enemy nation may be no different from risking your life to preserve yourself. The preservation of each individual is bound up with the preservation of the society if, as is Locke's view, slavery is not necessarily better than death (2T.17). To surrender to a tyrannical power does not bring safety. The sensible course to take in self-defense may be to join in the defense of your community against the enemy.

This is persuasive only if you accept Locke's condition that a member of society has no right to renounce his membership and emigrate; the choice is to fight or to surrender. But to accept Locke's condition is to accept the point at issue. Why does the individual remain under a permanent obligation even when that obligation means he must sacrifice his life? And the issue is of course properly put in terms of sacrifice, not just in terms of risk. The case we began with is the case "where he is almost sure to perish" (2T.139).

It seems that Locke requires a man to sacrifice the end to the means—his own preservation to the preservation of the group—which makes the commitment to join a political society appear irrational. But there is a complication in the relation between ends and

44. Gary Glenn argues forcefully that if a man has a duty to sacrifice his life for his country, he has alienated his right to life. The soldier's duty is incompatible with the prohibition against suicide that is the basis of Locke's argument for limited government and therefore also incompatible with the right of resistance. You do not have a power over your own life that can be given to society. However, it is more correct to say that you do not have absolute, arbitrary power over your own life. Glenn acknowledges that governments have the rightful authority to order soldiers to their death. Where do they get it if not from the members of society? Moreover, there is no conflict between a duty to obey just commands and a right to resist unjust ones, though there is certainly a problem with the judgment of which is which. Gary D. Glenn, "Inalienable Rights and Locke's Argument for Limited Government: Political Implications of a Right to Suicide," *Journal of Politics* 46 (February 1984): 80–105.

means in this situation. The decision to join a society is the result of a calculation that membership in a society is the necessary means to secure your preservation.[45] Permanent obligation is, in turn, a necessary condition for the preservation of the society. And you cannot reasonably act to secure your ends while rejecting what is necessary to secure the means. The argument parallels Locke's argument concerning the necessity, and therefore also the justice, of majority rule for the preservation of the society (2T.96–99). In both cases the individual's consent creates new obligations so that he is no longer as free as he was before. And in both cases those new obligations have the effect of subordinating the individual to the group in certain respects.

Joining a political community is a calculated risk. You are likely to live longer and better with it than without it. But the price of the protection of the community may be the ultimate sacrifice, since the community cannot maintain itself without the right to demand this of its members. The sacrifice itself clearly cannot be defended on the grounds of self-interest. Although it is reasonable as a matter of calculation of self-interest to make the bargain, like all other bargains, it is a matter of justice to keep up your part of it. When a man makes an agreement expecting it to be to his advantage and later finds that it is not, he is not free to break his word.[46]

The bargain is made with the initial act of consent to membership in the society. And this is "not only necessary, but just." Keeping your part of the bargain is a moral matter.[47]

> For being now in a new State, wherein he is to enjoy many Conveniences, from the labour, assistance and society of others of the same Community, as well as protection from its whole strength; he is to part also with as much of his natural liberty in providing for himself, as the good, prosperity, and safety of the Society shall require: which is not only necessary, but just; since the other Members of the Society do the like. (2T.130)

45. See 2T, chap. 9. Laslett argues that this chapter is unconnected to the preceding chapter and was probably written and added to the text in 1689. *Two Treatises*, note to 2T.123, p. 395. But there is certainly a logical connection: chapter 8 makes the case that political society is formed out of individual consent; chapter 9 answers the question, Why do men part with their natural freedom and consent to political obligation? See also chap. 3, note 24.

46. This is a juridical, not psychological, argument. The question of what motivates men to do the right thing, and in this case to obey dangerous military commands, is a different question.

47. Hobbes also argues for the duty to keep your promises and on the basis of the self-contradictory character of bad faith. Nevertheless, no contract can oblige you not to run to save your life. Hobbes, pp. 191, 199, 268–70.

If you wish to enjoy the benefits of social life, you must be willing to make the necessary sacrifices. If you expect others to be willing to make those sacrifices, you must be willing to do the same. The bargain is necessary to obtain the benefit you seek and just in the sense that it is equitable.[48]

But the passage suggests another interpretation: the sacrifice for the group is just because you owe it in return for benefits received. In addition to the notion of reciprocity and equity here, there is the notion that duty arises from privilege or enjoyment. This thought is also suggested when Locke argues that enjoyment of any part of a country's dominion is tacit consent to obey its government's laws (2T.119). But no obligation is owed simply on account of receiving benefits; rather, one chooses to accept benefits and in so doing accepts the conditions associated with them.[49] Locke argues that obligations to obedience arise from consent rather than from a duty to one's benefactor. No man owes obedience to the society he is born to, and the debt to one's parents is limited to honor and gratitude (2T.66, 113–22; see also 1T.43).

The contribution of the society as a whole to the individual's well-being is not taken by Locke to be grounds for a claim on the individual. Though the thought is suggested by the passage quoted above (2T.130), it would be a misinterpretation of it. The sacrifice is just, "since the other Members of the Society do the like." The individual may owe a great deal of his own ability to preserve himself to his society and owe a great deal of his security to their protection; and it is in exchange for these benefits of society that the individual parts with his natural liberty to the extent necessary to preserve the society. But the individual is in no way obliged to render political obedience merely as a result of benefits received. That obligation arises only from his freely given consent to be so obliged.

48. See John Locke, MS. c.28 f.139, "Morality," where Locke argues as follows: since man did not create himself, other men, or the world, "no man at birth can have a right to anything." Men must either enjoy all things in common or settle their rights by compact. The former leads to unavoidable want. The latter is therefore preferable. But contracts are either to be kept or to be broken. If they are to be broken, then the compact is made for nothing; if to be kept, justice is established and a duty that is the first rule of our happiness. Objection: it may be to a man's advantage to break his word. Response: all men are under the same rule. If I am permitted to break my word, so are all other men. Then everything is subject to force or deceit and no man can be happy unless he is stronger and wiser than all mankind. "For in such a state of rapine and force it is impossible any one man should be master of those things whose possession is necessary to his well being."

49. See chap. 3, note 36, and accompanying text. The element of choice is crucial even when the implications of the choice are not conscious. Simmons argues, mistakenly I think, that tacit consent in Locke's thought is nothing other than fairness or gratitude (p. 91).

We have seen both that the obligation that arises in this way is binding and permanent and that it is limited in its extent. The bond of obligation to society or to government is dissolved at the point of illegitimate action. A man has a duty to fight only just wars and a duty to join only just resistance. A member of society, unlike a slave, retains his right to life also in that he retains the right to judge whether the power he has entrusted to his governors is used properly or whether his governors have become indistinguishable from slavemasters.

But political society is an arrangement where each relinquishes his private judgment. Consent is not retractable. And private judgment is relinquished to a public judge, which is either the majority or one or a few appointed by them. Consent need not be unanimous in every case. Nonetheless, the obligations created by consent are at some point no longer binding, and there must be some means of judging when the public judge has forfeited the right to be obeyed. Who does judge the limits of obedience and by what criteria?

This is the last question that Locke must answer in order to respond fully to Filmer's criticisms of consent theories. The charge is that if the people judge, then there are no criteria of judgment in practice. Disobedience can occur unchecked and at will. Without a satisfactory answer to the question, Who judges? and without certain criteria for judgment, Locke's interposition of society between the individual and the established government through his dual theory of obligation will not serve as the basis for a doctrine of resistance without anarchy.

We can anticipate some of the complications involved in Locke's response to these charges. Having seen Locke's several criteria for legitimate government in chapter 2, the problems of conflicts among the criteria and their relative weight should reappear in considering Locke's view of how to recognize illegitimate government action: conquest, tyranny, or usurpation. Having seen Locke develop a two-stage theory of consent in which the individual obligates himself to the society and the society establishes a government, any question of a right of disobedience is complicated by questions of the possibility of collective action and collective responsibility.

Earlier we noted the practical difficulty of collective action: Can the society continue to function when the established government is dissolved? Can it lay claim to the obedience of its members on the grounds that it continues to act as an umpire between them? Here we find further complications with the claims of the society and government on the individual. The individual is obliged to obey the decisions of the majority or the established government whether or not those are decisions he "did actually consent to" (2T.97). But his obligations dissolve if those decisions are unjust. Does this mean that the individual is the final judge of his obligations, the final judge of what conduces to the preservation of himself and his rights? If not, and the individual remains obligated to the judgment of the society as a body, does the final judgment of right remain with the majority? In one case it seems that Locke would fail to secure individual obedience; in the other, that he would fail to secure individual freedom.

In dealing with this dilemma, it is critical to determine when and whether the dissolution of government also dissolves society. This determination will clarify the obligations of the individual in the various circumstances in which his community may be threatened. The same determination is necessary to resolve the practical question of whether resistance immediately produces anarchy. And last, one must know the conditions for the dissolution of the society in order to know whether we can maintain, as we argued above, that Locke, with Rousseau, finds that the people are always right though the majority may be wrong. Locke distinguished between society and government, and thus between dual corresponding levels of obligation, in order to establish a ground for both obedience and resistance, and for a resistance that could claim to be more orderly than anarchic. It remains to be seen whether he succeeded.

Resistance

Locke argues that a successful political theory helps to maintain the peace by establishing a clear standard of legitimate power and a clear designation of who is to exercise it. In the absence of either, the peace is threatened both by rebels of all sorts justified by the lack of any secure ground for obedience, and by ambitious men encouraged to fulfill their ambitions by establishing their claims to rule on the basis of force. But Locke also argues that even when the legitimacy of authority is clear, the claims of an established legitimate ruler to the obedience of his subjects are meaningless without a concomitant right to resist illegitimate authority. In establishing that there is legitimate authority, that there is a way of knowing who is to exercise it, and that illegitimate claims may be resisted, does Locke establish the foundation for a peaceful politics or does he plant the seeds of instability and frequent rebellion?

To put the matter differently, an effective standard always requires both a law and a judge. Locke considers three types of cases where the law or rule is broken: conquest, usurpation, and tyranny. These three taken together compose the set of illegitimate government actions. In Locke's terms, the set could be described as the set of acts of war, foreign and domestic, undertaken by governments. We will consider each of the three types of illegitimate actions first with respect to the rule or law—that is, what makes it illegitimate— and then with respect to who is to judge its illegitimacy in practice and who is capable of acting on that judgment. In other words, we will consider the possibilities for maintaining or restoring the peace.

In all cases the basic standards for legitimacy and hence for these three classes of illegitimate actions are the same: preservation and consent. But the effects of the various violations of these standards on government and society differ. In some cases it appears that only a part of the government or a single action loses its binding authority; in others, that the bonds of society and government are altogether dissolved. These differing effects determine the possibilities, both in fact and in right, for recourse against illegitimate government action. Locke's doctrine of resistance includes a full range of responses to the various kinds and degrees of abuse of government power.

After elaborating what his doctrine of resistance is, we will be able to determine whether Locke has responded to those who charge that a doctrine of popular resistance is incompatible with a stable political order and whether he has responded to the problem as he set it for himself, to establish a theory of political power that cannot be reduced to "might makes right."

THE DISSOLUTION OF SOCIETY AND GOVERNMENT

Men in a political society are bound to obey a "common judge with authority," and this common obligation is a part of their bond to one another as members of a political unit. When the authority of the common judge is lost, these bonds are clearly threatened. What kinds of actions undermine or destroy the authoritative character of a government, and what effects do these actions have on the unit and its members?

We begin with the case of conquest. Locke's consideration of conquest is intended to correct the error of those who "reckon Conquest as one of the Originals of Government" (2T.175). The victory of a conqueror can never be the source of political authority to govern the vanquished, whether or not the conqueror has justice on his side. Locke treats the case of the unjust conqueror as an obvious one: force can never be the basis of right, and consent given at the point of a sword cannot convert force to right.

> For the Law of Nature laying an Obligation on me, only by the Rules she prescribes, cannot oblige me by the violation of her Rules: Such is the extorting any thing from me by force. Nor does it at all alter the case, to say I *gave my Promise*, no more than it excuses the force, and passes the Right, when I put my Hand in my Pocket, and deliver my Purse my self to a Thief, who demands it with a Pistol at my Breast. (2T.186; see 2T.176)

Though attempts to compel submission by force may succeed in fact, the right to resist aggressors and to overthrow successful ones remains, even from one generation to the next. (2T.176).

Victory in resisting an aggressor that extends to vanquishing him in his own territory makes a just conqueror of the victorious defender. But just conquest also gives no right to political authority over conquered peoples or to ownership of conquered territory. The first of these claims is more simply defended than the second. A just conqueror does gain power over those who have forfeited their rights by actual participation in or collaboration with the unjust attack, and the power he gains over these is despotic power; he may kill or enslave them. But

> all the rest are innocent; and he has no more Title over the People of that Country, who have done him no Injury, and so have made no forfeiture of their Lives, than he has over any other, who, without any injuries or provocations, have lived upon fair terms with him. (2T.179)

Noncollaborators and children remain free. Even supposing that all members of the society can be taken as responsible for the unjust aggression of their government and that the just conqueror can then rightly subdue the entire society and rule them despotically without their consent, this authority still would not extend beyond one generation. The next generation would have a right to overthrow the government thus established and replace it with one of their choosing (2T.188–89). Even just conquest, then, cannot be the foundation for lasting authority to govern.

How is it that a just conqueror can rightfully enslave the guilty but cannot take possession of their lands? This Locke admits might well be considered a "strange Doctrine" (2T.180). Locke defends his doctrine with a series of arguments more than sufficient to make his case. First, he argues that the claim to an aggressor's person arises from his unjust use of force against you, but a claim to his possessions can arise only from the damage sustained in the attack.[50] On this basis the just conqueror does have a claim on the property of the conquered, but only as the source of reparations. And the wife and children of the conquered aggressor also have a claim on his property. His unjust action does not forfeit their rights. This situation of joint claims is resolved in favor of the inheritance rights of the children, if the property is insufficient to satisfy all claims. Since by the law of nature,

> all, as much as may be, should be preserved, it follows that . . . he that hath, and to spare, must remit something of his full Satisfaction, and give way to the pressing and preferable Title of those who are in danger of perishing without it. (2T.183)[51]

Next, Locke grants for the sake of argument that the conqueror's claims for reparation should be satisfied before all other claims. Even in this case the conqueror will not gain the right to dispossess the posterity of the vanquished. Where all land is possessed and none is waste, the value of possession in perpetuity far exceeds the amount of damages that might have been sustained in war. Where there is very little landownership and a great deal of wasteland, the value of an inheritance is minimal. But in these situations conquerors rarely bother to claim the lands that were owned by those they conquered. Though Locke is silent on the matter, it seems that the just conqueror could claim these lands by right if he wished to recoup his losses in this way[52] and that he would be entitled to claim any wastelands that he could put under cultivation, just as any individual or nation can claim uncultivated lands out of the common.

But for any lands to be of use to a conqueror, they must be cultivated. Once those whom the conqueror can justly enslave are dead, he must distribute the land among their free children in order to get any benefit from it. But any agreement by which this distribution could take place would be a binding compact establishing full property rights for free men. Any attempt to take their property or

50. This distinction seems to rule out the use of fines as punishment in criminal cases and punitive damages in civil cases, although such penalties may be justified as deterrents to others. See 2T.8–11.

51. See 2T.181–83. For another example of the natural law duty of charity see 1T.42. And for family rights in property see chap. 2, note 15, and accompanying text.

52. Though the value of the crop alone would be worth more to him in this case. Also, Locke's first argument, that the natural law requires that the children of the conquered have an opportunity to enjoy their inheritance, would cover this case. Locke has granted the priority of the conqueror's claims only for the sake of argument.

any part of what they manage to accumulate as a result of the cultivation of the land without their consent would be an act of tyranny that the populace would have every right to resist (2T.193–95). So even if one accepts the notion that a just conqueror has a right to the property of the conquered, a position that has already been shown to be false, "Nothing of *Absolute Power* will follow from hence, in the continuance of the Government" (2T.193).

In arguing that the just conqueror cannot claim the lands of the conquered, Locke establishes in a negative sense what he had established earlier in a positive sense; the connection between the consent of the governed and legitimate government jurisdiction over territory (2T.116–22). If your ancestors did establish a government on the basis of their consent, you may ordinarily claim your inheritance under the lawful jurisdiction of that government only by accepting that government. The alternatives in each generation where government is established on a legitimate foundation are emigration or obedience to the government supported by the majority. If this were not so, no government would have any secure continuation or secure territorial jurisdiction. And this is exactly what a government established by right of conquest lacks. Whatever the rights of the just conqueror over the generation that actually waged the war, future generations may claim their rightful inheritance by throwing off the conqueror's yoke and establishing a government on the basis of consent, the only foundation for legitimate jurisdiction over men or their property (2T.191–92).[53]

In sum, Locke demonstrates that any claims to establish a government or to take possession of a country by right of conquest are illegitimate, even if the conqueror enters the country with right on his side. The first violates the principle of consent, derived from natural freedom, while the second violates the rights of inheri-

---

53. Gauthier suggests that Locke could maintain a consistent relation between inheritance and consent without denying that political power can be acquired through just conquest. If the just conqueror acquires the jurisdiction that the defeated commonwealth forfeits, then he could require consent to his government as a condition of the children's enjoyment of their inheritance in the same way that any legitimate government does. But victors do not *acquire* all forfeited rights of defeated aggressors; those rights are lost. See 2T.182. Jurisdiction, the right to regulate property by law, dissolves when the government dissolves. Legitimate jurisdiction can belong only to an already legitimate government. Gauthier also puts the cart before the horse when he argues that a conqueror is not a usurper, since a usurper is one who gains power by means not prescribed by the laws of the community and the conqueror has destroyed the community and its laws. Precisely so! The children of the vanquished have the right to form a community with rules for the distribution of power within it. See Seliger, *Liberal Politics*, pp. 112–13.

tance, derived from the natural right of preservation (2T.190). Without a foundation in consent the government is a usurpation, and without respect for property rights it is a tyranny (see 2T.192).

> As Conquest may be called a Foreign Usurpation, so *Usurpation* is a kind of Domestick Conquest, with this difference, that an Usurper can never have a Right on his side, it being no Usurpation, but where one *is* got into *the Possession of what another has Right to.* (2T.197)

And since the laws of the community designate who has the right to rule as part of the form of government established by the consent of the people, anyone who comes to power "by other ways, than what the Laws of the Community have prescribed, hath no Right to be obeyed" but is a usurper (2T.198). Usurpation violates the constitutive laws of the community, which are the sole source of authority within it.

Tyranny is also apparently defined as a violation of the laws of the community, of those substantive laws directed toward the public good.

> As Usurpation is the exercise of Power, which another hath a Right to: so *Tyranny* is *the exercise of Power beyond Right,* which no Body can have a Right to. And this is the making use of the Power any one has in his hands; not for the good of those who are under it, but for his own private separate Advantage. When the Governour, however intituled, makes not the Law, but his Will, the Rule; and his Commands and Actions are not directed to the preservation of the Properties of his People, but the satisfaction of his own Ambition, Revenge, Covetousness, or any other irregular Passion. (2T.199)

A ruler who sets himself above the law asserts both absolute and arbitrary power, in every sense of these terms. His tyranny is here identified with willful action for private ends and contrasted to lawful action, which is reasonable action for the preservation of the public.

But the relation between the positive law and the natural law dictate of preservation is no less ambiguous here than it was when Locke discussed legitimate political power. Certainly there is no simple identity between law and right. Locke recognizes the possibility of tyrannical laws (2T.201, 221–22), and he does not retract his defense of prerogative as justified by its tendency to promote the public good despite its violation of the law. The identification of tyranny with the violation of the law is conditional: *"Where-ever Law ends Tyranny begins,* if the Law be transgressed to another's harm" (2T.202).

But this conditional statement is the exception rather than the rule in the rhetoric of Locke's discussions of tyrannical actions. Law and the public good together are repeatedly placed in opposition to force and to private will or appetite (2T.206, 209, 226, 232). The impression of Locke's rhetoric is, then, something of a distortion of his position. Tyranny includes any violation of right, and there are some violations of the law that are not tyrannical.

Technically, Locke's statements may be reconciled with one another if the term "law" is considered in both a particularly precise and a rather general sense. Because no positive law is valid unless it accords with the natural law, when a legislature acts to advance its own interests at the expense of the public good, its action is called not a "tyrannical law," but an act of war (2T.222). The expression "tyrannical law" makes as little sense as "illegitimate political power" in Locke's usage. Again, because the fundamental standard of right is called the natural law, tyranny is always a violation of the law in this general sense. Contrariwise, an act of prerogative in accord with that standard is lawful in the same general sense. "Lawful" is here taken as equivalent to "rightful" (see, for example, 2T.18, 24, 165, 207). Prerogative powers are certainly rightful in that they derive from the natural law and depend on the consent of the people (2T.159, 163–64). The ambiguity might also be explained with the thought that Locke need not always mention the exception, prerogative, each time he states the general principle, rule of and by law.

Nonetheless, no technical explanation should be allowed to obscure the rhetorical emphasis of Locke's discussion of tyranny. He gives the impression that tyranny is largely an executive phenomenon, that it can ordinarily be recognized by its violation of the standing law, and that the law alone authorizes the use of government power and defines its extent (2T.200, 202). At the same time, we must remember that tyranny can be identified with illegality to the extent that the laws of the community may be identified with the public good, and only to that extent.

Tyranny and usurpation (foreign and domestic) comprise all cases of unlawful power where the principles of legitimacy are preservation and consent and where each principle is joined to a fundamental law.

> The *first and fundamental positive law* of all Commonwealths, *is the establishing of the Legislative Power;* as the *first and fundamental natural Law,* which is to govern even the Legislative it self, is *the preservation of the Society,* and (as far as will consist with the publick good) of every person in it. (2T.134)

But the simple correspondence between usurpation and breaches of consent and the fundamental positive law, on the one hand, and tyranny and breeches of preservation and the fundamental natural law, on the other, is too simple. First, usurpation is not the only possible violation of the fundamental positive law. And second, violations of this positive law are violations of the natural law as well.

> *Usurpation,* is a change only of Persons, but not of Forms and Rules of the Government: For if the Usurper extend his Power beyond what of Right belonged to the lawful Princes, or Governours of the Common-Wealth, 'tis *Tyranny* added to Usurpation. (2T.197)

Since no one has a right to change the forms and rules of the government established by its fundamental positive law, to do so is an act of power beyond right, which is the very definition of tyranny, even though a change in the forms of government might bring good government in every other way. And despite Locke's distinction between usurpation and alteration of the forms of government, the latter involves the former as well. To be sure, a usurper might not try to change the forms of government, and a change in those forms might be attempted by the duly authorized rulers of the community, men who are not usurpers in the strict sense. But a successful attempt necessarily would be a usurpation, for to alter the forms and rules establishing the legislative is to give this power to others or to take it for yourself when it was to be placed elsewhere by the laws of the community (2T.212–23). Change in the forms and rules of the government looks like a double evil: tyrannical and usurping.

Change in the constitutive rules of the government obviously alters the legislative established by the community, but other forms of usurpation and tyranny also have this effect. When a tyrant sets his will in place of the laws of the community, he sets himself up as legislator in place of the legislators authorized by the community. When a usurper makes the laws, he does the same (2T.212–17). Any action that has this effect is illegitimate because the legislative is "sacred and unalterable in the hands where the Community have once placed it" (2T.134). Neither the society as a whole nor the governors appointed by it may change the form of an established government (2T.134, 141, 149, 212, 227, 243).

In establishing a government, the society obligates all its members to obey those men who are authorized to govern by the agreement of the society. An agreement is not an agreement if its terms may be changed at any time. The society may not change its government at will for the same reason that the individual may not dissolve his allegiance to the society at will. Consent freely given is binding and not retractable.[54]

The legislators may not themselves alter the established legislative power because they hold this power as a trust. They cannot transfer their authority because it is not theirs to give away; there is no property right in political power. They have been entrusted with the authority to make laws, but not to make lawmakers (2T.141). Only the consent of the people can establish the authority to make laws. and without that authority no law is binding. To replace the established legislative with a new legislative power is to introduce force without authority, or the state of war, and to remove the only umpire the people were bound to obey. To violate the first and fundamental positive law is, then, to violate the natural law dictate that the society is to be preserved.

This means that there is no legitimate alteration of the legislative even if the alteration brings good government. A usurper who rules well is not on that account a legitimate ruler with a right to the obedience of his subjects. Locke is consistent in insisting that a judge with power to execute his judgments is not sufficient to establish legitimate government; it must be a judge with authority, and authority arises only from consent where men are by nature free.

Again, the question is raised of the relation between Locke's two principles, freedom and preservation, in a situation where they might conflict. Is the first merely instrumental to the second? May the "first and fundamental positive law" be abrogated in the name of the natural law? Do formal requirements give way to substantive ones? And again, it is Locke's discussion of prerogative that supplies ammunition for an affirmative response to these questions.

Locke recognizes authority in the executive to reform electoral districts and the number of representatives when he exercises his prerogative of convoking the legislature (2T.157–58). If this change in the forms and rules of government is considered by Locke as the equivalent of altering the legislative, Locke is indeed giving to the executive the right to dissolve the fundamental constitution of the government and to justify the act by an appeal to the maxim, "*Salus Populi, Suprema Lex.*" But Locke makes clear that this power of electoral reform is not equivalent to a right to change the original con-

---

54. The people may establish a government in such a way that they may periodically alter it by authorizing it for a distinct period of time. See 2T.243.

stitution. Rather, such a reform must produce a representation "suitable to the original Frame of the Government" by restoring the old and true legislative according to the original principles of representation. Maintenance of the constitution in its original form despite the inevitable changes brought about by changes in the distribution of population and wealth is the "*Salus Populi*" that this prerogative serves.[55]

Martin Seliger has argued that Locke contradicts himself here in a manner "unusual even by Lockeian standards."[56] He contends that Locke first asserts that electoral reform alters the legislative and that he does this in order to exclude the legislative body in principle from engaging in electoral reform itself. Seliger then claims that Locke must reverse this position to maintain an executive prerogative of electoral reform. But Locke never identifies electoral reform and alteration of the legislative: he merely says that "most think it hard to find" a remedy to the problem of rotten boroughs because *they* make that identification. If they were right, the people could not act to remedy the situation because they can act only if the government is dissolved, and no government authority could act because its power cannot reach the constitution. Because just electoral reform does not alter the constitution, government bodies may engage in electoral reform. Nothing in Locke's assertion of an executive prerogative to do so prejudices the legislative right to do so. In fact, he insists more than once that "whoever" restores a just representation is to be applauded. No doubt Seliger is correct that Locke did not expect much from the legislature in this regard; they have a "private interest" in "keeping up Customs and Priviledges, when the reasons of them are ceased." They have an interest in inaction in this area, but this does not mean they have no right to act.[57] Locke's discussion of this prerogative does not, after all, threaten our assertion that there is no legitimate claim to alter the fundamental positive agreement according to which men in society have submitted to government, and that an alteration in that agreement cannot serve to preserve the society.

The bonds of obligation established in political communities are

55. See 2T.216. Reapportionment is alteration of the legislative only when it is contrary to the public good and without the consent of the people.

56. Seliger, *Liberal Politics*, p. 348. For his complete argument on this question, see pp. 343–49.

57. A defense of both executive prerogatives and legislative rights in this area accords with Whig practice as Seliger himself describes it. See *Liberal Politics*, pp. 343–44. See also Ashcraft, *Revolutionary Politics*, pp. 238–39.

dissolved only as the result of the various forms of illegitimate action that we have been considering here. There is no authority, and thus no obligation, where men rule without consent or contrary to the public good. But this cannot mean that any action lacking authority dissolves all the bonds of government and society immediately, or Locke would have a theory that defined anything less than perfectly just government as grounds for revolution and as generating immediate anarchy. Conquerors, usurpers, and tyrants in all their forms violate the standards of legitimacy and consequently may be resisted. But a practicable theory of resistance requires considerably more than this.

A theory of popular resistance requires both that the dissolution of government and the dissolution of society be distinguished and that no distinction be made between the dissolution of a part of the government and the dissolution of the whole. It has been argued that Locke included both of these elements in his solution to the political problems presented by the conflicts England experienced under a mixed constitution. Locke's constitutional theory envisions a mixed government in which the executive has a share in the legislative and the branches are coequal under the constitution (2T.151). Neither branch has authority to alter the constitution by which it is empowered. This is to say that Parliament is not supreme and may not undertake constitutional change in reaction to abuses of executive power. Instead, the dissolution of the authority of one part of the government dissolves the government entire, thus freeing the people from their obligations under the constitution so that *they* may act to establish a new government. For legitimate popular resistance to occur, the government must be dissolved; for it to occur without anarchy, the society must remain intact.

Theoretically, the right of resistance belongs to the people as a political unit, and each member remains obligated to the unit. But these matters of right depend upon the maintenance of the society in fact. When society can no longer maintain itself as a unit, the members are released from their obligation (2T.211). Thus both the right to and the possibilities for recourse against illegitimate government actions depend on how those actions affect society in practice. We have seen that Locke does not expect a political society to last long once its established government is destroyed, and his theory of resistance must meet this difficulty. We begin to see the import of Locke's assertion that

> he that will with any clearness speak of the *Dissolution of Government,* ought, in the first place to distinguish between the *Dissolution of the Society,* and the *Dissolution of the Government.* (2T.211)

The precise effects of conquest, usurpation, and tyranny on the bonds of government and society must be considered in order to know who has the right to respond to abuses of power and who might have some possibility of success.

Locke states clearly that in the case of conquest, government and society are destroyed together.

> For in that Case, (not being able to maintain and support themselves, as *one intire* and *independent Body*) the Union belonging to that Body which consisted therein, must necessarily cease, and so every one return to the state he was in before, with a liberty to shift for himself, and provide for his own Safety as he thinks fit in some other Society. Whenever the *Society is dissolved,* 'tis certain the Government of that Society cannot remain. Thus Conquerors Swords often cut up Governments by the Roots, and mangle Societies to pieces, separating the subdued or scattered Multitude from the Protection of, and Dependence on that Society which ought to have preserved them from violence. (2T.211)

No distinction is made between just and unjust conquest, since the society of the conquered as a unit capable of defending its members is dissolved by the destructive effects of the war, regardless of who is in the right. Defeat frees each individual member from any obligation to the others, and this allows for the incorporation of the conquering and conquered peoples into one community. It "seldom happens, that the Conquerors and the Conquered never incorporate into one People, under the same Laws and Freedom" (2T.178).

But when Locke speaks of the right to resist subjection to the government imposed by a conqueror, he seems to imply that this is a right that belongs to the people as such—that conquest does not destroy society.

> But the Conquered, or their Children, . . . may *appeal,* as *Jephtha* did, *to Heaven,* and repeat their *Appeal,* till they have recovered the native Right of their Ancestors, which was to have such a Legislative over them, as the Majority should approve, and freely acquiesce in. (2T.176)

> For the first *Conqueror never* having *had a Title to the Land* of that Country, the People who are the Descendants of, or claim under those, who were forced to submit to the Yoke of a Government by constraint, have always a Right to shake it off, and free themselves from the Usurpation, or Tyranny, which the Sword hath brought in upon them, till their Rulers put them under such a Frame of Government, as they willingly, and of choice consent to. Who doubts but the Grecian Christians descendants of the ancient possessors of that

Country may justly cast off the Turkish yoke which they have so long groaned under when ever they have a power to do it? For no Government can have a right to obedience from a people who have not freely consented to it. (2T.192)

Locke seems to be speaking of a national right of self-determination, a right belonging to a distinct people with political and territorial claims that continue through the generations. And here again there is no distinction between just and unjust conquest that might clarify the matter, since those who were defeated by a just conqueror but who did not join in the initial unjust attack, and also their children, have the same status as victims of an unjust conqueror and their children.

Appearances to the contrary notwithstanding, Locke's manner of speaking of the right to resist the impositions of a conqueror, just or unjust, does not contradict his straightforward assertion that conquest dissolves society and the government with it. Society is dissolved when it is no longer capable of providing defense for its members, and they may join a new society. But they may also choose to incorporate together again as a society that excludes the conquering peoples; as a society that is ethnically, linguistically, culturally, religiously, and in any other way similar to the original conquered group. The right to be governed by a government of your choosing is inseparable from the right to belong to a society of your choosing.[58] Conquered peoples have not forfeited their right to exist as a separate society despite their defeat in battle.

In this way Locke's theoretical position regarding the rights of the conquered allows for a right to reinstate a political society with its own government but also allows for a peaceful amalgamation of the conquered people with the conquerors. There is a right, but no duty, to resist the conquerors and to try to reinstate your original society once it has dissolved. Because conquest dissolves society, each individual is free to make his own choice.

Usurpation was defined as domestic conquest, but it hardly seems to involve in every case the extreme effects of foreign conquest. In fact, Locke treats both the various forms of usurpation and the various forms of tyranny under two different headings—alteration of the legislative (2T.212–20) and breach of trust (2T.221–22)—and these are distinguished by their effects on the bonds of society. Both alteration of the legislative, the first case, and breach of trust,

58. In fact, the latter is the operable extent of the requirement. See p. 121 above.

the second case, dissolve the government, but the first is accompanied by dissolution of the society and the second is not.[59]

Alteration of the legislative dissolves the government because, in that case,

> no one Man, or number of Men, amongst them, can have Authority of making Laws, that shall be binding on the rest. When any one, or more, shall take upon them to make Laws, whom the People have not appointed so to do, they make Laws without Authority, which the People are not therefore bound to obey; by which means they come again to be out of subjection, and may constitute to themselves a *new Legislative,* as they think best, being in full liberty to resist the force of those who without Authority would impose any thing upon them. (2T.212)

In a mixed government structured like the English one, the legislative is altered when the prince "sets up his Arbitrary Will in place of the Laws" (2T.214); "when the Prince hinders the Legislative from assembling . . . or from acting freely" (2T.215); when the prince, without consent and contrary to the public good, alters the electors or modes of election (2T.216); and when the people are subjected to a foreign power by either the prince or the legislative (2T.217). The government is also dissolved in a manner that destroys the society as well, and consequently in a manner that belongs with this group of examples of alterations of the legislative, when the executive abandons his charge and fails to execute the law (2T.219).[60] In each of these cases the change in the government is clear and complete, "plain" and "visible" (2T.214, 219).[61]

In these cases the dissolution of the society follows upon the dissolution of the government. The authorized legislators of the society and the laws made by them are no longer the functioning legislative. There is no one whom all members of the society are

---

59. The analysis that follows relies heavily on Tarcov, "'Best Fence against Rebellion.'" It is Tarcov's argument, modified only slightly here, that the first case dissolves society and the second does not, and that the distinction is significant for Locke's theory of resistance. Locke is justifying and advocating resistance when tyranny is intended but not fully accomplished; he argues for the right to a domestic "preemptive strike."

60. It should be clear that some of these examples are of usurpation, some of tyranny, and some of both. The distinction between alteration of the legislative and breach of trust does not correspond precisely to that between usurpation and tyranny. Contrast Tarcov, "'Best Fence against Rebellion,'" p. 210.

61. When the prince alters electors or ways of election it will be clear that there has been a change, though it may be unclear whether it is a change for the good. If the change restores the "original Frame of the Government" and the people consent to it, it is just prerogative. See 2T.158.

bound to obey. The "Umpirage, which they have provided in their Legislative, for the ending all Differences, that may arise amongst any of them" is broken, and when this is "broken, or dissolved, Dissolution and Death follows." Society dissolves when it can no longer function as a unit to preserve the group and its members, and it cannot do so without an established legislative acting as the will of the society and authorized to punish breaches of the peace (2T.212, 220, 227).

Consequently, a successful alteration of the legislative leaves each individual free and in the state of nature. "Every one is at the disposure of his own Will" (2T.212; see 2T.219). The dissolution of government from within, when it takes the form of an alteration of the legislative, is no different from the dissolution of government from without, or conquest, in its consequences. And one of the examples of the former is delivery of the people into subjection to a foreign power (2T.217). In these circumstances the people have a right to reconstitute their society by reinstating a new legislative "umpire" if they can, but the society is dissolved and its members are free of all political obligation.

To advocate resistance only in these circumstances is to tell the people that

> they may expect Relief, when it is too late, and the evil is past Cure. This is in effect no more than to bid them first be Slaves, and then to take care of their Liberty; and when their Chains are on, tell them, they may act like Freemen. This, if barely so, is rather Mockery than Relief; and Men can never be secure from Tyranny, if there be no means to escape it, till they be perfectly under it: And therefore it is, that they have not only a Right to get out of it, but to prevent it. (2T.220)

When the legislative has been altered and government and society have been dissolved, the chance of mounting a successful resistance is slim indeed. (Similarly, we can infer that Locke is not optimistic about the prospects of overthrowing a successful conqueror.)[62]

If there is to be an effective right of resistance, then, the people must be freed from their obligation to their government while there is still time to prevent tyranny. That is to say, the government must be dissolved, since the people cannot act to alter their legislative within the constitution, but only extraconstitutionally, on default of the established government. The government, therefore, must be dissolved as a matter of right when tyranny and subversion

62. See his pessimistic remarks at 2T.176, 179, 180.

of the legislative are intended, attempted, endeavored, or designed, but not in fact accomplished.[63]

This is the feature that most clearly distinguishes the second case, breach of trust, from the first.[64] Breaches of trust are attempts by the legislature or the prince on the properties and liberties of the people. Power is abused to further ends contrary to those for which it was entrusted (2T.239). Examples include what we would call tyrannical laws that would give the legislators or others an arbitrary and absolute power over the properties of the subjects; attempts by the executive to set his arbitrary will in place of the laws; attempts to further this aim by corrupting representatives and preengaging electors, thus destroying the free action of the legislature; and similar corruption of the administration of the laws in order to crush his opposition (2T.221–22).[65] These attempts, unlike the examples given in the first case, do not clearly and completely change the government. For example, corrupting representatives is considerably less visible than preventing the legislature from meeting at its appointed time. And a single tyrannical law would not obviously dissolve the government in its entirety. In these cases the duly authorized rulers of the community have not been replaced by others but are themselves functioning in a manner subversive of the ends of government.

But these abuses are sufficient to justify resistance. Locke's argument here is that any breach of trust forfeits the power that has been entrusted; that those who attempt to misuse their authority "cannot any longer be trusted" (2T.222). Consequently their authority is dissolved,[66]

> and it [the legislative power] devolves to the People, who have a Right to resume their original Liberty, and, by the Establishment of a new Legislative (such as they shall think fit) provide for their own

63. Because the people have the right to prevent tyranny, "There is therefore, secondly, another way whereby *Governments are dissolved*" (2T.221). Note the use of "therefore." See Tarcov, "'Best Fence against Rebellion,'" pp. 210–11.

64. At 2T.227–28, Locke's position is restated. To alter the legislative is to "unty the Knot"; society dissolves. Locke's doctrine is "to tell the People they are absolved from Obedience, when illegal *attempts* are made upon their Liberties or Properties"—breaches of trust (my emphasis).

65. See Laslett, *Two Treatises*, note to 2T.122, p. 461. The general example seems to fit the specific case of James II's attempts to enforce the Declaration of Indulgence.

66. The government is "dissolved" in the same sense that we say that Parliament is "dissolved": its members lose their public authority and return to the status of private individuals.

Safety and Security, which is the end for which they are in Society.
(2T.222)

In this case society is not dissolved, and it is not too late for it to act
to preserve itself.[67]

Why is it that the dissolution of government in the first case is
quickly followed by the dissolution of society, but the dissolution of
government does not dissolve society in the second case? Societies
are dissolved when they are no longer able to preserve themselves
as distinct units with the ability to protect their members from violence. In the first case the tyrants have succeeded in establishing
their power, and the government has lost all authority. There is
thus no longer any bar to the state of war among men (2T.212,
227; see 2T.20–21), and the society is incapable of maintaining an
authority that can accomplish this purpose. Moreover, the society
cannot protect its members from the tyrannical violence of the
rulers. As in the case of conquest, the fact of defeat dissolves obligation to society. In the second case, the society is still capable of
resisting abuses of authority and of providing itself with a new legislative or protecting the old from continued subversion. In this
sense, the society remains by definition when the government is
dissolved by attempts at oppression rather than by successfully consolidated oppression.

But if in the second case the government is dissolved and without authority, is not the bar to the state of war between individual
members of the society as effectively destroyed as in the first case?
Where is the "umpire" that all members of the society are bound to
obey? No one is obligated to obey unjust actions of the government
or to obey further commands of those persons who have promulgated them. But the obligations of each to the laws that are legitimate and to their enforcement by the duly authorized persons
remains. These public actions have been authorized by the consent
of the society, and their continued authority is necessary to the
preservation of the society, something to which each member is
committed. Locke's theoretical position is not incompatible with the
obvious practical political observation that laws passed by regular
procedure and the administration of justice under them can continue to operate while resistance is mounted against a king and
certain of his actions—an oppressive tax, for example.

This is the practical manner in which society remains though
government has dissolved. It is an alternative to the vision of a

---

67. The duty to resist operates here, but not in the first case or in the case of
conquest. See chap. 3, note 42, and accompanying text.

situation where society remains and governs as a direct democracy in the times of revolution. If Locke did envision a viable operating majoritarian democracy in these circumstances, there would have been no need for him to elaborate the distinction between the first and the second case; even alteration of the legislative would not dissolve the society. Locke's theory of resistance does not depend on the "legal fiction" of direct majority rule any more than did his discussion of the origin of governments. In neither case does he maintain that men actually govern themselves as pure democracies, nor does his argument depend on his making such a case. The theory requires a historically practicable condition compatible with the analytically derived right of the society to a government authorized by the consent of the majority and operating for the public good, and to which all members are obligated, and in both cases this theoretical requirement is met.

The practical reality of Locke's second case might be described as one where the authority of the abusive part of the government dissolves while the healthy portions remain. But it is imperative that it not be so described. If it were, and given Locke's constitutional theory according to which the people cannot act while the government stands, Locke would be left with two alternatives: either he would have to accept a right in the healthy parts to alter the government in response to the abuses, or he would have to accept a situation where there would be no right to act against government abuses until it is too late, the entire government is subverted, and all are returned to the state of nature. To accept the first alternative would be to abandon the theoretical ground for a mixed monarchy with constitutionally coequal parts. It would throw Locke back to the alternatives of parliamentary supremacy or monarchical absolutism—the Scylla and Charybdis of the constitutional debate. Locke avoids this dilemma as well as the second alternative by arguing that attempted oppression dissolves the government entirely and frees the people to alter their legislative. Locke's constitutional theory is consistent with an effective right of resistance to abuses in a mixed and balanced government.

The interpretation outlined above of Locke's distinction between the first case, alteration of the legislative, and the second, breach of trust, and of the effect each has on the bonds of society helps to explain certain textual problems. The two cases are not clearly distinguished in the text as classes of illegitimate actions. Certainly alteration of the legislative is also a breach of trust, for example, and Locke says as much (2T.239). Just as with the distinction between usurpation and tyranny, certain cases overlap;

changes in forms and persons violate the ends of government as much as do changes in the substantive policies of government that further the private interests of the governors. In addition, some of the particular examples used seem to belong to both cases; for example, the prevention of free legislative action by the executive and setting his arbitrary will in place of the laws (2T.214, 215, 222). But in the first case the executive sets his will in place of the laws, and in the second he "goes about to." The relevant distinction is how successful he is at it. Actions of the second category tend to become actions that belong in the first, and with the same disastrous effects. That is, after all, the reason for the discussion of the second category; unless you resist actions that tend toward a subversion of the legislative, it will be too late.[68]

The variety of illegitimate government actions form a continuum in terms of their effects on rights and duties and their effects in a practical sense. At one extreme, the total abdication of the executive reduces the people to a "confused Multitude, without Order or Connexion" (2T.219); all political obligations are dissolved. Similarly, an attempt by the legislative or the people to alter a legitimate legislative is "open and visible Rebellion, apt enough to be taken notice of; which *when it prevails,* produces Effects very little different from Foreign Conquest" (2T.218, my emphasis). The middle range includes various forms of hindering the legislative from acting freely, some more radical than others. But all of these dissolve the government, and if nothing is done soon the society will also dissolve.[69]

At the other extreme are tyrannical actions that dissolve neither government nor society, a situation not yet considered here. The action of a constable who arrests a man at a time or in a place other than that specified in the king's writ, for example, is a tyrannical act against which there is legal recourse in the system Locke recommends, and which therefore does not produce a dissolution of government (2T.205–10). The constable has no authority in acting against the law, but because his is a delegated authority, his abuse

68. "It is not specifiable acts that constitute breach of trust but the end or design." Tarcov, " 'Best Fence against Rebellion,' " p. 215.

69. See 2T.215, 222. At 2T.155, Locke speaks as if hindering the legislative from meeting does not dissolve the society even though at 2T.215 this is given as an example of the first case. Whether it dissolves the society depends on whether the people in fact are able to act in response. Even if the society is dissolved, the people retain the right to reconstitute it by acting together to reinstate their legislative. In other words, a resistance movement constitutes a political society, and as a political society the people exercise their right of resistance. Contrast Tarcov, " 'Best Fence against Rebellion,' " p. 206.

does not dissolve the government so long as appeal to his superiors is available. Availability of recourse, as well as intention and severity, distinguishes Locke's categories of analysis. Tyrannical actions of this sort are acts of war that do not bring back the state of war, because an effective judge between the parties remains. Where there are remedies within the government (and incidentally, remedies such as these do not unbalance the coequal status of executive and legislative), the government is not dissolved, nor is popular resistance justified on every occasion of injustice.

For the variety of injuries, Locke recommends a variety of remedies, both for their justice and for their practicability. We begin with the thought that to know what the possibilities are for justifiable and successful resistance, we had to determine when and whether government and society dissolve. We found that in all cases there is no authority without consent and against the public good. But we found also that whether recourse is possible within the framework of government is the criterion for dissolution of government and that whether extraconstitutional recourse is still possible is the criterion for dissolution of society. It is dissolution of the society that is to be avoided at all costs, and the greatest threat to the society is an alteration of the constitution of its legislative that leaves no recognized authority. Resistance against illegitimate government actions is meant to forestall this possibility, and where this is too late resistance is still justified, though less likely to be successful. We turn now to the various forms of resistance, keeping in view that resistance is justified only on default of the government and that therefore legitimate resistance depends upon a just estimate of the government's actions.

THE DOCTRINE OF RESISTANCE

Locke makes the claim that his doctrine encourages peace, whereas Filmer's doctrine lays the groundwork for incessant strife. Properly stated, the claim in question is that the doctrine encourages and helps to preserve a just peace. Those who support peace at any price in the end permit greater bloodshed.

> If the innocent honest Man must quietly quit all he has for Peace sake, to him who will lay violent hands upon it, I desire it may be consider'd, what a kind of Peace there will be in the World, which consists only in Violence and Rapine; and which is to be maintain'd only for the benefit of Robbers and Oppressors. Who would not think it an admirable Peace betwixt the Mighty and the Mean, when the Lamb, without resistance yielded his Throat to be torn by the imperious Wolf? (2T.228)

The more precise question to be asked of Locke is not, Will his doctrine encourage peace? but Will his doctrine discourage aggressors?

Two elements of Locke's doctrine are open to charges that would undermine his claim to be able to give a positive answer to the question. The first is his contention that all governments derive their authority from the consent of the people. When conquerors, usurpers, tyrants, or rebels unsettle governments and new ones are established, how is the consent of the people given and recognized? If genuine consent cannot be distinguished in practice from passive acquiescence, Locke is subject to the same criticism he leveled at Filmer: he establishes a standard of right with no practical efficacy. This is tantamount to providing no standard at all but leaving the matter to be determined by force. To say that the consent of the majority authorizes rule is useless without a way of knowing who has the consent of the majority (compare 1T.106–7). Locke's doctrine, in this event, would simply legitimate the power of the prevailing forces in any contest for political power.

The second element is the right to resist abuses of power. Locke must respond to the charge that a doctrine of popular resistance is destabilizing. Who is to judge abuses, and is there reason to expect that the judgment will be made correctly? An unjust rebellion is no less an act of war than is conquest, usurpation, or tyranny. Locke must argue that his doctrine of a right in the people to resist illegitimate exercises of power will lead to resistance only when there is cause and not on every slight occasion.

Locke defends a variety of legitimate responses to the variety of abuses of power involved in conquest, usurpation, tyranny, and their combined forms. In any given case, the appropriate response is determined in part by whether the society remains obligated to its government and by whether the individuals remain obligated to their society. We must look more closely at each case of abuse and the responses to it in order to evaluate the claim that Locke's doctrine discourages aggressors and encourages only just resistance to them.

In the case of conquest, two responses are legitimate: the government of the conqueror may be resisted and replaced, or it may be legitimated by the consent of the conquered. The society has been dissolved by the total defeat of its legislative, and therefore each individual is free to join with any others in any political society. How is it known in practice when the society is dissolved and with it the individual's obligation to fight to defend it? At what point is a collaborator no longer a traitor but simply a free individual making his choice? Since the society is dissolved when it can no longer maintain itself as an independent unit and protect its members, a practical judgment must be made by each individual in the circumstances as to the society's capacity for defense, and there will often be times when the matter might reasonably be argued both ways.[70] But such times ordinarily do not last long; the victory or defeat of the conqueror or usurper will determine the question.

If a conqueror or usurper has consolidated his power, his rule cannot become legitimate in any other way than by receiving the consent of the people. The establishment of a peaceful and prosperous regime under the conqueror's or usurper's rule is not sufficient to establish its legitimacy, even if such a regime has prospered for a very long time. There are no prescriptive rights in Locke's political theory.[71] The passage of time does not in any way prejudice the rights of the children to the last generation to rise up and establish a government of their choosing and to reclaim their birthright. Only consent of the current subjects forecloses the option of resistance in future generations.

Since there can be no legitimate rule without consent, it is very important to be able to recognize what constitutes consent in these situations: "Yet such has been the Disorders Ambition has fill'd the World with, that in the noise of War, which makes so Great a part of the History of Mankind, this *Consent* is little taken notice of" (2T.175). If tacit consent of a sort that may be "little taken notice of" is sufficient to provide legitimacy to the rule of a conqueror or usurper, Locke's doctrine is open to the charge that the requirement of consent is meaningless. The mere passivity of the subjects would meet it—a passivity that can, of course, be the sign of successful oppression rather than the consent of the governed. What is it in practice that distinguished consent from mere acquiescence to brute force, which Locke explicitly argues cannot be taken for the true basis of obligation (2T.176, 186)?

The dimensions of the difficulty are diminished considerably by recalling that there are certain governments that can never have the legitimating consent of the people. No government can be given a right to "destroy, enslave, or designedly to impoverish the

70. See Franklin, pp. 61–62, for an interesting discussion of the controversy in 1650 over whether men should comply with the requirement to pledge allegiance to the government. Taking the Engagement to the Commonwealth was considered by some to be collaboration with a usurpation, but justified nonetheless.

71. This he shares with Filmer. See Daly, pp. 119–23.

Subjects" for the same reasons that no man can consent to slavery (2T.23, 135, 149). Consequently, obedience to oppressive rulers is never a sign of consent to their rule.

In addition to this negatively stated standard, Locke indicates positive criteria as well.

> For no Government can have a right to obedience from a people who have not freely consented to it: which they can never be supposed to do, till either they are put in a full state of Liberty to chuse their Government and Governors, or at least till they have such standing Laws, to which they have by themselves or their Representatives, given their free consent, and also till they are allowed their due property, which is so to be Proprietors of what they have, that no body can take away any part of it without their own consent, without which, Men under Government are not in the state of Freemen, but are direct Slaves under the Force of War. (2T.192)[72]

Representation in a legislative body is the minimum indication of consent sufficient to legitimate the rule of a government that is otherwise legitimate, protecting the property of its citizens and governing by standing laws. On these terms the conquered and the conquerors might well incorporate into one people "under the same Laws and Freedom" (2T.177).[73]

Locke does not unsettle the peace by casting doubt on the legitimacy of every government that has a conqueror somewhere in its history. The possibility of consent to a conqueror provides the same security for existing regimes that a doctrine of prescriptive right does, but only so long as those regimes meet certain basic standards of justice.

But does Locke unsettle the peace by encouraging would-be conquerors? To the extent that theoretical arguments make a difference in these matters,[74] Locke's discussion of the rights of conquerors and the rights of the conquered certainly must be discouraging. Conquest, even when it results from just self-defense, gives no claim to expanded territory and no right to rule. And con-

---

72. "Nor can such an *Usurper*, or any deriving from him, ever have a Title, till the People are both at liberty to consent, and have actually consented to allow, and confirm in him, the Power he hath till then Usurped" (2T.198).

73. This the Normans, Saxons, and Britons did, whereas the Turks and Grecian Christians did not. See 2T.176, 192.

74. Though Locke certainly did not expect to discourage conquerors by appealing to their moral scruples, he clearly believed that theoretical argument does make a difference; "There cannot be done a greater Mischief to Prince and People than the Propagating wrong Notions concerning Government" (2T, Preface). See 2T.1, 163, 226.

querors are threatened indefinitely with the legitimate resistance of the conquered peoples. If "the properest way to prevent the evil" of domestic oppression "is to shew them the danger and injustice of it who are under the greatest temptation to run into it," there is no reason to think that the same approach would not be useful in dealing with foreign oppression as well (2T.226).

But the right to resist conquerors is balanced by the right to consent to their rule if it be just. The net effect of Locke's teaching is to civilize conquerors. They are taught that their rule will be secure only if they rule by standing laws, with the consent of the people, and without violating property rights. And this is a lesson that one might reasonably expect to have some effect.

The same two-pronged argument applies to usurpations (2T.198). Locke makes a clear showing that these actions are illegitimate and may be resisted. There is certainly no encouragement of usurpation there. On the other hand, when usurpations do occur, there is a way to permanently put a stop to the violence and settle the legitimacy of the regime. The problem with this argument, in both the case of conquest and the case of usurpation, is that the second part of the argument may undermine the discouraging effects of the first if the message transmitted is that an attempt to overturn an existing government is worthwhile in a situation where there is a good chance of winning the approbation of the people. This is perhaps not a serious problem in the case of conquest, since men generally do not like to be ruled by foreigners. In the case of usurpation, the problem is more or less serious depending on your estimate of the people's capacity to recognize, and give their loyalty to, a good government. If the people have also learned their lessons from Locke, they are not likely to be ready to trust anyone who would displace by force even tolerably decent authorities in a tolerably decent government. In each case Locke makes the illegitimacy of aggression clear, maintains a right to resist it, but holds out the possibility that just rule will receive the consent of the people. These moral arguments support prudential calculations that discourage violence and oppression.

There is one possible exception; the colonization of wastelands. This is a practice that Locke not only does not discourage, but actively encourages. Far from considering colonization as aggression, Locke considers it a practice that increases "the common stock of mankind" (2T.37) by developing and exploiting the productive capacity of the earth. There can be no objection to the morality of English colonization of America, for example, if one accepts Locke's argument concerning the manner in which land comes to be property and the corresponding view of what lands remain waste and part of the common.

Locke describes three stages of development. Men first lived in nomadic communities as hunters and herdsmen. Later they settled in cities and cultivated the land. And last, they enlarged and increased their possessions with the use of money and commerce (2T.38, 45–50). At the first stage, ownership of the land is not claimed by anyone; all land is waste, and there are no territorial nations. In Locke's view, this is the way of life of the American Indians (2T.30, 41, 46, 49).[75] The Indians do use money, but without agriculture money will not lead to unequal possession of land (2T.49, 46, 184). At the second stage, territorial boundaries are set between nations by consensual agreements, but much of the land still remains waste within those boundaries and is not claimed by the inhabitants because they are not capable of using it. Locke uses biblical examples to illustrate this stage, where men could wander freely with their flocks from one territory to another. Since land is not yet scarce at this stage, there "could be no doubt of Right, no room for quarrel" (2T.38–39, 51). With the development of money and commerce, it becomes reasonable for men to enlarge their possessions, and land becomes scarce. Wastelands begin to disappear. At this third stage, the boundaries between nations are also settled by consent. Each nation relinquishes its claim to that portion of the common inheritance of mankind that is claimed by another. This is done either expressly, by leagues, or tacitly, by consent to the use of common money. To agree to trade in a certain coin is to agree to the unequal division of possessions that results from that trade where people produce unequal amounts. In every case, labor *begins* a property in land, but consent settles the division of property both between and within communities (2T.45–51).

As nomadic peoples, the Indians cannot lay claim to the lands over which they wander. To do so is to claim a greater portion of the common grant to mankind than they can make use of for the greatest benefit of mankind. If they fight to keep settlers out of their hunting grounds, they are the aggressors.[76] The settlers lay claim to land that is waste, that they can put to use, in a situation where there is ample room for the Indians to live as wanderers.

---

75. There were, of course, American Indian tribes that were agricultural and claimed territory. There would be no right to disturb these tribes and no reason to do so with so much available land. See 2T.184. Locke's position could also be challenged with an argument that territorial rights can be established by hunting on the land.

76. See Seliger, "Locke, Liberalism and Nationalism," p. 28.

And "he that leaves as much as another can make use of does as good as take nothing at all" (2T.33). The life of the settlers resembles that of men in the biblical times of the second stage. The settlers would, then, also have no right to keep the Indians from hunting or grazing animals on uncultivated lands that they claimed as within their territories. America is a place with much wasteland and no scarcity, so it should be a relatively simple matter to settle what territorial differences there are by agreement and to live in peace. From a Lockean point of view, there is certainly no injustice in the spread of agriculture and commerce where there is "enough, and as good left" (2T.33), and colonization is not a case of conquest.

Although conquest and usurpation can be ratified after the fact by the consent of the people, tyranny never can be. But because abuses of prerogative are tyrannical acts[77] and acts of prerogative are legitimated after the fact by the tacit consent of the people, similar problems arise here. May the prince legitimately use his prerogatives to do anything that the people will tacitly allow? Is tyranny understood as nothing other than those actions that the people in fact resist? In every case, power either is used for the public good or it is not, and the judgment of the people cannot alter the objective moral status of the action. Abuse of prerogative is tyranny whether or not the people recognize it as such (2T.166, 168). But a legitimate use of prerogative must both serve the good of the public and be accepted by the people (2T.164).

If the first of these conditions is met, the second is also likely to be. Locke contends that the people are not too scrupulous in judging the prince if the general tendency of his administration is to their benefit. This is why prerogatives tend to be enlarged in the reign of a good prince (2T.161, 165). But Locke goes further than this. In the case of the use of prerogative powers to reapportion the legislature, for example, if the action "cannot but be acknowledged to be of advantage to the Society, and People in general, [it] will always, when done, justifie it self . . . it cannot be doubted to be the will and act of the Society" (2T.158).

When a measure like a reapportionment clearly serves the general good, the consent of the people can be assumed. No additional indication of consent is necessary, as it is to legitimate the just rule of a conqueror or usurper. The difference is that in the case of prerogative the people have already entrusted the person holding

77. Prerogative is power to act for the public good. Abuse of prerogative is to act against it, which is "power beyond right," which is tyranny. See 2T.160, 164, 199.

office with the powers of the office, including certain prerogatives. So the consent of the people can be assumed unless and until they exercise their right to limit and redefine prerogative powers in response to abuses.

Locke seems confident that the people will recognize and oppose abuses as readily as they will recognize good government. Those who would attempt tyrannical abuses are threatened with the danger of resistance from a people who can recognize tyranny when they see and feel it, whose leaders have been taught to watch out for it, and who know they have a right to resist it. Wise princes can easily avoid opposition to their rule by ruling well and letting the people feel the benefits of good government (2T. 168, 209). The security of a ruler's power is tied to the justice of his rule. Again, Locke's moral argument has the practical consequences of both discouraging abuses and encouraging rulers to do well by doing good.

The primary challenge to Locke on the question of keeping the peace comes not from the charge that he encourages tyranny, usurpation, or conquest in any form, but from the charge that his case for the legitimacy of popular resistance will encourage anarchic conditions. There are two forms of this charge: first, that any individual may then disobey the law whenever he believes it is unjust, and second, that the people as a whole will be too quick to overturn their governments.[78]

> May the *Commands* then *of a Prince be opposed?* May he be resisted as often as any one shall find himself aggrieved, and but imagine he has not Right done him? This will unhinge and overturn all Polities, and instead of Government and Order leave nothing but Anarchy and Confusion (2T.203)

> To this perhaps it will be said, that the People being ignorant and always discontented, to lay the Foundation of Government in the unsteady Opinion, and uncertain Humour of the People, is to expose it to certain ruine; And no Government will be able long to subsist, if the People may set up a new Legislative, whenever they take offence at the old one. (2T.223)

Locke tells us that "in all States and Conditions the true remedy of *Force* without Authority is to oppose *Force* to it" (2T.155). But he also tells us that "*Force* is to be *opposed* to nothing, but to unjust and unlawful *Force*" (2T.204); and

> where the injured Party may be relieved, and his damages repaired by Appeal to the Law, there can be no pretence for Force, which is

78. The two are discussed in two sections, 2T.203–10 and 2T.223–43.

only to be used, where a Man is intercepted from appealing to the
Law. For nothing is to be accounted Hostile Force, but where it
leaves not the remedy of such an Appeal. And 'tis such *Force* alone,
that *puts* him that uses it *into a state of War*, and makes it lawful to
resist him. (2T.207)

Therefore abuses of power for which there is an appeal do not
dissolve the government, introducing a state of war between prince
and people, and certainly do not dissolve society, reintroducing the
state of nature among everyone. The bar to the state of war remains in the form of legal redress against executive officers who
may be "questioned, opposed, and resisted" (2T.206).

Legal avenues for redress against tyrannical abuses give effect to
the right of resistance without destabilizing the government. This
combination is ensured in the wisest constitutions by the responsibility of inferior executive officers coupled with the lack of personal responsibility of the prince. Challenges can be raised against
particular abuses without jeopardizing the head of the body politic
(2T.205). There are a variety of possibilities for institutional embel-
lishments on this theme, some of which provide recourse against
unjust laws when duly executed by the executive as well as against
unauthorized executive actions or abuses of prerogative. Impeachment, judicial review, a constitutional amendment procedure, and
trial by jury could all be seen in this light. Trial by jury is a second
chance, after initial passage of the law by their representatives, for
the people to give or withhold their consent to a law through representatives of the community; it is a kind of "popular judicial review." An example certainly known to Locke's readers is a jury's
acquittal of seven bishops who were charged with publishing a sedi-
tious libel because they petitioned James II to be relieved of the
duty of proclaiming his Declaration of Indulgence, which they
charged was illegal. Procedures for appeal to the law against executive abuses are, to use Locke's characteristic metaphor, "fences"
against constitutional crisis and civil war. An umpire between government and people serves the same function as an umpire among
the people. Where there is a right of appeal within the government, an "appeal to heaven" cannot be justified (2T.204).

Locke's response to the first charge, then, is that individuals
ought to have legal recourse available to them against executive
officers to redress individual abuses (2T.203–7). There is an orderly way of handling these sorts of injustices. This line of argument suggests that, for those cases where legal appeals are available, Locke justifies extralegal resistance only as a last resort.

But there are many abuses for which there may be no appropriate legal remedy. Executive interference with the meetings of the legislature is a clear case. Or the abuses in question may include perversion or obstruction of the legal process of appeal (2T.20, 208, 222). And though the people have a right to limit executive prerogatives by law when they believe these powers have been abused, this approach is likely to be ineffective where the executive has a veto power. Under this form of constitution, the executive

> has no distinct superior Legislative to be subordinate and account-
> able to, farther than he himself shall joyn and consent: so that he is
> no more subordinate than he himself shall think fit, which one may
> certainly conclude will be but very little. (2T.152)

The scope of executive prerogative is likely to be successfully limited by law either when one executive is replaced by another or when the executive is so politically weakened in a contest with the legislature and the people that he accepts the limitation as the price of the throne. Locke seems to have in mind a prince who rejects such a bargain when he writes:

> If a Controversie arises betwixt a Prince and some of the People, in a
> matter where the Law is silent or doubtful, and the thing be of great
> Consequence, I should think the proper *Umpire*, in such a Case,
> should be the Body of the *People*. . . . But if the Prince, or whoever
> they be in the Administration, decline that way of Determination,
> the Appeal then lies nowhere but to Heaven. (2T.242)

Controversies like these, which go beyond a few individual cases, cannot be settled within the constitution, and disturb the peace of the nation, are not likely to arise without good cause. Locke's response to the second charge is that the people are unlikely to overturn their government on account of some frivolous change in their "unsteady Opinion, and uncertain Humour" (2T.223). The people are so attached to their forms of government that they are reluctant even to repair obvious defects. Evidence for the attachment of the people to their constitutions and their aversion to change in them is to be found in the fact that England still has its king, Lords, and Commons with kings from the original line, despite the many revolutions that have taken place in its history (2T.223). A general desire for a change in the constitution is an unlikely cause for disorder in the state.

But in all governments and regardless of the various hypotheses concerning rights of resistance, the people will resist if

> the mischief be grown general, and the ill designs of the Rulers be-
> come visible, or their attempts sensible to the greater part, [other-

wise] the People, who are more disposed to suffer, than right themselves by resistance, are not apt to stir. (2T.230; see 2T.208–9, 224–
25)

Popular uprisings occur if and only if

a long train of Abuses, Prevarications, and Artifices, all tending the
same way, make the design visible to the People, and they cannot but
feel, what they lie under, and see, whither they are going. (2T.225)

The best way to prevent popular uprisings is to give the people
good government. Instability in the commonwealth is most often
the fault of oppressive rulers who have made themselves the object
of the general suspicion of their people,

wherein they are the less to be pitied, because it is so easy to be
avoided; It being as impossible for a Governor, if he really means the
good of his People, and the preservation of them and their Laws
together, not to make them see and feel it; as it is for the Father of a
Family, not to let his Children see he loves, and takes care of them.
(2T.209; see 2T.230)

Locke's response to the charge that his doctrine creates instability is that instability is most often the result of resistance that is
justified, and that at least his doctrine teaches the true rebels, the
tyrants and usurpers who reintroduce the state of war, that they
cannot expect to do so with impunity (2T.226–27).

In this, Locke's doctrine is clearly superior to the alternative,
and he concludes his case with an attack on the opposition. One
cannot argue consistently that there is no right to resist the violence
of rulers if there is a right to resist the violence of foreigners and
subjects. Even Barclay must admit a right of resistance in some
circumstances, and if he were to speak consistently, they would be
the same circumstances recognized by Locke (2T.228–39). Most
important, without a right of resistance, the field is open to tyrants.
If there is peace under tyranny in any sense, it will be one that is
worse than "pure Anarchy" (2T.225; see 2T.13). And in the long
run, peace is less secure when men believe that there is no right to
resist oppressors. Then "Men live together by no other Rules but
that of Beasts, where the strongest carries it, and so lay a Foundation for perpetual Disorder and Mischief, Tumult, Sedition and
Rebellion" (2T.1). Only to the extent that potential tyrants, conquerors, and usurpers are discouraged by the threat of resistance
to their rule does Locke's doctrine minimize rebellions by minimiz-
ing the occasions for them.

But this is not an argument that rebellions will be less frequent when there is just cause for them. In effect Locke argues for justice over peace in any given situation, though the argument is not made in these stark terms. The quiet that may prevail under tyrants is not called "peace" but is called by its analytically correct name, "the state of war." Analytically and rhetorically, it is injustice that shatters the peace. To be on the side of justice, then, is to be on the side of peace, even if it requires warfare to restore justice. Locke's doctrine is more radical than he makes it sound.

Far from providing an argument that would discourage popular resistance, Locke implies that resistance is not likely to occur as often as it should. Locke reassures his critics with the observation that the people will not rise in defense of a few private men unless the "Precedent, and Consequences seem to threaten all" (2T.208). And even "manifest Tyranny" will not disturb the state if the "Body of the People do not think themselves concerned in it" (2T.207). But the fact that the people will not react until abuses have become general and obvious is not necessarily a virtue. And it is Locke who teaches the people and their leaders that the body of the people *is* often concerned in the abuses that affect a few private men.

When a question does arise whether the executive has abused his prerogatives, Locke maintains that "the tendency of the exercise of such *Prerogative* to the good or hurt of the People, will easily decide that Question" (2T.161). The problem here is that the question may be raised and answered too late or not at all. This concern is, after all, the reason for Locke's distinction between those abuses that dissolve the society and government together and those where the government dissolves but the society can still act to maintain its legislative. Evidently Locke does not believe that the people will spontaneously and accurately judge the use of executive prerogatives. "The tendency of the exercise of such *Prerogative*" is not always easy to discern. The people must be awakened to the danger, the tendency of a chain of abuses must be made visible to them, so that they may act to prevent the dissolution of their society.

Moreover, where the tyrannical nature of an action is easiest to discern, there is also least likely to be any timely recourse or any recourse short of civil war. For example, if the executive should use the force at his disposal to hinder the legislative from meeting at a time duly appointed by law, the abuse would be clear and indisputable; there could be no legitimate debate whether the action was undertaken for the public good (2T.155, 215; contrast 2T.216). But there would also be little likelihood of an effective response.

To prevent tyranny and to act in time requires the ability to recognize the beginning of a long train of abuses in the early attacks on a few. Locke teaches his readers that an attack on a few may become an attack on the whole and that they must be the watchful guardians of their liberties and properties against government abuses.[79]

Nonetheless, Locke cautions his readers that they must judge carefully whether their cause is just; whether the abuses suffered by a few are in fact the early signs of a general oppressive design; and whether they are "worth the Trouble" that an appeal for redress may cause the entire society.

> If it be objected, this would cause endless trouble; I answer, No more than Justice does, where she lies open to all that appeal to her. He that troubles his Neighbor without a Cause, is punished for it by the Justice of the Court he appeals to. And he that *appeals to Heaven,* must be sure he has Right on his side; and a Right too that is worth the Trouble and Cost of the Appeal, as he will answer at a Tribunal, that cannot be deceived, and will be sure to retribute to every one according to the Mischiefs he hath created to his Fellow-Subjects; that is, any part of Mankind. (2T.176)

Just as the right of resistance does not justify the use of force if peaceful adjudication of disputes is available, neither does it justify any "Mischief" that is not both just in its claim and a reasonably proportionate means to secure justice.

Locke's advice to those who would preserve their lives, liberties, and property from the abuses of tyrants is twofold: if there is a genuine means of redress within the government, it is the only legitimate avenue of protest; but if there is not, and if they have a reasonable possibility for success, men need not wait until "their Chains are on" before they "may act like Freemen . . . they have not only a Right to get out of it [tyranny], but to prevent it" (2T.220).

"Preventive resistance" or "anticipatory resistance" covers the class of situations where the government is dissolved but the society is not. In these cases there have been abuses of government power sufficient to indicate an attempt to subvert the government and establish a tyranny, but the society is still capable of acting to preserve its freedom under the government of its choosing. But who is it that acts for the society in these situations, and what right do they have to speak for the whole?

When a contest arises between the executive and legislative lead-

---

79. See Tarcov, "'Best Fence against Rebellion,'" pp. 213–17.

ers, how is it known which side speaks for the majority of the body of the people? Again, since there can be no legitimate government without the consent of the people, it is critical to know who has that consent. The success or failure of resistance is not a sufficient test for the presence or absence of the support of the majority. A legitimate popular opposition may be crushed by a tyrant, and a factious rebellion may succeed in becoming a usurpation. The question is the same as that raised in considering conquest, usurpation, and prerogative. Peace and quiet do not legitimate tyranny. When the peace is broken, there will no doubt be cases where the sentiments of the majority are clearly shown in their willingness to take up arms. In the absence of this kind of clear evidence, the new government established as the result of successful resistance would have to be legitimated in the same way that a conqueror's or usurper's is. Either the people must be free to choose their government through some kind of representative assembly established for the purpose, or they must be represented in the assembly of a government operating by standing laws that get their authority from the consent of that body.

But Locke has a particular form of resistance in mind. He envisages legislators and other prominent public men leading an opposition to executive abuses. When the government is dissolved and the right of resistance comes into play, legislators have no right as legislators to speak for the society. Yet they do have a role as leaders of the opposition.[80] Locke explicitly states his reasons for fearing that the danger is most likely to come from the executive under a constitution like the English one. The prince has the resources at hand and may easily be persuaded that he may use them with impunity to

> *make great Advances toward* such changes [alteration of the legislative] under pretence of lawful Authority, and [he] has it in his hands to terrifie or suppress Opposers, as Factious and Seditious, and Enemies to the Government. Whereas no other part of the Legislative, or People is capable by themselves to attempt any alteration of the Legislative without open and visible Rebellion, apt enough to be taken notice of; which when it prevails, produces Effects very little different from Foreign Conquest. (2T.218, emphasis added)[81]

Not only is the threat to the government most likely to originate with the executive, but his plans are likely to proceed invisibly and

---

80. See Ashcraft, *Revolutionary Politics*, pp. 327–29.
81. See Hamilton, Jay, and Madison, no. 48, pp. 308–13, for a complementary argument that legislative abuses are more likely in the American system.

by degrees in a manner that might successfully be thwarted by an alert opposition.[82] We have already noted the continuity between Locke's two categories, breach of trust and alteration of the legislative, in the case of the executive's attempts to set his arbitrary will in place of the law. Legislators have a duty to prevent executive breaches of trust from becoming a consolidated and successful alteration of the legislative. Insofar as legislators promote or do not hinder executive designs, "they are guilty, and partake in this, which is certainly the greatest Crime Men can be guilty of one towards another" (2T.218).[83]

Locke's explicit warnings against the executive and his relative silence throughout concerning legislative abuses could lead the reader to conclude that he was simply more trusting of legislative representatives than of monarchs. The entire chapter "Of Tyranny" focuses on executive abuses, and nowhere is there a systematic treatment of tyrannical laws and the possibilities for recourse against them. But Locke reminds the reader that tyranny is not a fault of monarchies only and that power may be used tyrannically "whether those that thus use it are one or many" (2T.201). Legislative abuses are also given as primary examples of the second case, breach of trust (2T.221–22). It is not that legislators are less likely to be inclined to abuse their power, but that they are at an institutional disadvantage in the English system and therefore less likely to have good opportunities to do so.

Legislators cannot proceed "under pretence of lawful Authority" without the concurrence of the executive. Where executive and legislature cooperate in schemes of oppression, there may be little likelihood of successful resistance regardless of which of the two initiated the scheme. But where the executive opposes legislative designs, he has formidable weapons at his disposal in the form of prerogative powers and the command of the combined forces of the community. Even an executive with no legislative veto may have power to prorogue or dissolve Parliament. And this prerogative is one that Locke does not justify by the impossibility of conveniently regulating the sitting of the legislature in any other way. Legislators certainly could have the sole right to determine when to bring their proceedings to a close. But if they did, "long Continuations of their Assemblies, without necessary occasion, could not but be burthensome to the People, *and must necessarily in*

---

82. "Locke presents a theory of opposition as well as of resistance." Tarcov, "'Best Fence against Rebellion,'" p. 208.

83. See chap. 3, notes 42 and 67 and accompanying text on the duty to resist.

time produce more dangerous inconveniences" (2T.156, emphasis added; see 2T.218).[84] Locke is quite willing to leave to the executive sufficient authority to discourage and to oppose legislative abuses. But given the context in which the *Second Treatise* was written, it is not surprising that Locke emphasizes the need for and legitimacy of concerted opposition to executive encroachments.

This is not, however, simply a matter of rhetoric appropriate to the Exclusion Crisis and the Glorious Revolution. Where the executive shares in legislative power, the legislature does not have the weapons within the constitutional structure to hinder executive encroachments as effectively as the executive may hinder legislative ones. Locke's solution is to alert political leaders to the need for watchfulness against the executive on behalf of the people so that they may act in time to prevent tyranny. If the executive's tyrannical designs have gone far enough, the government is dissolved and legislators may act not as legislators, but as leaders of resistance.

This doctrine of resistance is the counterpart to Lockean prerogative in the sense that the first allows for a politically effective right to respond to executive abuses and the second allows for a politically effective right to respond to legislative defects and abuses, while neither establishes a superiority of one branch over another within the constitution. Ordinary times are sharply distinguished from extraordinary ones. Both legislators and executive have the right and the duty to recognize extraordinary occassions and to use their powers on those occasions in extraordinary ways on behalf of the public good.

In the case of executive abuses, extraordinary times may look deceptively like ordinary ones. Even if the captain of the ship "often" and "for some time" steers away from Algiers, his settled destination may nonetheless be the slave markets (2T.210). The king is the captain in question, and his "Algiers" the establishment of absolute monarchy and the Catholic religion. The friends of the commonwealth who can see the tendency of his actions must "make the design visible to the People" before the destination is reached (2T.225).[85] This was the role of the Whig leaders in 1688; the Glorious Revolution fits the model of Lockean resistance.

But if this is Locke's interpretation of the events of 1688, his

---

84. That Parliament was not to be prorogued or dissolved without its own consent was one of the "essentials of the revolutionary program." Ashcraft, "Revolutionary Politics," p. 485 n.13. Locke evidently did not support the program of the radical Whigs in this particular.

85. Tarcov, "'Best Fence against Rebellion,'" pp. 215–16.

view is at odds with the dominant Whig interpretation of those events.[86] The Whigs had rejected the theory of parliamentary supremacy that had justified resistance to the king in 1640 and replaced it with a theory of forfeiture. This was their solution to the problem of providing an avenue for resistance without anarchy under a mixed constitution. With no dissolution of the government, Parliament declared that James II had forfeited the throne and proceeded, as a convention Parliament, to fill the vacancy. But this theory of forfeiture does not solve the problem of parliamentary supremacy. There is no effective distinction between parliamentary supremacy and a right in Parliament to both "find" and fill a vacancy on the throne. Parliament remains the final judge.[87] Locke speaks of these events in his preface to the *Second Treatise* with no mention of the role of the Parliament. Legitimate resistance occurs only on the dissolution of the government and is undertaken by the body of the people. Locke considered the convention Parliament to be not a "formal Parliament," but "something of another nature" whose business it was to mend "the great frame of the government."[88]

Locke remains opposed to alterations of the legislative by any part of the government or even by the entire government. Such alteration can take place only when the government is dissolved and the people act. This is a position that seems to conflict with Locke's support of the Exclusion Bills. The Tory opponents of those bills argued that no act of the government can take precedence over the fundamental law establishing the succession to the throne,[89] and one might expect Locke to agree with them. The Whigs replied that no law is superior to the act of the established government. Again, Locke did not share the theoretical ground of many of his Whig political allies. If it would have been legitimate in Locke's view for the entire legislative to alter the succession so as to forestall the danger represented by the prospect of James on the

86. See Ashcraft, *Revolutionary Politics*, chap. 11.

87. Franklin, pp. 98–126.

88. John Locke to Edward Clarke, 8 February 1689, in *The Correspondence of John Locke and Edward Clarke*, ed. Benjamin Rand (Plainview, N.Y.: Books for Libraries Press, 1927; reprint ed., 1975), pp. 288–90. Franklin suggests that Locke wished for a broader representation in the convention Parliament than in an ordinary Parliament precisely because it was to exercise a constitutional function and ought to be able to speak for the majority of the society. See pp. 119–22. See also Ashcraft, *Revolutionary Politics*, postscript. Throughout chapter 19, Locke rhetorically emphasizes that the people resist while deemphasizing the role of legislators as leaders of resistance, perhaps in order to stress that resistance is a right belonging to private men as members of society and not a right authorized within the government.

89. Daly, p. 144.

throne, then it can only be that alteration of the succession in these circumstances is not equivalent to alteration of the legislative. The appropriate analogy in this case is to reapportionment.[90] No dissolution of the government is involved. The original constitution of the legislative is maintained by changes that preserve it in response to unforeseen and unforeseeable circumstances that threaten it.

The right of resistance belongs to the people as such and can be exercised only when the government is dissolved. But if the people are the judges of when it is dissolved, do they not have this right as often as they wish? The criticism is analogous to the criticism of the Whig theory of forfeiture as a replacement for parliamentary supremacy. If Parliament judges when there is a vacancy, the Parliament is supreme; if the people judge when the government is dissolved, the people are supreme. And in the latter case, the supremacy is tantamount to anarchy. Locke's defense against the charge that his doctrine of resistance encourages frequent rebellion is not yet complete.

Locke concludes the *Second Treatise* by reintroducing the question of unjust rebellion in the form of the question, Who judges?

> Here, 'tis like, the common Question will be made, *Who shall be Judge* whether the Prince or Legislative act contrary to their Trust? This, perhaps, ill affected and factious Men may spread amongst the People, when the Prince only makes use of his due Prerogative. (2T.240)

Locke's first response is that the people have the right to make this judgment, just as a private individual has the right to judge the performance of his trustee or deputy. In fact, the right is particularly important in this case since "the evil, if not prevented, is greater, and the Redress very difficult, dear, and dangerous" (2T.240; see 2T.242). But this right is often an ineffective one. If the rulers "decline that way of Determination," or if the question concerns the prerogative of convening the legislature, or if either the executive or the legislature goes about to destroy the people, then the people cannot act as a judge on earth to decide the question (2T.168, 241–42).

Instead, they have the right to make the judgment that they will "appeal to heaven." To say that there is no judge on earth with authority is not to say that there is no right and wrong. God in heaven remains the final judge. And each individual always has the right to judge in his own conscience whether to "appeal to heaven." That is to say, he has the right to judge whether any other man has

90. See pp. 144–45 above.

put himself into a state of war with him. The right "to appeal to heaven" is a right of war—a right to take up arms in defense of life and liberty whenever there is no judge on earth to whom he can appeal. This is an inalienable right; without it, a man would be a slave subject to absolute power (2T.13, 19–21, 168, 181, 241–42).

When the people judge that their rulers have introduced the state of war with them, they judge that their authorized public judge has lost the right to be judge on earth. The people determine the limits of their obedience. This determination is an aggregate of individual judgments. But the appeal to arms will not be worth the trouble and cost to an aggrieved individual unless he can persuade his fellows to join him. He must appeal to the majority for support, and there is a presumption that a discontented majority is in the right.

But if the majority judges wrongly, the fact of majority consent will not make the rebellion justified. Might does not make right whether the mighty are few or many, and in both cases the wrong side sometimes wins. When the majority is in the right in a controversy where the society has not been dissolved, the individual is bound by his obligation to the society to join in the resistance. But the individual is also the ultimate judge of whether the majority is in the right. When they are in the wrong, there is no longer any obligation to the society. The society is dissolved by unjust popular rebellion; the people as such are always guiltless (2T.218; pp. 129–30 above). Each individual must judge whether private individuals or the government initiated the state of war. In addition, and regardless of the justice of the cause, the individual is the ultimate judge of whether his society has in fact dissolved. This is the case that arose in our consideration of conquest and usurpation. The individual must determine at what point his society can no longer function as a defensive unit, at what point he would be free to consent to the government of a conqueror or a usurper. Thus the individual is, in every case, the judge of the limits of his obligations to society as well as to its government.

Ultimately, there is no common judge with authority between rulers and people or between an individual and the group. There is no absolute obedience; might does not make right; and each individual is judge in his own case. Locke ends with the same problem with which he began. He started by recognizing the problems that result in the state of nature because each individual is judge in his own case. Civil government is the proposed solution to those problems (2T.13, 136). But the solution is not of the sort that definitively and eternally overcomes the problem; Locke is no utopian.

Conflicts between government and people bring back the state of nature (2T.226–27). And each individual is judge in his own case when he makes the judgment that this has occurred.

Locke's argument comes full circle. If you begin with the premise that each man has the inalienable right to judge the means to his preservation, and if this natural right must be preserved, then you end with the conclusion that each man has an inalienable natural right to judge the limits of his obedience to a government established to secure his preservation. Does this mean that Lockean civil government is no solution at all to the problems that arise in the state of nature where free and equal individuals each judge of their rights in relation to one another? Can the right of each individual to judge the limits of his obligations be distinguished from a right to retract his consent at will? Does Locke's doctrine of resistance fatally undermine his case for the ground of obligation?

It should be said first that the difference is great, in terms of the principle involved, between the claim that men have a right to break their agreements at will and the claim that no individual need perform his part of a contractual obligation if the other partner has defaulted. In the latter case, the contract is broken. This situation is analogous to that between men and their government when government is dissolved. But in that situation, since the compact is a trust, one party has the right to judge when the compact is no longer binding. Judging according to clear standards whether a breach of trust has occurred is very different from withdrawing consent or obedience at will. The first requires rational argument. There is evidence to be weighed and considered and opposing evidence and arguments to take into account. An exercise of judgment is called for, rather than an exercise of pure will. There can be political argument over the question, Has there been a breach of trust on the part of the government? As a practical matter, men who believe that this determination cannot be made at pleasure but only upon showing cause, men who are convinced by Locke of the meaning of the principle of consent, will take their obligations more seriously than men who believe otherwise. This is not a negligible consideration, though Locke does not rely on an expectation of principled behavior alone. The understanding that change in the government is justified only when the government is dissolved is bolstered by the consideration that resistance must be worth the trouble and cost.

Moreover, Locke's political solution depends on the claim that men are able to judge when the government is dissolved, that they are more likely to judge their rights and duties correctly under government than they are in the state of nature, and that their misjudgments are less likely to have disastrous consequences. Locke seems fairly confident that the people are capable of making some of the most important political judgments correctly. They are not likely to resist their government without just cause, and they cannot be prevented from resisting manifest oppression when they have the opportunity to do so. The people can see and feel sufficiently well to judge the performance of their governments. Men can adequately judge government because they experience its benefits or burdens directly. Unjust rebellion is unlikely because most men will not be misled as to their true rights and interests. The errors of a few will not cause general chaos under government, as they will in the state of nature, because the force of many will be united against them. Confidence in the people's capacity to judge government on the basis of their true rights and interests is the ground for the confidence that unjust rebellions, seditions, and tumults are not a serious cause for concern.

Yet Locke does not deny their possibility. The people or some part of them may attempt an alteration of the legislative, for example, though such an attempt may be blocked or deterred by the power of the prince in the same way a legislative attempt may be (2T.218). And Locke concedes that "the Pride, Ambition, and Turbulency of private Men have sometimes caused great Disorders in Commonwealths, and Factions have been fatal to States and Kingdoms" (2T.230) though he lays the blame for the initiation of such troubles at the feet of the rulers rather than the people. The people are less likely to mistakenly jettison good government than to mistakenly acquiesce to a government that threatens to become tyrannical. Unjust rebellion, though unlikely, is not impossible and, as we have seen, just rebellion may come too late. In either case a doubt remains as to the people's capacity for judgment, and there is reason to consider more carefully the people's role as judge.

The people are capable of judging clear cases clearly. Preservation, or the public good, is the sort of standard against which experience can be tested easily at the extremes. But when the case is clearest, the possibilities for action are often least promising. And the people cannot adequately judge the long-range tendencies of their ruler's policies. Locke's insistence that the people will recognize and resist oppression and that they will recognize the benefits of good government might give the impression that he is too optimistic concerning the people's capacities. But the rhetorical effect on the reader is rather to emphasize the responsibility of political leaders in making the effects of government policies clear to the

people. Rulers who wish to keep order and stability in the state
need only make the people feel that they rule for their benefit.
Leaders who wish to oppose a potential tyrant must make his designs visible to the people. And potential tyrants are forewarned
that the people are perfectly capable of being intelligent followers.

There are two problems, then, with the doctrine that the people
are ultimately judge of their rights under government. First, in the
extreme case, there is no common judge for the entire community.
The right of the people to judge may leave government in a position that is too precarious. Locke must rely on the people's capacity
to judge well. And second, the people are not capable of judging
well in doubtful cases, in the "gray areas" where conflicts are most
likely to arise.

The law and the formal, legal institutions of government are
major elements of Locke's response to both of these difficulties.
Legal forms and institutions can guide the people's judgment in
determining whether resort to arms is justified. Most important,
there can be no resort to war if there is an impartial judge to whom
appeal is available and whose decisions the parties are obligated to
accept on the basis of their consent. While certain institutions of
government are operating, any disturbance of the peace is unjustified. The operation of a system of legal appeals acts as a fence
against the ultimate case where the people act as the final judge.
Locke is interested in establishing "fences" against the worst case.
Laws are a fence to property, freedom is a fence to preservation,
civil society is a bar to the state of war. These are Locke's characteristic metaphors (see, e.g., 2T.17, 136, 222). "When push comes
to shove," "ultimately," and "in the end" there is no judge on earth
between rulers and people, but it is possible to put a lot of distance
between ordinary times and the "final analysis." Recognized common authorities and modes of procedure for resolving conflicts do
just that.

But when the formal channels of authority are circumvented or
altered by those in power, resistance is justified. And these usurpations are visible abuses precisely because they are violations of formal procedures. Interference with the meeting of the legislature or
levying a tax without legislative approval are clear examples. Formal criteria can serve as signs of legitimacy as well. For example,
the participation of a representative body is a clear sign of consent
to a newly established regime. Laws and formal procedures and
criteria serve to diminish the "gray areas." Where all public authority derives from the consent of the people, violations of the formal
processes for making decisions are clearly suspect. Consent, like

preservation, is the sort of standard whose violation is often clearly recognizable.

This is one of the reasons for Locke's rhetorical identification of tyranny with lawlessness and of law with the public good. Where the law is "silent or doubtful" (2T.242), there may be more latitude for unquestioned discretion; but certainly where a law is violated, the action is immediately suspect. Prerogatives must be defended as necessary and conducive to the public good. It is not a sufficient defense to claim prerogative powers as rights of office.

This is also one of the reasons for Locke's extraordinary emphasis on preserving the form of government. The form of government designates the authorized adjudicators for the community and the processes by which they operate. It provides the visible and obvious legitimate mode of resolving disputes and enforcing their resolution. Locke so emphasizes the character of government as an authorized common judge that he characterizes tyrannical actions as the prelude to alteration of the legislative when one would ordinarily expect exactly the reverse; a discussion of usurpation as the prelude to tyranny. Instead, "*overturning* the Constitution and Frame of *any Just Government*" is "the greatest Crime" (2T.230; see 2T.218).

Throughout this discussion of the *Second Treatise* we have repeatedly been struck by the importance of formal requirements and criteria in Locke's political teaching. Consent is not subordinate in status to preservation. Both are necessary, and neither is a sufficient condition for legitimate government. The extent of legitimate authority is determined by both its end and its origin. A usurper who rules well is not a legitimate ruler. Violations of the first and fundamental laws of the community are violations of the natural law as well.

Why is an authorized common judge so critical? The immediate answer is that it is the response to the problems of the state of nature where each judges for himself. The capacity of men to judge for themselves in this situation is insufficient to regulate their common life. But establishing a judge with authority on earth is a fragile human solution. Conventions cannot overcome the natural human condition, but can only introduce improvements that allow men to manage it. Men are always threatened by the possibility of a return to their unimproved state.

Locke's political solution is that of an anxious realist but not that of a cynic. He develops an analytically sound solution to the practical problems posed by critics of consent theories. He can explain in a practically plausible manner how territorial nations can come into being and how their governments both establish order and undergo radical change in accord with the fundamental natural law dictates of freedom and preservation. But order and authority are conventional creations, "fences" against the worst. There is no permanent solution to the problems posed by natural freedom.

4

Reason and Politics Reconsidered

Introduction

Locke begins the *Second Treatise* by defining the political problem as that of establishing a judge to settle disputes among men. He ends the *Second Treatise* by again raising the question, Who shall be judge? He ends with the possibility of revolution, with the breakdown of the peace. There is no absolute guarantee against the reintroduction of the state of war once civil society has been instituted. And in the end, each individual is judge of whether the government has violated its trust and placed itself in a state of war with the people. The right to make this judgment is an inalienable one. Ultimately, there is no common judge on earth between ruler and ruled. To acknowledge a right of revolution is to acknowledge that there is no permanent solution to the political problem. Political institutions are necessary because it is not sufficient for each man to be judge in his own case; the political solution is imperfect because each man must ultimately judge in his own case.

Locke's characterization of the government as common judge and of the people as final judge suggests that a more general inquiry into the relations of knowledge, judgment, law, and politics in Locke's thought is warranted. This inquiry is also suggested by the strong resemblance between the general conclusions from our consideration of the *Second Treatise* and the general conclusions from our consideration of Locke's *Essay*. In both cases Locke defends standards that can be demonstratively known at the same time that he emphasizes the necessity for judgment. In both cases Locke attempts to avoid both absolutism and relativism. His effort is to explain and allow for a wide variety of conventions in different communities while arguing that there are rational and natural principles of right that apply everywhere and always.

It is this double emphasis in his thought that provoked certain kinds of questions concerning both his epistemology and his politics. For example, his claim that mixed modes and relations are arbitrarily constructed ideas seemed to conflict with his claim that men can know the natural law with certainty. In his political treatises, his claim that many forms of government are legitimate seemed to conflict with statements that all legitimate government must rule by standing laws and that the rule of law requires separation of powers, representative assemblies, and so forth.

Considering Locke's epistemology, we came to the conclusion that politics is possible, necessary, and imperfect because reason is both sufficient to guide men's conduct and limited in significant ways. We cannot know all things with certainty, and the principles that we can know do not automatically govern our behavior. Principles must be applied in practice to particular cases, and there is always a need for judgment between competing principles. In governing our conduct there is an essential role for judgment, practical and moral. Considering Locke's political theory, we found that the political question is posed as the question, Who shall judge? in those circumstances that must be governed by judgment. And we found that this is the question that finally does not have a perfectly satisfactory answer.

When men make judgments in cases where their own interests are involved, they cannot be expected to be impartial. Interest, passion, and partisan loyalties all interfere with the reasonable resolution of a controversy. Yet Locke describes legitimate government as an impartial judge or umpire. Government, properly structured, can be disinterested, dispassionate, nonpartisan. It is the impartiality of such a government that allows Locke to characterize it both as rational and as free government. There is a connection between Locke's view of human reason and his particular vision of liberal politics. There is a connection between the meaning of reason and the meaning of freedom in Locke's work, whether the subject is free and rational government or the free and rational individual. Considering further Locke's characterization of government as an impartial judge should yield both a clearer picture of his political vision and a better understanding of the relation between his epistemology and his politics.

Government as Judge

Governments are established to provide an impartial common judge and so "avoid, and remedy those inconveniencies of the State of Nature, which necessarily follow from every Man's being Judge in his own Case" (2T.90). Where every man is his own judge, judgments are not likely to be reasonable because men will be partial to themselves and because there is no certain established way of applying rules to particular cases. To remedy the inconveniences that follow from this state, government must somehow be capable of greater rationality in resolving men's disputes than men themselves exercise on their own behalf. And this capability depends decisively on the disinterestedness and impartiality of the government. Impartiality is the key to the distinctive character of Locke's liberalism. Locke's political solution must be understood in the light of his analysis of the problem as the need to overcome impediments to rational judgment.

Our difficulties arise only because our behavior is not sufficiently guided by reason. The foundation of vice itself is wrong measures of good, incorrect ideas of what will produce the greatest good or evil for ourselves (Essay IV.20.16). Criminals are those who have "renounced Reason, the common Rule and Measure, God hath given to Mankind" (2T.11; see 2T.10, 16). Moreover, where there is no common established judge, men will not act reasonably in punishing the transgressions of others.

> Men being partial to themselves, Passion and Revenge is very apt to carry them too far, and with too much heat, in their own Cases; as well as negligence and unconcernedness, to make them too remiss in other Mens. (2T.125; see 2T.13)

Passion and self-love will produce the "inconveniencies" of the "irregular and uncertain" exercise of the power of punishment (2T.127). Only an impartial, unbiased man can determine rationally what actions deserve punishment—what the rules of reason are—and only an impartial, unbiased judge can mete out reasonable punishments and thus put an end to the state of war (2T.20). Ignorance, as well as interest, partiality, and passion, contributes to our difficulties, and all of these are understood as failures of reason.

> For though the Law of Nature be plain and intelligible to all rational Creatures; yet Men being biassed by their Interest, as well as ignorant for want of study of it, are not apt to allow of it as a Law binding to them in the application of it to their particular Cases. (2T.124)

A prince may be "led by Reason, Mistake or Passion" (2T.13), but mistake and passion both would be considered failures of his rational faculties, defects in the conduct of his understanding. In Locke's work there is almost no systematic discussion of the various passions; there is almost nothing that we would call a psychology.[1] Instead, the passions are discussed in general terms as one kind of hindrance to rational conduct.

Whereas the *Second Treatise* emphasizes interest, bias, and passion as sources of controversy, the argument of the *Essay* raises the possibility that uncertainty too can be a source of controversy among men. That argument indicates that even if all men were perfectly rational, the limits of reason are such that there would still be cause for controversy and need for an authoritative determination of questions that have no certain and demonstrable answers. For example, the difficulty of knowing with certainty in every case who is and is not a man leads to controversy over baptisms and infanticide.[2] Similarly, without conventional authoritative determinations of what counts as a contract, how to transfer title to property, the relative values of coins, and so on, the opportunities for controversies, even among men of good will, would expand enormously. These are matters that can only be determined arbitrarily, by convention, and they must have some determination if men are to have a functioning society.

The crucial political question of determining who has a right to rule is also affected by this sort of problem. In the *First Treatise*, Locke criticizes Filmer's claim that Adam's heir is the sole legitimate ruler by pointing out that we cannot know who that person is without divine designation, which we do not have. Filmer's principle is of no practical value and opens the way to endless political controversy because it leaves men in doubt as to the most important thing (1T.81, 106–7, 119–27; see 2T.113). Where there is no clear and certain objective determination of a question and the only way to settle it is by a commonly accepted convention, there had better be a legitimate means to settle the question in that way. Government is a remedy for the defects of reason in this respect as well.

But Locke makes it clear that the greatest source of unreasonable behavior is not this inevitable uncertainty but men's tendency to be partial to themselves. Yet he does not provide a systematic discussion of what is meant by partiality or by impartial judgment in a political context. To understand the importance of impartiality for rational judgment and therefore also for good government in Locke's view, we must turn to his *Conduct of the Understanding*, a

---

1. See Essay II.20 for Locke's brief discussion of the passions. It includes the remarkable statement that some men do not feel anger and envy.

2. See Essay III.9.13: "Or who shall be the judge to determine?" the right signification of a word for a substance. See also pp. 29–31 above.

piece originally intended to be a new chapter in the fourth edition of the *Essay*. Here Locke deals explicitly with all those things that interfere with rational judgment. The piece is a guide to the conduct of reason "in the search of knowledge and in the judgments it makes," and it is therefore also a guide to conduct itself.

> No man ever sets himself about any thing but upon some view or other which serves him for a reason for what he does: and whatsoever faculties he employs, the understanding, with such light as it has, well or ill informed, constantly leads; and by that light, true or false, all his operative powers are directed. (CU.1)

Anything that interferes with a clear understanding of the truth interferes with rational behavior, and partiality is the greatest interference with both.[3]

We are apt to be partial in our judgments through either passion, interest, or an unwarranted trust in the opinions of others. A single passion can establish a tyranny in the mind so that our thoughts are no longer free to consider a wide variety of things (CU.45), or we may simply ignore rational argument and evidence in areas where we have allowed our passions to dominate (CU.3; Essay IV.20.6, 12). Interest also can lead men to stop their inquiries at the point where they have reached an opinion suitable to their interest or lead them to adopt the opinions of a party that suits their interest without ever subjecting those opinions to a reasoned examination (Essay IV.20.15, 18). Custom, education, and the constant influence of their party also blinds whole societies and sects, even where men are sincere and are not influenced by their own interests (Essay II.33.18). Party loyalty is an example of placing an unwarranted trust in others' opinions. But whether we subject our minds to the opinions of party leaders, to those of our friends, neighbors, parents, or nurses, or to those of men of great reputation, the effect is the same; our reasoning is then based on false foundations.

> Such foundations are these and the like, namely: the founders or leaders of my party are good men, and therefore their tenets are true; it is the opinion of a sect that is erroneous, therefore it is false; it hath been long received in the world, therefore it is true; or it is

3. See also John Locke, MS. c.28 f.2, "Study," 25 March 1677. This manuscript touches many of the same themes as the *Conduct of the Understanding:* that the end of knowledge is to guide conduct; that our opinions should be formed independent of other men's opinions; that ignorance is preferable to false opinions.

new, and therefore false. (CU.6, 24; Essay IV.15.6, IV.20.8–10, 17–
18)

Rational conduct requires unprejudiced consideration of all the evidence and arguments involved in a question.

Partiality is an impediment to acquiring knowledge and judging
well, an obstacle to rational conduct, and a source of the controversies among men that lead to the necessity for government. And this
is true of the partiality associated with blind adherence to authoritative opinions as well as the partiality associated solely with
passion and interest. The *Second Treatise* emphasizes passion and
interest as the sources of the political problem. The political problem is portrayed as a problem of how to identify and punish criminal behavior in order to keep the peace, and how to establish an
authority with sufficient power to do this without becoming criminal itself in relation to the people.[4] But in the *Essay* and the *Conduct
of the Understanding*, Locke suggests that blind partisanship also has
a political bearing and can be a source of conflict in established
societies at least as dangerous as ordinary criminal behavior.

According to Locke, if men were to take nothing as true on authority—to accept nothing beyond the evidence as it appears to
them—and if they were to use their words with clear and consistent
significations, the prospects for peace in the world would increase
considerably. Men who accept orthodox opinions without examination substitute faith for reason and, in so doing, establish a tyranny
over their own minds (Essay IV.18.1; CU.12, 34).[5] These sorts of
men would tyrannize over the minds of others as well (Essay
IV.19.2). They are suspicious of those who do examine their opinions carefully and who remain indifferent until they have examined them, accusing these men of heresy or apostasy, especially in
matters of religion. Locke's response to this attitude is that a reasoned examination should be no threat to a good and true cause
and that God certainly does not require men to misuse their rational faculties in order to accept religious truths (CU.14, 35).

The proper use of our faculties serves "Knowledge, Truth, and
Peace," while their misuse makes a man a "Slave of Vain-glory,

---

4. The criminal is used repeatedly as an analogue to the absolute ruler. For
example see 2T.176, 202, 228.

5. Relying on faith in matters that can be settled by reason is a major source of
difficulties: "The Measures and *Boundaries between Faith and Reason:* the want where-
of, may possibly have been the cause, if not of great Disorders, yet at least of great
Disputes, and perhaps Mistakes in the World. For till it be resolved, how far we are
to be guided by Reason, and how far by Faith, we shall in vain dispute, and endeav-
our to convince one another in Matters of Religion" (Essay IV.18.1).

Ambition, or a Party" (Essay III.11.7, III.9.21, III.10.22). The abuse of words by learned men has

> invaded the great Concernments of Humane Life and Society; obscured and perplexed the material Truths of Law and Divinity; brought Confusion, Disorder, and Uncertainty into the Affairs of Mankind; and if not destroyed, yet in great measure rendred useless, those two great Rules, Religion and Justice. (Essay III.10.12)

> I leave it to be considered, whether it would not be well for Mankind . . . that the Use of Words were made plain and direct; and that Language, which was given us for the improvement of Knowledge, and bond of Society, should not be employ'd to darken Truth, and unsettle Peoples Rights; to raise Mists, and render unintelligible both Morality and Religion? (Essay III.10.13)

The cause of truth and the cause of peace are both furthered by the progress of reason in the world. Increased reasonableness will decrease controversy and party strife, and vice versa (see Essay IV.3.20). Locke condemns partisanship because those who act on the basis of party loyalty have abandoned the use of their rational capacities.

It is possible for an individual to train himself to be impartial in his judgments. Every question must be approached with indifference, without wishing that any particular opinion on the question should turn out to be true, and each of one's own opinions must be subjected to thorough examination. "In these two things . . . consists that freedom of the understanding which is necessary to a rational creature, and without which it is not truly an understanding" (CU.12; see CU.11; Essay IV.19.1). To truly understand is to see with your own eyes, and not to blindly adopt the opinions of others as your own, and it is to see with eyes that are clear of the "cataracts" of prejudice (CU.10, 24).

A man who can examine opinions, arguments, and evidence thoroughly and indifferently will give his assent to the position that is in fact most probable. We are not able to agree to a position that seems less probable to us than its alternative. So the only hindrances to our accepting the proposition that is truly most probable is our refusal to consider some of the possibilities and cutting off our inquiries through passion or interest (Essay IV.20.15–16; CU.33). Any predisposition to accept one position as true because it is the position of one's party or group is an enemy to the truth. And conversely, a full examination of a question necessarily leads us to reasonable and correct opinions.

Some men do overcome the effects of passion, interest, and

orthodoxy and become truly impartial and reasonable. But is there a political analogue for the personal effort to overcome the defects of reason? Is it possible to institute an impartial, indifferent, reasonable government? Certainly, absolute monarchy is no solution, for it institutionalizes the problems of partiality that arise where each man is judge in his own case.

> *Absolute Monarchs* are but Men, and if Government is to be the Remedy of those Evils, which necessarily follow from Mens being Judge in their own Cases, and the State of Nature is therefore not to be endured, I desire to know what kind of Government that is, and how much better it is than the State of Nature, where one Man commanding a multitude, has the Liberty to be Judge in his own Case. . . . Much better it is in the State of Nature wherein Men are not bound to submit to the unjust will of another: And if he that judges, judges amiss in his own, or any other Case, he is answerable for it to the rest of Mankind. (2T.13)

Absolute monarchy does not solve the problem of the state of nature, but only exacerbates it. Locke's view of the solution involves establishing nonpartisan government, and he justifies all the characteristic institutions of the liberal state on this basis. What does it mean, then, to say that legitimate government serves as an impartial judge?

As we have seen, when Locke speaks of the government as a judge, he is not referring exclusively, or even primarily, to the operation of the courts. A commonwealth is established by setting up a

> Judge on Earth, with Authority to determine all the Controversies, and redress the Injuries, that may happen to any Member of the Commonwealth; which Judge is the Legislative, or Magistrates appointed by it. (2T.89)

The first requirement is a common law to serve as "the Standard of Right and Wrong, and the common measure" by which particular judgments in particular cases can be made and then enforced (2T.124; see 2T.87). Legislative, executive, and judicial functions are all included in the conception of government as judge. And for the government to operate rationally, for its judgments to be impartial, all these functions must be exercised with indifference, without partisanship, and without the corrupting influence of personal interest or passion.

Any government that operates according to standing laws, rather than temporary, arbitrary decrees, has an impartial legislative in an important sense. Public judgments are made according to "settled standing Rules, indifferent, and the same to all Parties" (2T.87). These rules are

> not to be varied in particular Cases, but to have one Rule for Rich and Poor, for the Favourite at Court, and the Country Man at Plough. (2T.142)

Moreover, settled, standing rules make the boundaries of a man's freedom clear and limit the rulers to the punishment of the guilty. Standing rules or established, written laws eliminate uncertainty— uncertainty that men are likely to exploit for their own benefit.

> For the Law of Nature being unwritten, and so no where to be found but in the minds of Men, they who through Passion or Interest shall mis-cite, or misapply it, cannot so easily be convinced of their mistake where there is no establish'd Judge: And so it serves not, as it ought, to determine the Rights, and fence the Properties of those that live under it. . . . Men unite into Societies, that they may have . . . *standing Rules* to bound it, by which every one may know what is his. (2T.136; see 2T.124)

But standing laws also can be subverted to serve private interests. A great many of the positive laws of countries are nothing more than the "Phansies and intricate Contrivances of Men, following contrary and hidden interests put into Words" (2T.12). Locke suggests a variety of means to hinder rulers—princes or legislators—from pursuing their own interests at the expense of the public good. Laws are less likely to be designed to serve the hidden interests of governors where legislators serve in collective bodies whose members periodically return to their status as private citizens. Governors will be unable to exempt themselves from the laws where there is a separation of powers and a judicial appeal against executive officers. The right of the people to define the limits of the prerogative powers of the prince is also understood as a check against abuses that occur when rulers come to have "distinct and separate interests from their people" (2T.111). All of these institutional innovations are meant to secure disinterested government, to prevent the private interest of the rulers from taking the place of the public good (2T.91, 94, 107, 110–11, 143, 162, 205–6).

The theoretical conception that underlies these institutional arrangements is that rulers are public officers who exercise powers temporarily entrusted to them by the people. There is no property in office. Political power, unlike power over property, is not given for the benefit of the person holding that power. Political power is created as the result of a compact establishing a system of institutional relationships, a system of offices, and a means of authorizing certain persons to hold those offices and exercise their designated powers in accordance with the purposes of the trust. When the limits of the trust are violated, an officer of the government

> has no right to Obedience, nor can claim it otherwise than as the publick Person vested with the Power of the Law, and so is to be consider'd as the Image, Phantom, or Representative of the Commonwealth, acted by the will of the Society, declared in its Laws; and thus he has no Will, no Power, but that of the Law. But when he quits this Representation this publick Will, and acts by his own private Will, he degrades himself, and is but a single private Person without Power, and without Will, that has any Right to *Obedience*. (2T.151; see 2T.149–52, 202)

There is no private political authority, and there is no place for private interest in political judgment. Political authority is legal, impersonal, public authority.

Government composed of public officers operating according to standing laws is impartial, then, in several respects. All men are equally subject to the laws, including officers of the government. A formal system of institutional checks is established to prevent the sorts of abuses that arise from the personal interests or passions of government officers and to provide remedies for abuses when prevention fails. And there is a general understanding that political power is a trust from the people meant to be used for public, not private, purposes.

But are these remedies sufficient for abuses that are not so much the result of private interest or passion as the result of party prejudice? Locke emphasizes private motivation far more than party activity in the *Two Treatises*. He analyzes political rights and duties in the *Second Treatise* in terms of the relations between individuals, the people, and the government. He gives no recognition to parties or to any kind of subgroups within the society. Or to be precise, when parties are given any recognition, it is only negatively (2T.20, 158). In particular, Locke writes that the decisions of the government as an impartial judge are not to be based on the dogmas of any party, but are to be based on "mature debate." For the executive to attempt to corrupt legislators or electors to secure an assembly whose votes are predetermined is "as perfect a Declaration of a design to subvert the Government, as is possible to be met with" (2T.222). Such corruption of legislative judgment is cause for resistance.

Considering Locke's own political experience and his emphasis on the power of partisan passions and interests, it seems paradoxical that he might think it possible to establish nonpartisan government.[6] But for the same reasons, it is not surprising that he might wish to do so. His approach to the problem of blind party loyalties seems to be to try to exclude the influence of parties from government as far as possible rather than to incorporate party contests in the ordinary operations of government. The *Letter Concerning Toleration,* for example, as well as some of Locke's very early writings, attempts to clearly define the limits of civil authority and religious authority in order to isolate religious parties from the sphere of politics.[7]

Locke's hostility to party politics is an important component of his particular vision of government as an impartial judge. Rational judgment is impeded by party prejudice. Rational judgment requires a complete deliberation in determining what the law is to be and how it is to be applied to a particular case. Judgment is the process of balancing and weighing arguments and evidence against one another. And right judgment is possible only when all arguments and evidence are given consideration (Essay IV.14, IV.15.5; CU.7, 16). While it is true that the mere "Pretences, or Forms of the Law" will not ensure a just result (2T.20), it is also true that fair procedures are necessary for reasonable judgment. Locke quotes Seneca approvingly to the effect that "a man who decided a case after hearing only one side of it was in no way just, even if the decision was just" (CU.10). Impartial judgment requires a fair deliberative procedure where all sides get a hearing, and when such a procedure is honestly followed, the result is likely to be a reasonable decision. After complete consideration, a substantive judgment is reached that certainly may favor one party or position, but on a rational basis.

Locke measures government against the ideal of reasoned political deliberation. A good law is one that a disinterested observer would choose when presented with all the available facts and arguments. This means not that each individual legislator is expected to be disinterested, but that the legislative process is to be a process where arguments are presented and heard and issues decided by

6. The antiparty views of the American Founders have the same paradoxical quality. See Ruth Weissbourd Grant and Stephen Grant, "The Madisonian Presidency," in *The Presidency in the Constitutional Order,* ed. Joseph M. Bessette and Jeffrey Tulis (Baton Rouge: Louisiana State University Press, 1981), pp. 55–59; Richard Hofstadter, *The Idea of a Party System: The Rise of Legitimate Opposition in the United States, 1780–1840* (Berkeley: University of California Press, 1969).

7. See Abrams, ed., *Two Tracts.* See also Robert P. Kraynak, "John Locke: From Absolutism to Toleration," *American Political Science Review* 74 (March 1980): 53–69. Kraynak argues that the absolutism of Locke's early works and the toleration of the later works are alternative strategies for managing the problem of religious sectarian warfare.

men who have not committed themselves before hearing the debate. Even a compromise among competing interests at least ought to be discussed. Party commitments that predetermine legislative outcomes destroy the legislative process.

Moreover, Locke describes a process where a fair determination by the government is not necessarily understood as a compromise among all the parties or positions heard or one where the determination depends upon the direct representation and participation of each competing interest in the legislature. His view of the just result of legislative deliberation is not the compromise produced through legislative bargaining among interest groups, each represented roughly according to its strength in the society. Equality for Locke means equality under the law, and not necessarily equal representation in the lawmaking process. And a just decision is one that serves the public good, which is not always identical to a decision that gives some benefit to each member of a coalition of partial interests. Locke's political analysis does not presuppose a variety of competing groups within society. He does not rely on heterogeneity for protection against abuses of power.[8] Instead, he argues for legal and institutional restraints on government, for a right of resistance, and for a correct understanding of the extent of political power. In sum, Locke's liberalism is antiparty, antiauthoritarian, and constitutionalist, and not at all identical to a pluralist democratic liberalism.[9]

It is also far from a laissez-faire conception of the role of the state in liberal government. To conceive of government as an impartial judge or a common umpire is not necessarily to conceive of it as a mere arbitrator of whatever controversies happen to arise, taking a passive role. Government does more than settle civil suits and punish criminals. It also does more than supply a peaceful environment for competition among parties and private interest groups. Parties and interest groups are absent from Locke's political analysis, and the role of the state is not defined by its relation to such groups. Instead, the state serves positive public purposes by establishing authoritative conventions and formal procedures that are necessary for the conduct of daily common life, by protecting private rights, and also by making legislative judgments as to what actions will best promote the interests of the public. In doing so, legitimate government acts rationally in that it serves as an appro-

8. Similarly, Locke's argument in the *Letter Concerning Toleration* does not rely on religious heterogeneity as the security for religious freedom. Compare Hamilton, Jay, and Madison, no. 51, p. 324.

9. See Miller, p. 170.

priate means to an end in accord with the law of reason—the preservation, and certainly the comfortable preservation, of the society as a whole.[10]

Locke's solution to the problem of establishing a common judge on earth, an impartial umpire, is a particular vision of liberal government in accordance with a particular conception of rationality. Legitimate government involves a formal system of laws and institutions meant to ensure fairness, to provide checks against the influence of the personal interest of those in power, and to protect the possibility of nonpartisan deliberation that will produce decisions serving the good of the public. All legitimate government action is understood as an expression of the public will. And this public judge is capable of a reasonable determination of controversies that is not possible where each man is judge in his own case. It is capable of rational action to the extent that passion, interest, and prejudice are prevented from interfering with a complete consideration of each question and with enforcement of the final determination. To be sure, Locke recognizes the frailty of this system of institutions. He reminds his readers to be always watchful for encroachments motivated by the ambitions and interests of those holding power and for the disruptive influence of factions and parties. The people must have recourse to resistance when the system fails to prevent abuses, when legitimate government becomes illegitimate despotism, when reason gives way to tyrannical impulses.

Government as an impartial judge, as Locke understands it, is government according to reason, and it is liberal government. We should not be surprised to find that the institutions that allow Locke to characterize legitimate government as rational government are the same institutions that allow us to characterize it as liberal government. Locke's understanding of human reason is inseparable from his view of the possibilities and limits of liberal politics, and his understanding of human freedom is inseparable from his view of the possibilities and limits of reason. Failures of reasonableness and the necessary uncertainties that result from our limited capacities cause controversies. Yet reasonable government is possible largely through a system of standing laws and institutional checks that also preserve our freedom from the arbitrary will of

10. See John Locke, "Some Considerations of the Consequences of Lowering the Interest and Raising the Value of Money" and "Further Considerations Concerning Raising the Value of Money," in *Works*, vol. 5, for Locke's views on government economic policy. See also Locke, *Letter Concerning Toleration*, for discussion of the extent of civil authority.

powerful men. The relations among freedom, reason, and will are central to Locke's thought. We turn now to a consideration of Locke's understanding of those relations as they shape his views both of free government and of the free individual.

Reason, Freedom, Will

Locke's description of the free and rational man and his description of free and rational government are based on the same understanding of the relationships among freedom, reason, and will. There is a consistent view of the meaning of freedom and of reason that runs through all of his major work. To be ruled by reason, rather than by arbitrary will, is the very definition of freedom, personal and political. Locke defends liberal government as legitimate government on the grounds that liberal government institutionalizes the proper relations between reason and will and so preserves man's natural freedom.

Freedom, in its general sense, is a power to think or act according to your preference (Essay II.21.7–27). It is freedom from any necessity that imposes a restraint on your actions. This use of the term "freedom" can be appropriately applied to men and animals alike and permits no distinction between liberty and license. But human freedom, the freedom of an intellectual being, is the power to guide your preference according to reason as well as to pursue the course dictated by your preference (Essay II.21.47–53). Men have power to suspend the determination of the will until they have given full consideration to the consequences for their happiness of each proposed course of action. The end and use of our freedom is to attain the happiness we seek. For this reason, to subject the will to the dictates of reason in this way is the fulfillment of our freedom, not a limitation of it (Essay II.21.48–50).[11]

Because human freedom is defined in terms of the capacity to reason, the distinction between liberty and license is clear and significant.[12]

> If to break loose from the conduct of Reason, and to want that restraint of Examination and Judgment, which keeps us from chusing or doing the worse, be *Liberty*, true Liberty, mad Men and Fools are the only Freemen. (Essay II.21.50)

> The *Freedom* then of Man and Liberty of acting according to his own will, is *grounded on* his having *Reason*, which is able to instruct him in

11. See pp. 44–47.
12. See pp. 92–93.

that Law he is to govern himself by, and make him know how far he is left to the freedom of his own will. To turn him loose to an unrestrain'd Liberty, before he has Reason to guide him, is not the allowing him the priviledge of his Nature, to be free; but to thrust him out amongst Brutes, and abandon him to a state as wretched, and as much beneath that of a Man, as theirs. (2T.63; see 2T.22, 57)

The capacity to reason distinguishes men as free creatures from the beasts.

When a man fails to exercise his freedom to suspend his will and to act only after rational deliberation and instead acts in response to unrestrained desires, Locke says that he has descended to the level of the beasts and may be treated as a beast.[13] But unlike a beast, the man can be held responsible for what he has done. He can be considered guilty because he has a duty to use his rational faculties to guide his actions (Essay II.21.47, 52, 56). The possibility of free and rational action is the grounds for the duty to act reasonably.

It is also the grounds for the right to govern your own conduct. Nobody can rightfully subject another human being who is capable of governing his own actions according to his own reason. Men are free, then, in the additional sense that they have a right to govern themselves as their reason dictates. Because they are rational beings, they have a "Title to perfect Freedom"; it is the "great priviledge of finite intellectual Beings," the "priviledge of his Nature, to be free" (2T.87; see 2T.63; Essay II.21.52).

Freedom is identified with subjection to reason, and reason is identified with law. The rule of reason is the law of nature, and the free man is governed both by the law of nature and by positive laws that implement that higher law. Through this identification of freedom with reason and reason with law, the two notions of freedom—as the power to act as you will without restraint and as the power to guide the will itself—appear to be complementary notions.

For *Law*, in its true Notion, is not so much the Limitation as *the direction of a free and intelligent Agent* to his proper Interest, and prescribes no farther than is for the general Good of those under that Law. . . . So that, however it may be mistaken, *the end of Law* is not to abolish or restrain, but *to preserve and enlarge Freedom;* For in all the states of created beings capable of Laws, *where there is no Law, there is no Free-*

13. But see 1T.56–58. Man is capable of sinking to a level below that of the beasts when he "quits his reason" (1T.58). Men, not beasts, are capable of "unnatural" acts (1T.56).

> *dom.* For *Liberty* is to be free from restraint and violence from others which cannot be, where there is no Law: But Freedom is not, as we are told, *A Liberty for every Man to do what he lists:* (For who could be free, when every other Man's Humour might domineer over him?) But a *Liberty* to dispose, and order, as he lists, his Person, Actions, Possessions, and his whole Property, within the Allowance of those Laws under which he is; and therein not to be subject to the arbitrary Will of another, but freely follow his own. (2T.57)

Freedom is subjection to the law, and subjection to the law is contrasted with subjection to the arbitrary will of another man. A free man must be governed neither by another man's will nor by his own unguided will. A free man is restrained, but only by the rules of reason.

And to be truly free, he must be guided by his own reason. It is not enough to do the reasonable thing. A man must have reached the conclusion on his own that it is the reasonable thing to do.

> And therefore every Man is put under a necessity by his constitution, as an intelligent Being, to be determined in willing by his own Thought and Judgment, what is best for him to do: else he would be under the determination of some other than himself, which is want of Liberty. (Essay II.21.48)

To govern yourself according to the opinions of others accepted on faith or authority without examining the evidence is to subject yourself to intellectual tyranny (Essay IV.18.1; CU.12, 34). The free man is master of his own thoughts and is independent of party prejudices, religious authorities, or the dominant customs of his society. To truly understand something, a man must make it his own (CU.24; see CU.11–12, 20). Locke prefers a man who is wholly ignorant to one who accepts opinions without examination (CU.13, 34–35).[14] To accept opinions without examination, even if they are correct opinions, is a perversion of the rational faculties and is consequently a perversion of freedom.

Locke acknowledges that no man can fully consider the evidence and arguments concerning every one of his many opinions (Essay IV.16.4). Most men, in fact, have very little leisure for the pursuit of knowledge and inquiry, though all have sufficient time to give some thought to the condition of their souls (Essay IV.20.3). But those who are in the worst position by far are those who are constrained by the positive laws of their country to accept a given religion and restrict their own inquiries (Essay IV.20.4).

14. Compare Hobbes, p. 106, and Plato, *Republic,* trans. Allan Bloom (New York: Basic Books, 1969), 478d.

Locke's emphasis on independence of mind is further evidence of his seriousness about the status of freedom as something more than merely instrumental to preservation. For example, there is a parallel between the thought that it is not enough to be right—that the opinion must be your own—and the thought that it is not enough for government to govern well—that it must be grounded in consent. Freedom means to govern yourself according to reason. But this means not only that you are guided to act in a manner consistent with the rational end of preservation and happiness, but also that you are guided by your own reason and not by authority, or force, or arbitrary will in any form.

The freedom of the individual understood in this way has a natural basis, both in the capacity to reason and in the desire for freedom, a desire for self-mastery present in every human being. Men want to act independently and to be masters of their situation. A generalized desire for mastery over people and things could be seen as the root of all injustice. But when it is limited to a desire for self-mastery and controlled by the rational faculty, it becomes indistinguishable from a desire for freedom.[15] This desire can find its satisfaction in a political state where no man is the master of another, but where each is equally subject to general laws, and by his own choice.

Locke's treatment of consent illustrates his general understanding of reason, freedom, and will as they operate in a single individual and in political relationships. Only a free man has the capacity to give his consent to form an agreement. To make a promise, a man must be a free agent; one who can be held responsible for his actions, who can determine what he wills, and who has the power to do as he wills so that he can perform whatever actions are required of him to fulfill his obligation. Freedom is a precondition for the creation of binding obligations. But there are also limits on the sorts of obligations that a free man can create for himself. No man has the right to consent to enslave himself to a tyrant, for example. Moreover, submission to tyranny can never be a rational means to the rational end of preservation. Freedom is limited by the requirement that a man's will be determined by his reason. And in fact this is not a limitation, but a fulfillment of human freedom. The freedom of a rational being is to be guided by reason. And so, to bind your will and create a nonretractable obligation for yourself

15. See Locke, "Some Thoughts Concerning Education," pars. 35–38, 41, 73, 76, 81, 107; Nathan Tarcov, *Locke's Education for Liberty* (Chicago: University of Chicago Press, 1984), pp. 7–8, 89–90.

to legitimate government does not conflict with natural freedom, but is instead an exercise of it.

The liberal state—legitimate government as Locke describes it—is the political state that embodies the proper natural relations among freedom, reason, and will. The authority of the government is grounded in the freely given consent of each individual member and not in forced subjection to the will of powerful men. And while consent cannot simply be assumed because the government in question is good government, all obligation to government ceases when it ceases to govern according to reasonable rules. In submitting to legitimate authority, each individual determines his will according to his own reason and continues to guide his actions according to a will guided by reason in the form of positive laws and according to his own reason in areas left untouched by the laws.

Under legitimate government, subjection to will gives way to subjection to the law, and in this legitimate government conforms to the moral conditions of the natural state.

> The *Natural Liberty of Man* is to be free from any Superior Power on Earth, and not to be under the Will or Legislative Authority of Man, but to have only the Law of Nature for his Rule. The *Liberty of Man, in Society*, is to be under no other Legislative Power, but that established, by consent, in the Common-wealth, nor under the Dominion of any Will, or Restraint of any Law, but what the Legislative shall enact, according to the Trust put in it. . . . *Freedom of Men under Government, is,* to have a standing Rule to live by, common to every one of that Society, and made by the Legislative Power erected in it; A Liberty to follow my own Will in all things, where the Rule prescribes not; and not to be subject to the inconstant, uncertain, unknown, Arbitrary Will of another Man. As *Freedom of Nature* is to be under no other restraint but the Law of Nature. (2T.22)

Legitimate government is grounded in consent and ruled in such a way that there is no governing private will. Each man remains equal to his fellows in their equal status under the law. And because legitimate government is an instrument of peace and security, it also serves the natural, rational end of preservation. Free government is in accord with man's natural condition.

Locke's liberalism, and particularly the premise of his political argument, that men are naturally free, depends on his view of men as uniquely capable of governing their actions according to the dictates of reason. Moreover, free government is like a free individual writ large; all arbitrary will is voluntarily subordinated to rational rules of conduct. In short, Locke's model for legitimate government is not the patriarchal family, but the free and rational individual. His view of legitimate government is of free government understood as government where reason rules in the form of general laws, while his view of illegitimate government is of tyranny understood as the rule of unrestrained private will. A man who uses his natural faculties as he should voluntarily submits his will to the dictates of reason. Legitimate government is government where men have voluntarily submitted themselves to be governed by reasonable rules. Legitimate government is government that embodies our best natural possibility.

Conclusion: Locke and Liberal Theory

The general presupposition of Locke's political theory is that demonstrative normative theory is possible. Locke's *Second Treatise* deduces a theory of rights and duties from a clearly stated premise, and the argument proceeds logically to conclusions that are meant to be as certain as conclusions of a mathematical proof. The particular presupposition of Locke's political theory is the premise that men are by nature free. On the basis of this premise, Locke seeks to establish standards that distinguish legitimate political power from illegitimate despotism.[1] The general framework for his argument is set by the question of legitimacy. The primary task of any political theory is to identify the criteria by which legitimate and illegitimate power may be distinguished. The argument is further shaped by the need to show that these normative criteria are applicable in practice, and especially that the criteria elaborated by liberal theorists on the basis of the premise of natural freedom can be defended against the charges made by those who criticize such theories as impracticable. Locke proceeds to show that, on the basis of liberal principles, legitimate governments can be stable and continuous over time in many different communities, each with its own territorial jurisdiction. Moreover, one can clearly know who ought to be obeyed and to what extent. Locke responds to the critics by showing that liberal theory can provide a justification for the duty to obey legitimate authorities while allowing for a right to resist illegitimate power.

---

1. "For example, if it be demanded, whether the grand seignoir can lawfully take what he will from any of his people? This question cannot be resolved without coming to a certainty, whether all men are naturally equal; for upon that it turns, and that truth, well settled in the understanding and carried in the mind through the various debates concerning the various rights of men in society, will go a great way in putting an end to them and shewing on which side the truth is" (CU.44).

It is in Locke's *Essay* that his argument for the possibility of his theoretical enterprise can be found. There he attempts to establish that the truths of morality, personal and political, are available to unaided human reason. Beginning with self-evident propositions, men can link these propositions into demonstrations that will lead to sound conclusions about the moral basis and moral limits of political relations. The certainty of this sort of reasoning follows from the fact that the ideas that are its elements are mixed modes, ideas that men create as models by which to order and understand experience rather than ideas meant to serve as copies of things in our experience. Abstract reasoning affords access to truths of which we can be certain, particularly in the area of ethics. In political theory, such reasoning can provide us with knowledge of the rights and duties of men in society.

Moreover, sound theoretical knowledge of political right, of political legitimacy, has important practical consequences. If the distinction between legitimate authority and power simply is not established theoretically, political authority is undermined, tyrants and usurpers are encouraged, and civil peace is threatened. This is the central failure of theorists of absolute monarchy. By teaching subjects that they have an absolute duty of obedience to whoever is in power, they justify the rule of the strongest and support challengers to established rulers who think they might succeed in establishing a new order. They fail to understand that a duty to obey rightful authority is inseparable from a right to resist the wrongful use of force, and that both are necessary to secure the peace. Political theory, by defining the distinction between legitimate and illegitimate power, supports both a duty of obedience and a right of resistance. In doing so, successful political theory serves the cause of peace as well as the cause of truth.

Political theory, then, can discover the standards by which governments are to be judged, and it should direct itself to that task above all. But the abstract theoretical argument will be successful only if it can be demonstrated that the standards are applicable to political reality. One must know what the standards are, and also how to recognize when they have been met. For example, whether the right to rule is based on divine gift, consent, or heredity, the legitimate claimant of that divine grant, consent, or hereditary position must be clearly identifiable. The right to rule must also be a right that can be legitimately exercised simultaneously by different men in different political communities but cannot be legitimately claimed simultaneously by many men within the same political community. Moreover, it must be possible to distinguish in practice not only between legitimate government and tyranny, but also between legitimate resistance and anarchy. With these requirements met, a political theorist could claim to have contributed to just and peaceful political life.

Locke's is a liberal political theory. He attempts to meet these requirements for political theory with an argument that begins with the premise that men are by nature equal. The premise of natural equality is identical to the premise of natural freedom. Both can be negatively stated in the same way: there is no natural political authority. Locke's argument proceeds from its premise with the additional understanding that there can be no political authority without a reason for it. Power can be rightfully exercised only as a means to legitimate ends. These ends also are to be inferred from man's natural condition. Men have an equal natural right of preservation, and political authority must consequently be directed toward the preservation of the members of the political community.

These two principles, freedom and preservation, drawn from the natural law, are the touchstones for distinguishing legitimate and illegitimate exercises of power in all social relationships, including political relationships. Any government that sacrifices the safety and prosperity of its citizens for the benefit of its rulers is a tyranny. Any government that operates without the consent of the people is equally illegitimate, a usurpation. The requirement of consent follows directly from the principle of freedom, since with no natural basis for authority, authority can arise only from agreement among equals. In no case can a government be considered legitimate unless it fulfills both requirements. It must be based on consent and serve the public good.

Although Locke recommends a certain sort of government with separated powers and an elected representative assembly, a wide variety of institutional arrangements could meet these requirements for legitimate government. Locke seeks to identify not the best political order, but the basic minimal conditions that every political society must satisfy if it is to have legitimate rule. And there can be legitimate rule in democracies, aristocracies, hereditary monarchies, and tribal kingdoms. But in any form of legitimate government it must be understood that political power is a trust from the community as a whole and that all members of the community, including those in authority, are subject to its laws.

These two ideas taken together are the essential components of the constitutionalist conception that Locke adopts to replace more traditional conceptions of sovereignty. Once it is understood that the law is supreme over any private will and that the people are supreme in the sense that they determine when their trust has been violated, the central issue for political theory no longer is to identify whose will is sovereign.

This dual supremacy is related to Locke's distinction between society and government, and that distinction is the basis for his solution to the practical problem posed by liberal theory. To say that the people are supreme as final judge of the fulfillment of their trust is to say that political authority reverts to the society as a whole when the government is dissolved by a violation of its trust. The supremacy of the law follows from the notion that all members of the society without exception, by consenting to membership in it, obligate themselves to the government of that society so long as the government operates according to its trust.

The distinction between political society and the government created by it permits Locke to argue that a theory based on natural equality can nonetheless justify true political obligation. It is also the basis for his solution to the practical problem of justifying a right of resistance without at the same time justifying anarchy. Because men are by nature equals, political societies can be formed only by unanimous consent of their members. But neither the decision to form a particular sort of government nor the actual legislative decisions of the community need be unanimous. The agreement of each member to join the society entails an agreement to abide by the decisions of the government. Such obligation is necessary to maintain the society, and it can be assumed that no rational man would seek to establish a political unit without the conditions necessary for its continuation. An individual's natural right is exercised not by participation in government, but by the decision to become a member of society. Consent can provide a practical means of determining who is to rule and of establishing lasting obligation to the authorized government without any abridgment of natural freedom. But when the government is dissolved, either through actions harmful to the public good for which there is no legal redress or through alterations of the authorized form of government itself, then all obligation to the government ceases. Yet each individual member remains obligated to the society, if the society remains and can act as a functioning unit to halt the subversion of the government or to establish a new one. A situation of anarchy arises only in the case where government and society have both dissolved and all return to a state of nature. A right of resistance can be exercised by the people in circumstances of clear abuse and before the authorities have been completely transformed without immediately introducing a condition of anarchy.

In making this case, Locke offers his solution to the theoretical problem confronting theorists of his time. One alternative had been to defend a right in Parliament to act on behalf of the people in resisting abuses of the king. But this alternative was incompatible with a defense of mixed and balanced government where king and Parliament were independent and coequal. It tended to undermine the ordinary authority of the king. It also left unanswered the question of a right to resist parliamentary abuses. The second alternative was to locate the right of resistance with the people, keeping the balance within government intact but running the risk of justifying frequent rebellions or anarchy without the possibility of distinguishing between justified resistance to oppression and simple criminal disobedience.

Locke tries to show that mixed and balanced government is compatible with a popular right of resistance. The law rules while the government stands, and society can act to prevent its own dissolution once the government has dissolved. Neither legislative nor executive is given sovereign authority within the government, and the obligation to obedience is not undermined by the right to resist. The right of resistance is exercised by the people acting as a political unit, and it is a carefully limited right. Resistance is justified only when the basic minimal standards for legitimacy are being threatened. Revolution is described not as a step toward realizing an ideal of justice, but as resistance to political degeneration.

But Locke is not entirely successful in his resolution of this problem. The theoretical framework for its solution is in place in the form of a distinction between the dissolution of society and the dissolution of government, but Locke does not resolve all the difficulties presented by the practical application of his principles. Ultimately, each individual must judge for himself whether conditions are such that the government or the society has dissolved, and his obligations with them. This is the radical political individualism characteristic of liberal thought. Each individual is the final judge of his community and its government. And there can be no assurance that these judgments will be made correctly.

But there can be both clearly articulated standards of right and aids to correct judgment as to their applicability in the circumstances. For example, when a conquered people participates in the legislative assembly of a new government, this can be taken as an indication that they consent to the government. When rulers oper-

ate in violation of established legal procedures, this can be taken as
an indication that they may be overstepping their bounds. Established conventions and institutionalized procedures serve as indicators of legitimate and illegitimate action. They also serve as barriers
against the degeneration of a political situation to the point where
each individual is left to his own judgment. Resistance is not justified so long as there are legal channels for resolving a dispute. The
characteristically liberal emphasis on the legal order is a response
to the problems posed by liberal individualism. Or in Locke's
terms, an authorized common judge is the solution to the problems
posed by the condition where each is his own judge—the condition
of natural freedom.

It is a solution in the sense that it is a means of managing the
problem, but it cannot do away with the problem once and for all.
Locke cannot guarantee that there will never be unjust resistance,
just as he cannot assure that there will never be tyrants who manage to secure the allegiance of their subjects. But these are fatal
shortcomings only if political theory is expected to provide perfect
solutions or guarantees.

It is important to maintain a clear understanding of what political theory and political practice can and cannot do. Locke keeps the
reader constantly aware of the gravity of the political problem and
of the fragility of human solutions to it. The political problem
arises because there is no natural political order. All men are free
and equal, and some men are always willing to use force to impose
their will on others. There is no natural common authority to ensure that force is always coupled with right. The establishment of
such an authority according to principles of right that can be clearly demonstrated goes a long way toward solving the problem. But
men strong enough to impose their will in violation of the rights of
others always will be tempted to do so, and there will not always be
a common authority able to peacefully settle the dispute. We cannot finally overcome our problematic situation.

So Locke does not provide techniques for ensuring that correct
political judgments will always be made and enforced; that would
be beyond the scope of any political theory. Theory cannot simply
secure peace and justice. What it can do—its most important task—
is to let men know what political evil is. Or to put it positively,
political theory defines political justice, and this is itself the most
important prerequisite for keeping the peace.

Locke's attitude toward the political problem is the same as his
attitude toward the problem of human understanding. Men cannot
know everything, but they can know enough to govern their con-

duct rationally. Action need not be arbitrary; it can be guided by rational principles of conduct. But the application of those principles to practice will always involve an element of judgment and uncertainty. And some men will simply fail to submit themselves to the guidance of their rational faculties. Government is necessary because of these limits of reason. But government according to reason is possible. The premise of Locke's political argument, that men are naturally free, depends on his view of men as uniquely capable of governing their actions according to reason. His view of legitimate government is of free government understood as government where reason rules according to general laws. Liberal government, with the particular role of the law within it, is an attempt to provide the conditions for impartial, rational, and therefore free government. But Locke, always aware of the limits of human capacities, does not claim to provide a perfect solution. His liberal politics are supported by his estimation, positive and negative, of the extent of human understanding.

Locke's is a cautious liberalism. Unlike some more modern versions, it has not been coupled with a faith in the inevitable progress of human communities. There is instead a constant anxiety about the possibility of political degeneration. Consequently Locke's political theory contains two tendencies that are not entirely harmonious. On the one hand, there is what could be called Locke's conservative side. Locke recognizes that political order is precarious and that change might be for the worse. This is ground for caution concerning change in forms of government and tolerance of less than perfect justice if abuses have not grown general and severe. On the other hand, Locke appears as a radical, urging citizens to be ever watchful for abuses and ready to act before it is too late. Moreover, he chooses justice over the kind of peace that can be found under tyrannies, defining tyranny as a state of war.

This ambivalent attitude is an expression of the central axis of conflict within liberal theory generally. Every liberal theory must find some more or less uneasy reconciliation of the claims of order and revolution, society and the individual. Any theory whose premise is the equal individual rights of each, or natural freedom, must confront the difficulty of justifying stable and effective political authority without violating that premise. Although Locke argues that justification of political authority is the central task of political theory generally, it is clearly a task confronting liberal theory. If the starting point is natural freedom, the question is bound to be the grounds and extent of political obligation—of legitimate authority.

That Locke defines the political question as the question of legitimacy is also one indication of his generally moderate attitude. In both his epistemological and his political investigations, he seems to think it is dangerous both to expect too much and to aim for too little. Utopian expectations and a political theory that concentrates on perfect justice make every real political order appear unjust. This is not a perspective that can provide useful guidance for men who need to know whom to obey and to what extent. Moreover, when expectations are unrealistically high, inevitable disappointment produces nihilistic reactions. And if you simply expect the worst from men, the worst is what you will get. A political theory that finds it necessary to justify the absolute right to the use of force in the hands of one man will provoke in the end "perpetual Disorder and Mischief, Tumult, Sedition and Rebellion" (2T.1).

Locke's attitude, in contrast, gives men their due while recognizing their limitations. A just estimation of men's capacities must be the foundation for any theoretical effort that hopes to offer men practical guidance in managing the political problem and in avoiding the worst that can befall them. Locke demonstrates the necessity for limited horizons, but he also offers the possibility of limited success.

> When we know our own *Strength*, we shall the better know what to undertake with hopes of Success. . . . 'Tis of great use to the Sailor to know the length of his Line, though he cannot with it fathom all the depths of the Ocean. 'Tis well he knows, that it is long enough to reach the bottom, at such Places, as are necessary to direct his Voyage, and caution him against running upon Shoals, that may ruin him. (Essay I.1.6)

Bibliography

Aaron, Richard I. *John Locke.* 3d ed. Oxford: Oxford University Press, 1971.

Aaron, Richard I., and Jocelyn Gibb, eds. *An Early Draft of Locke's Essay: Together with Excerpts from His Journals.* Oxford: Clarendon Press, 1936.

Aarsleff, Hans. "Some Observations on Recent Locke Scholarship." In *John Locke: Problems and Perspectives*, ed. John W. Yolton. Cambridge: Cambridge University Press, 1969.

Albritton, Robert R. "The Politics of Locke's Philosophy." *Political Studies* 24 (September 1976): 253–67.

Aschcraft, Richard. "Faith and Knowledge in Locke's Philosophy." In *John Locke: Problems and Perspectives*, ed. John W. Yolton. Cambridge: Cambridge University Press, 1969.

———. "Locke's State of Nature: Historical Fact or Moral Fiction?" *American Political Science Review* 62 (1968): 898–915.

———. *Revolutionary Politics and Locke's "Two Treatises of Government."* Princeton: Princeton University Press, 1986.

———. "Revolutionary Politics and Locke's *Two Treatises of Government:* Radicalism and Lockean Political Theory." *Political Theory* 8 (1980): 429–86.

Brogan, A. P. "John Locke and Utilitarianism." *Ethics* 69 (January 1959): 79–93.

Cook, Thomas I., ed. *John Locke, "Two Treatises of Government" and Robert Filmer, "Patriarcha."* New York: Hafner, 1947; 5th printing, 1964.

Cox, Richard H. *Locke on War and Peace.* Oxford: Clarendon Press, 1960.

Cranston, Maurice. *John Locke: A Biography.* London: Longmans, Green, 1957.

Daly, James. *Sir Robert Filmer and English Political Thought.* Toronto: University of Toronto Press, 1979.

Danford, John W. *Wittgenstein and Political Philosophy: A Reexamination of the Foundations of Social Science.* Chicago: University of Chicago Press, 1978.

Dunn, John. "Consent in the Political Theory of John Locke." *Historical Journal* 10 (1967): 153–82.

————. *The Political Thought of John Locke*. Cambridge: Cambridge University Press, 1969.

Filmer, Sir Robert. *"Patriarcha; or, The Natural Powers of the Kings of England Asserted" and Other Political Works of Sir Robert Filmer*. Edited by Peter Laslett. Oxford: Basil Blackwell, 1949.

"The First Set of the Fundamental Constitutions of South Carolina: As Compiled by John Locke." In *Historical Collections of South Carolina*, 2 vols., ed. B. R. Carroll. New York: Harper, 1836.

Franklin, Julian H. *John Locke and the Theory of Sovereignty: Mixed Monarchy and the Right of Resistance in the Political Thought of the English Revolution*. Cambridge: Cambridge University Press, 1978.

Gauthier, David P. "The Role of Inheritance in Locke's Political Theory." *Canadian Journal of Economics and Political Science* 32 (1966): 38–45.

Gibson, James. "John Locke's Theory of Mathematical Knowledge and of a Possible Science of Ethics." *Mind* 5 (1896): 38–59.

————. *Locke's Theory of Knowledge and Its Historical Relations*. Cambridge: Cambridge University Press, 1917; reprint ed., 1968.

Glenn, Gary D. "Inalienable Rights and Locke's Argument for Limited Government: Political Implications of a Right to Suicide." *Journal of Politics* 46 (February 1984): 80–105.

Gough, J. W. *John Locke's Political Philosophy: Eight Studies*. Oxford: Clarendon Press, 1950.

Grant, Ruth Weissbourd, and Stephen Grant. "The Madisonian Presidency." In *The Presidency in the Constitutional Order*, ed. Joseph M. Bessette and Jeffrey Tulis. Baton Rouge: Louisiana State University Press, 1981.

Hamilton, Alexander, John Jay, and James Madison. *The Federalist Papers*. Edited by Clinton Rossiter. New York: New American Library, 1961.

Hartz, Louis. *The Liberal Tradition in America*. New York: Harcourt, Brace and World, 1955.

Hobbes, Thomas. *Leviathan*. Edited with an introduction by C. B. Macpherson. Harmondsworth, England: Penguin, 1968.

Hofstadter, Richard. *The Idea of a Party System: The Rise of Legitimate Opposition in the United States, 1780–1840*. Berkeley: University of California Press, 1969.

Hume, David. "Of the Original Contract." In *Essays: Moral, Political and Literary*. Oxford: Oxford University Press, 1963.

"Instructions from the Board of Trade to Governor Nicholson," 13 September 1698. Virginia Colonial Records Project, Virginia State Library, Richmond. Microfilm. Classification number COS/1359/266–303.

Kemp, J. *Reason, Action and Morality*. New York: Humanities Press, 1964.

Kendall, Willmoore. *John Locke and the Doctrine of Majority Rule*. Urbana: University of Illinois Press, 1941.

————. "John Locke Revisited." *Intercollegiate Review* 2 (January–February 1966): 217–34.

King, Lord Peter. *The Life of John Locke with Extracts from His Correspondence, Journals and Common-Place Books*. 2 vols. London: Henry Colburn and Richard Bentley, 1830.

Kraynak, Robert P. "John Locke: From Absolutism to Toleration." *American Political Science Review* 74 (March 1980): 53–69.

Locke, John. "An Magistratus Civilis possit res adiaphoras in divini cultus ritus asciscere easque populo impovere? Affirmatur." In *John Locke: Two Tracts on Government*, ed. Philip Abrams. Cambridge: Cambridge University Press, 1967.

———. *Conduct of the Understanding.* 2d ed. Edited by Thomas Fowler. New York: Lenox Hill/Burt Franklin, 1971.

———. *An Essay Concerning Human Understanding.* Edited by Peter H. Nidditch. Oxford: Clarendon Press, 1975; reprinted with corrections, 1979.

———. *Essays on the Law of Nature.* Edited by W. von Leyden. Oxford: Clarendon Press, 1954.

———. *A Letter Concerning Toleration.* 2d ed. Introduction by Patrick Romanell. Indianapolis: Bobbs-Merrill, 1955.

———. *On the Reasonableness of Christianity as Delivered in the Scriptures.* Edited by George W. Ewing. Chicago: Henry Regnery, Gateway Editions, 1965.

———. "Question: Whether the Civil Magistrate may lawfully impose and determine the use of indifferent things in reference to Religious Worship." In *John Locke: Two Tracts on Government*, ed. Philip Abrams. Cambridge: Cambridge University Press, 1967.

———. "Some Thoughts Concerning Education." In *Educational Writings of John Locke*, edited with an introduction by James L. Axtell. Cambridge: Cambridge University Press, 1968.

———. "Some Thoughts Concerning Reading and Study for a Gentleman." In *Educational Writings of John Locke*, edited with an introduction by James L. Axtell. Cambridge: Cambridge University Press, 1968.

———. *Two Treatises of Government.* Edited by Peter Laslett. New York: New American Library, 1960; revised ed., Cambridge: Cambridge University Press, 1963.

———. *The Works of John Locke.* 10th ed., 10 vols. London: Churchill and Manship, 1801.

———. *The Works of John Locke in Ten Volumes.* 12th ed. London: Thomas Davison, 1823.

The Locke Newsletter, no. 13 (Autumn 1982). Edited by Roland Hall. Published by Roland Hall, University of York, Heslington, England.

Macpherson, C. B. *The Political Theory of Possessive Individualism: Hobbes to Locke.* Oxford: Clarendon Press, 1962.

Miller, Eugene F. "Locke on the Meaning of Political Language: The Teaching of the *Essay Concerning Human Understanding.*" *Political Science Reviewer* 9 (Fall 1979): 163–93.

Monson, Charles H., Jr. "Locke and His Interpreters." *Political Studies* 6 (1958): 120–33.

Pateman, Carole. *The Problem of Political Obligation: A Critical Analysis of Liberal Theory.* Chichester: John Wiley, 1979.

Perry, David L. "Locke on Mixed Modes, Relations and Knowledge." *Journal.of the History of Philosophy* 5 (July 1967): 219–36.

Petzäll, Åke. "Ethics and Epistemology in John Locke's *Essay Concerning Human Understanding.*" *Götesbörgs Högskolas Årsskrift* 43 (1937): 5–83.

Pitkin, Hanna. "Obligation and Consent—I." *American Political Science Review* 59 (December 1965): 990–99.

——. "Obligation and Consent—II." *American Political Science Review* 60 (March 1966): 39–52.

Plamenatz, J. P. *Consent, Freedom and Political Obligation.* London: Oxford University Press, 1938.

——. *Man and Society.* 2 vols. London: Longmans, Green, 1963.

Pocock, J. G. A. *The Ancient Constitution and the Feudal Law.* Cambridge: Cambridge University Press, 1957.

Pole, J. R. *Political Representation in England and the Origins of the American Republic.* Berkeley: University of California Press, 1966; California Paperbacks, 1971.

Polin, Raymond. *La politique morale de John Locke.* Paris: Presses Universitaires de France, 1960.

Riley, Patrick. "On Finding an Equilibrium between Consent and Natural Law in Locke's Political Philosophy." *Political Studies* 22 (December 1974): 432–52.

Rousseau, Jean-Jacques. "On the Social Contract." In *On the Social Contract with Geneva Manuscript and Political Economy,* ed. Roger D. Masters, trans. Judith R. Masters. New York: St. Martin's Press, 1978.

Seliger, Martin. *The Liberal Politics of John Locke.* London: George Allen and Unwin, 1968.

——. "Locke, Liberalism and Nationalism." In *John Locke: Problems and Perspectives,* ed. John W. Yolton. Cambridge: Cambridge University Press, 1969.

——. "Locke's Natural Law and the Foundation of Politics." *Journal of the History of Ideas* 24 (July–September 1963): 337–54.

Simmons, A. John. *Moral Principles and Political Obligations.* Princeton: Princeton University Press, 1979.

Singh, Raghuveer. "John Locke and the Theory of Natural Law." *Political Studies* 9 (1961): 105–18.

Skinner, Quentin. "History and Ideology in the English Revolution." *Historical Journal* 8 (1965): 151–78.

Spragens, Thomas A., Jr. *The Irony of Liberal Reason.* Chicago: University of Chicago Press, 1981.

Stephen, Sir James Fitzjames. *Horae Sabbaticae: Reprint of Articles Contributed to the Saturday Review.* 3 vols. 2d ser., essay 9. London: Macmillan, 1892.

Stephen, Sir Leslie. *History of English Thought in the Eighteenth Century.* 2d ed., 2 vols. London: Smith, Elder, 1881.

——. *History of English Thought in the Eighteenth Century.* 3d ed., 2 vols. New York: Peter Smith, 1902.

Strauss, Leo. "Locke's Doctrine of Natural Law." *American Political Science Review* 52 (June 1958): 490–501.

———. *Natural Right and History.* Chicago: University of Chicago Press, 1953; 7th printing, 1971.

———. *The Political Philosophy of Thomas Hobbes: Its Basis and Its Genesis.* Translated by Elsa M. Sinclair. Oxford: Clarendon Press, 1936; reprint ed., Chicago: University of Chicago Press, 1952.

Tarcov, Nathan. *Locke's Education for Liberty.* Chicago: University of Chicago Press, 1984.

———. "Locke's *Second Treatise* and the 'Best Fence against Rebellion.'" *Review of Politics* 43 (April 1981): 198–217.

———. "A 'Non-Lockean' Locke and the Character of Liberalism." In *Liberalism Reconsidered,* ed. Douglas MacLean and Claudia Mills. Totowa, N.J.: Rowman and Allanheld, 1983.

Tully, James. *A Discourse on Property: John Locke and His Adversaries.* Cambridge: Cambridge University Press, 1980.

Vaughan, C. E. *Studies in the History of Political Philosophy.* 2 vols. Edited by G. A. Little. Manchester: Manchester University Press, 1939.

Walzer, Michael. *Obligations.* Cambridge: Harvard University Press, 1970.

Woolhouse, R. S. *Locke.* Minneapolis: University of Minnesota Press, 1983.

———. *Locke's Philosophy of Science and Knowledge: A Consideration of Some Aspects of "An Essay Concerning Human Understanding."* Oxford: Basil Blackwell, 1971.

Yolton, John W. *Locke and the Compass of Human Understanding: A Selective Commentary on the "Essay."* Cambridge: Cambridge University Press, 1970.

———. "Locke on the Law of Nature." *Philosophical Review* 67 (1958): 477–98.

Zuckert, Michael P. "The Garden Died: An Interpretation of Locke's *First Treatise.*" Ph.D. diss., University of Chicago, 1974.

Index